SECURITY and **RISK** Technologies in **CRIMINAL** **JUSTICE**

SECURITY and **RISK** Technologies in **CRIMINAL JUSTICE**

Critical Perspectives

EDITED BY

Stacey Hannem, Carrie B. Sanders,
Christopher J. Schneider, Aaron Doyle,
and Tony Christensen

CANADIAN
SCHOLARS

Toronto | Vancouver

Security and Risk Technologies in Criminal Justice: Critical Perspectives
Edited by Stacey Hannem, Carrie B. Sanders, Christopher J. Schneider,
Aaron Doyle, and Tony Christensen

First published in 2019 by
Canadian Scholars, an imprint of CSP Books Inc.
425 Adelaide Street West, Suite 200
Toronto, Ontario
M5V 3C1

www.canadianscholars.ca

Library and Archives Canada Cataloguing in Publication

Security and risk technologies in criminal justice : critical perspectives
/ edited by Stacey Hannem, Carrie B. Sanders, Christopher J. Schneider,
Aaron Doyle, and Tony Christensen.

Includes bibliographical references and index.
Issued in print and electronic formats.
ISBN 978-1-77338-094-0 (softcover).--ISBN 978-1-77338-096-4 (EPUB).--
ISBN 978-1-77338-095-7 (PDF)

1. Criminal justice, Administration of--Technological innovations--Canada.
2. Criminal investigation--Technological innovations--Canada. I. Hannem, Stacey,
1979-, editor II. Sanders, Carrie B., 1978-, editor III. Schneider, Christopher J., editor
IV. Doyle, Aaron, editor V. Christensen, Tony, 1979-, editor

HV9960.C2S43 2018   364.971   C2018-904805-0
                                                                  C2018-904806-9

Text design by Elisabeth Springate
Cover design by Rafael Chimicatti

19   20   21   22   23   5   4   3   2   1

Printed and bound in Ontario, Canada

MIX
Paper from
responsible sources
FSC® C103423

CONTENTS

SECTION III: CHANGING RISK PRACTICES IN CRIMINAL JUSTICE INSTITUTIONS

ACKNOWLEDGEMENTS

The editors gratefully acknowledge the generous financial support of the Social Sciences and Humanities Research Council of Canada (SSHRC). The SSHRC Connections Grant program provided funding for a workshop that allowed our contributors to gather and spend a fruitful two days presenting their work and discussing the newest trends and theory in risk technology and criminal justice. This volume is the outcome of those discussions. We also received financial support from Wilfrid Laurier University's conference grant program, the Office of the Vice-President Academic and Provost, and the Dean of Human and Social Sciences at Wilfrid Laurier University, the Dean of Arts at Brandon University, and the Department of Sociology and Anthropology at Carleton University. Thank you to all of the workshop attendees who contributed their thoughts and ideas and engaged in lively discussions. At the risk of forgetting someone, we would like to acknowledge the attendance and contributions of Davut Acka, Lyria Bennett Moses, Philip Boyle, Janet Chan, Karine Côté-Boucher, Vanessa Iafolla, Debra Langan, Laura McKendy, Kelly Hannah-Moffat, Marcia Oliver, Pat O'Malley, James Popham, Dominique Robert, Silvian Roy, James Sheptycki, Gavin Smith, Shannon Speed, Kenneth Werbin, and Crystal Weston.

We were also fortunate to have the assistance of a group of excellent graduate students from the MA Criminology program at Wilfrid Laurier University. We wish to acknowledge the assistance and insight of Victoria Baker, Amanda Boyd, Sarah Fiander, Amanda Lancia, Emma Mistry, Jenniffer Olenewa, and Samantha Stycznski.

A very special mention and thank you to Marg Harris, who made all of the travel arrangements for our workshop and assisted cheerfully with many financial and administrative tasks. Many thanks are also due to Dr. Shane Dixon, the very hard-working research officer at Wilfrid Laurier University who assisted with our grant applications—your contributions do not go unnoticed. Also thanks to the anonymous reviewers who provided constructive feedback on our proposal and draft manuscript, and to Kerrie Waddington and Lizzie Di Giacomo, the helpful and patient editorial staff at Canadian Scholars, and our excellent copy editor, Caley Clements, who worked to see this volume come to fruition.

FOREWORD

The Unarticulated Political Appeals of Security-Related Risk Technologies

Kevin D. Haggerty

We are in the midst of monumental changes in the technological profile of national and international security, something that promises to alter almost all aspects of policing, security, criminal justice institutions, and the day-to-day routines of citizens.

The contributors to this excellent volume have commendably identified some of the more notable of such developments. In bringing these chapters together, the editors will help educate wider critical audiences about technological developments of which they would likely otherwise have little awareness. But beyond simply questioning the instrumental utility of these devices and related process of preventive security, the authors also detail how these phenomena can contribute to our understanding of risk, governance, and security.

What else might connect the many devices and practices outlined in this book? In this brief foreword, I focus on risk technologies to accentuate one additional association, which might provide a useful analytical strategy for contemplating how and why many such devices appeal to different security agencies.

First we must distance ourselves from the stories told by advocates for new security technologies. Small armies of supporters (and investors) stand ready to proclaim that big data, or brain imaging, or social media, will produce monumental gains in efficiency and cost savings. Decades of research in science and technology studies, however, have accentuated that technology is always also a social, organizational, and cultural phenomenon. To appreciate how or why a new technology is taken up, one must go beyond such advocacy to also investigate how new devices might mesh with other ostensibly "non-technological" challenges faced by potential users, and how technologies can help solve broader political problems for stakeholders (Bijker and Law 1992; Winner 1986).

To fully appreciate why criminal justice actors in North American and other Western democracies find a plethora of security devices appealing, one must harken back to a series of developments that coalesced in the early 1960s. At that time, research in the social sciences—particularly in social psychology—was drawing attention to limitations in human perception and the operation of implicit bias. Three related strands of empirical findings were—and continue to be—vital here. First were the recurrent early demonstrations that human perception could be faulty. Generations of undergraduate students have subsequently learned how our senses (particularly sight) are notoriously suspect, often providing demonstrably false impressions of the world. The second insight is that humans compensate for faulty perception by relying upon a range of informal heuristics and cognitive shortcuts to fill in and make sense of what they see (Jenkins 1997). Finally is the realization that such heuristics frequently draw upon and reproduce a range of often unpalatable and inaccurate stereotypes.

In relation to our assessments of other humans, such biases can involve assumptions about gender, physical ability, class, and any number of other variables. The highest profile and most politically volatile factor, however, has clearly concerned racial bias. It was hardly a revelation in the United States in the 1960s that criminal justice practitioners could be biased or outright racist. Perhaps more consequential was the insight that the perceptual schemes and ultimate decision making of individuals who would not be self-evidently racist (and who would likely vociferously disavow such insinuations) could still be racially biased (Banaji and Greenwald 2016).

Racial bias has been documented in decisions pertaining to medical treatment, hiring and promotion, university admissions, and a plethora of other domains. But it is in criminal justice where such concerns have been perhaps most high profile and politically charged. Almost any criminal justice decision is now open to suspicion that it might have been

shaped by explicit or latent racism. This would include street-level decisions about who to investigate, who to detain, and what (if any) charges
to lay, as well as decisions about what criminal laws are passed, where
financial resources are allocated, where police officers are deployed, how
pleas are negotiated, what sentences a judge delivers, where prisoners
are incarcerated, and who receives probation or parole and under what
conditions. Indeed, concerns about bias extend all the way to questions
about life-and-death decisions, given the racial dynamics surrounding
police shootings and the well-documented racial disparity in capital
cases in the United States.

Criminal justice actors now routinely face blunt, politically charged,
and often unanswerable questions about, for example, whether this law
was passed in part because it criminalized the preferred illicit drugs used
in visible minority communities (ignoring the illicit drugs preferred by
other ethnic groups); whether this Muslim woman would have been
searched at the airport if she was Christian; if this Latino man would
have had his car pulled over if he was white; or if this police officer
would have been more reluctant to shoot a white citizen as opposed to
a black citizen.

Bias in the criminal justice system has occasionally been traced
to racial enmity in a straightforward and unambiguous manner. In a
much larger number of cases, the influence of racial bias is harder to
discern, particularly if one recognizes that there can be a disjuncture
between attitudes and actions, and that any individual decision is typically overdetermined by a range of personal, organizational, attitudinal,
and interactional factors. Notwithstanding these difficulties of attribution on a case-by-case basis, concerns about bias continue to motivate
activists and a subset of politicians. Criminal justice practitioners have
been put on the defensive, particularly in the context of the Black Lives
Matter movement.

For decades, officials have recognized that bias—both the reality
of bias as well as public perceptions of bias amongst criminal justice
actors—could harm the legitimacy of criminal justice institutions. In
a democracy, such institutions rely on a minimum level of public trust
in order to operate legitimately. If a subset of the population comes to

suspect that how they are treated by security operatives is a function of the categories they fall into, and not simply due to their behaviour, trust is eroded and democracy suffers.

Officials frame these concerns as the problem of "discretion." In their eyes, *discretion* became something of a dirty word: a phenomena that had to be "tamed" and exercised in a rational and non-partisan manner (Gottfredson and Gottfredson 1987; Walker 1993). Unfortunately, the tools available to manage the discretion problem were frequently quite crude, often focusing on greater sensitivity training for criminal justice practitioners or efforts to hire visible minorities. Some of these initiatives were heartfelt while others were simple tokenism. No matter their sincerity, public concerns about discretion have continued to reverberate amongst certain (often racialized) segments of society, and in some jurisdictions have reached a crisis point.

It is in this context that I believe new risk technologies have an acute although often unarticulated appeal for a range of criminal justice agencies. A considerable subset of new technologies provides security-related decisions a veneer of objectivity and scientism, helping to shelter individual practitioners and organizations from accusations of bias. This insight follows from Ted Porter's (1994, 1995) study of the US Army Corps of Engineers, which documented the historical rise of a "trust in numbers" in that profession. As Porter's research shows, decisions about the location of bridges, dams, and roadways traditionally relied on the professional judgment of engineers. However, as engineers faced increasing accusations that their decisions were shaped by political considerations and served the interests of some groups over others, their profession embraced a series of quantitative and standardized accounting rules to help guide/determine the scope and location of engineering projects. For Porter, the problem that such numerical accounting rules solved was not about where to build bridges, but how to insulate a profession from accusations that its members were making politically partisan decisions in arriving at such determinations.

My sense is that part of the latent and unacknowledged appeal of a subset of security technologies lies in precisely this process: they help organizations counter or finesse accusations of bias. In a political climate where concerns about racism and other forms of discrimination have become inescapable and potentially incendiary, officials see this as a particularly appealing attribute.

One can see this operating in relation to several of the technologies highlighted by contributors to this volume. For example, Pat O'Malley draws our attention to a number of "preventive justice" technologies, including roadside alcohol Breathalyzers, mobile radar speed detectors, and, more recently, fixed photo radar systems that automatically record speeders and sometimes also cars running red lights. To varying degrees, all such devices help transform decisions previously based on a police officer's subjective professional judgment into automated decisions grounded in technological systems. While citizens can and do continue to question the value and utility of such devices, it has become harder (although by no means impossible) to claim that the decisions are related to officer bias.

The second example concerns the ion scanners studied by Stacey Hannem. These devices are used to identify levels of chemicals that could indicate the presence of illicit drugs or explosives. Hannem's focus is on the introduction of these devices into Canadian prisons, but they are more familiar as a component of airport security screening. In the aftermath of 9/11 such screening has become more intense, and also more controversial. Travellers and civil liberties organizations often insinuate that decisions about who is subjected to more thorough searches are informed by the racial biases of security personnel. Here, again, these scanners appeal to officials because they allow practitioners to justify their decisions to conduct enhanced searches as the determination of a scientific device, not as a result of the subjective judgment of security operatives. This performance of neutrality in pre-flight screening is further enhanced through the use of technologies that randomly tell officers which travellers should be subject to greater scrutiny—although officers still have the authority to single out travellers they deem to be suspicious.

The big data "predictive policing" models outlined by Janet Chan and Lyria Bennett Moses also fit into this pattern. For the police, one prominent use of the increasingly large data sets available to them about calls for police services has been the development of statistical models of geographical crime patterns. Used in many jurisdictions to predict where crimes might occur in the future, such models are also used to make decisions about where to deploy police officers in anticipation of crimes being committed (Brayne 2017). While cynical line officers often observe that they don't need a computer program to tell them to dedicate extra attention to historically "high-crime areas," such grumblings miss the larger point. Predictive policing algorithms allow officials to justify, for example, intensive police crackdowns in certain neighbourhoods on the grounds that the decision was the outcome of evidence provided by an objective technological tool, and not the result of a subjective and potentially suspect or racist police decision-making process. Chan and Bennett Moses are attuned to this process, noting in passing how such technologies create "an aura of neutrality. Because the patrol areas are determined 'scientifically' rather than through human discretion, law enforcement agencies have a response to public accusations of bias as to where police patrol."

None of this is to say that any such devices have banished bias. In some cases, it has certainly been significantly curtailed, but in others subjective decision making appears to have been relocated: it is now embedded in inscrutable computer algorithms (Brayne 2017) or operating in the dynamics of how practitioners deploy new technologies or interpret the outputs of these devices. Indeed, many of authors in this volume highlight precisely this process.

To reiterate, this collection does an excellent job of drawing critical attention to a range of new risk technologies and processes of prospective security, often raising questions about the extent to which these phenomena perform as advertised. My brief comments here are simply designed to encourage readers also to contemplate some of the broader social forces that could be at play in the introduction and embracing of such devices. This includes the extent to which new technologies can appeal to security operatives because they help solve complex social and political problems related to the operation of subjectively grounded discretion and bias—irrespective of whether they might or might not "work" according to the narrowly circumscribed claims of technology advocates.

REFERENCES

Banaji, Mahzarin R., and Anthony G. Greenwald. 2016. *Blindspot: Hidden Biases of Good People*. New York: Bantam.

Bijker, Wiebe E., and John Law, eds. 1992. *Shaping Technology/Building Society: Studies in Sociotechnical Change*. Cambridge, MA: MIT Press.

Brayne, Sarah. 2017. "Big Data Surveillance: The Case of Policing." *American Sociological Review* 82 (5): 977–1008.

Gottfredson, Michael R., and Don M. Gottfredson. 1987. *Decision Making in Criminal Justice: Toward the Rational Exercise of Discretion*, vol. 3. New York: Springer Science and Business Media.

Jenkins, Richard. 1997. "Rethinking Ethnicity." In *Rethinking Ethnicity: Arguments and Explorations*, 165–70. London: Sage.

Porter, Theodore. 1994. "Objectivity as Standardization: The Rhetoric of Impersonality in Measurement, Statistics, and Cost-Benefit Analysis." In *Rethinking Objectivity*, edited by Allan Megill, 197–237. Durham, NC: Duke University Press.

———. 1995. *Trust in Numbers: The Pursuit of Objectivity in Science and Public Life*. Princeton, NJ: Princeton University Press.

Walker, Samuel. 1993. *Taming the System: The Control of Discretion in Criminal Justice, 1950–1990*. Oxford: Oxford University Press on Demand.

Winner, Langdon. 1986. "Do Artifacts Have Politics?" In *The Whale and the Reactor: A Search for Limits in the Age of High Technology*, 19–39. Chicago: University of Chicago Press.

INTRODUCTION

*Stacey Hannem, Aaron Doyle, Christopher J. Schneider,
and Carrie B. Sanders*

Security and Risk Technologies in Criminal Justice: Critical Perspectives
offers a broad vision across, and critique of, contemporary preventive
practices and technologies for controlling risks of crime and terrorism.
Its eight chapters offer diverse views into multifarious preventive security
efforts in the 21st century across eight empirical sites, and the potential
for injustice in these justice measures. While the topics and sites explored here are deliberately very diverse, we see common themes that
help us examine the evolution of crime control and ramping up of preventive security more broadly in Western democracies. These empirical
studies allow the authors to revisit and update theoretical discussions of
"**actuarial justice**" (Feeley and Simon 1992), "policing the **risk society**"
(Ericson and Haggerty 1997), the rise of **surveillance** (Lyon 2007,
2015), or of "**pre-crime**" approaches to justice (Zedner 2007).

We are seeing the gradual accretion and proliferation of control measures, as documented in this volume. Organized thematically, the chapters
presented herein address forms of technology and classifications used to
identify "risky individuals." Drawing on Prus and Mitchell's (2009, 17)
broad definition of **technology** as "humanly engaged, conceptually achieved
instances of enabling devices," we encourage readers to think of **risk
technology** not merely in terms of electronic or computational devices, but
also as tools that mediate and shape human decision making with respect
to **risk** and **threat**. Some chapters address specific advances in electronic
surveillance, including traffic safety cameras (O'Malley, chapter 1) and ion
scanning machines searching for drug traces on prison visitors (Hannem,

chapter 3), while others provide an empirically grounded analysis of these technologies in practice. Collectively, the authors of this book address the move toward increasing reliance on risk prediction as crime prevention. For example, Doyle and McKendy (chapter 7) consider the slow but ultimately revolutionary ramping up of bail conditions tied to a massive increase in pretrial detention, Sanders et al. (chapter 4) discuss the use of community "hubs" for identifying high-risk individuals, and Dufresne, Robert, and Roy (chapter 5) describe the reification of risk prediction tools like the Psychopathy Checklist. Chapters on police use of big data (Chan and Bennett Moses, chapter 2) and social media (Schneider, chapter 6) and the integration of data collection into "smart" borders (Côté-Boucher, chapter 8) highlight how the proliferation and collection of data alter the practice of justice and security. The contributions in this book empirically document and analyze the myriad ways in which preventive security is evolving, expanding, and intensifying in various spheres of criminal justice, and the ways in which this paradoxically breeds new forms of insecurity, even as official crime rates decline.

While a shift to emphasizing prevention and risk-based approaches in criminal justice was becoming evident towards the end of the 20th century (Ericson and Haggerty 1997; Feeley and Simon 1992), recent years have seen such a proliferation of new technologies and practices, moving so rapidly on so many fronts, that it poses a challenge for critical analysts seeking to maintain an overview. In this brief introduction, we highlight four broad themes that crosscut the eight studies and chapters in this volume: (1) the shift to pre-crime and **preventive justice**, (2) the theatre and realities of technologies, (3) the **calculability** and incalculability of risks, and (4) the rhetoric and realities of cost savings and "justice on a budget."

PRE-CRIME AND PREVENTIVE JUSTICE

A notable shift in criminal justice is an increased emphasis on the future and on prevention, whether this is conceived in terms of risk, security, surveillance, or what Lucia Zedner (2007) calls "pre-crime."[1] While the move toward less individualistic, risk-based and future-oriented responses to crime in the form of the **"new penology"** (Feeley and Simon 1992) and "actuarial justice" was noted in the late 20th century, increasingly we see attempts to predict and respond pre-emptively to threats of harm. The ramping up of preventive security has occurred in response to what is seen as a changing risk environment, perhaps most notably in response to perceived risks of terrorism. Recent shifts to the war on terrorism have served as "the catalyst for a more pre-emptive approach to threats" (McCulloch and Wilson 2016, 2). "Pre-crime, like risk, is future oriented and linked to the pursuit of security. However, risk leans more towards prevention than pre-emption, and pre-emption is more forward than prevention" (McCulloch and Wilson 2016, 2). As pointed out by McCulloch and Pickering (2009), pre-crime is not crime prevention, in the traditional sense. While crime prevention focuses on identifying and targeting the root causes of crime, addressing its social causes, pre-crime, particularly in response to large-scale threats such as terrorism, is aimed at identifying potential perpetrators of harm on an individual level and intervening *before* they can act. The point of pre-crime then is not prevention, but rather pre-empting all forms of offending (McCulloch and Wilson 2016). Nevertheless, such shifts raise both practical and ethical questions. It is imperative that we "excavate the entrenched, often hidden assumptions that drive the security agenda by means of immanent critique, revealing the political and economic interests underlying the present pursuit of security as well as the intellectual assumptions upon which security policies are based" (Zedner 2007, 267).

The logic of pre-crime and preventive security is not only manifest in concerns about large-scale terrorism events, but it also underlies everyday social control mechanisms. O'Malley (chapter 1) points out that such "preventive offences" as driving while under the influence or speeding do not punish actions that have caused harm, but censure behaviour that carries the *risk* of harm in an effort to prevent such harms from occurring. Similarly, the explosion of the remand population, as described by Doyle and McKendy (chapter 7), is a by-product of judicial concern to pre-empt further criminal behaviour or evasion of justice. The ever-changing and volatile nature of crime and threats to security are creating conditions that are favourable to the exploitation of new risk technologies (Zedner 2007), yet, as evidenced in this collection, a myriad of technological, organizational, cultural, and user-capacity issues challenge the hype and mythology surrounding many of these technologies. In understanding diverse criminal justice apparatuses as part of a larger movement toward pre-emptive responses to threat, we can begin to see the proliferation of pre-crime logic in contemporary crime control practices and technologies.

THEATRE AND REALITIES OF TECHNOLOGIES

The expansion we are discussing is driven in part by techno-scientific advances, small and large: the advent of new surveillance technologies like traffic safety cameras (chapter 1) and ion scanners searching for drug traces (chapter 3), the rise of big data technology (chapter 2), the proliferation of social media and some of its unintended consequences for police (chapter 6), and the use of brain-mapping and attempts to link it to constructions of psychopathy (chapter 5). The place of technology is another key part of this storyline. Investment in new technologies is also, of course, tied to the perception that the integration of scientific practices in criminal justice settings enhances objectivity, accountability, and security (see Manning 2008; Sanders and Henderson 2013; Sheptycki 2004). Further, the integration of new technologies within the criminal justice sector is often associated with "smart," evidence-based initiatives; however, as noted by Public Safety Canada, many of these innovation investments have not been evaluated to confirm their benefits to objectivity, accountability, and security (Griffiths 2014).

Some of the research and theorizing available on risk technologies draws on the perspective of **technological determinism**, which focuses its attention and analysis on designer rhetoric concerning how these technologies ought to work, rather than attending to the ways in which the social gets inside of and shapes technological functioning (Sanders 2014). In other words, technological determinists rely on descriptions of how the technologies *should work* in an ideal sense, assuming that the technology determines user behaviour, without paying attention to how the technologies *actually function*, given the interpretation and engagement of individual and organizational users. Yet, research in science and technology studies has shown that "technology" also comprises knowledge about such systems as well as practices of handling them (MacKenzie and Wajcman 1985). Technology is constructed in the sense that it is "made" and also in the sense that it is interpreted and understood through social groups influenced by a range of physical, social, political, and organizational factors that may change over time (Bijker 2010; Orr 1996; Suchman 1987). Thus, risk technologies are not static entities, but instead are shaped by the meaning users ascribe to them and their "processes of production, translation, circulation, appropriation, experimentation and resistance" (Amicelle, Aradau, and Jeandesboz 2015, 294). In fact, research available on security technologies has found the technologies to reflect "the logics, rationalities and modes of reasoning of security practices" (Amicelle, Aradau, and Jeandesboz 2015, 297). In this way, technologies have "'cognitive effects'—wherein the normative and political ideals of their designers and users facilitate and constrain particular modes of interpretation and action (Grove 2015)" (Sanders and Condon 2017, 238). As evidenced by research conducted by both Chan and Bennett Moses (chapter 2) and Côté-Boucher (chapter 8), by focusing on technologies-in-practice, we can begin to understand how the structures inscribed in technologies shape "action by facilitating certain outcomes and constraining others" (Orlikowski and Robey 1991, 148; see also Orlikowski 2000). We must also consider how risk technologies, as a tool for "social sorting," may act to reinforce existing stereotypes about the "kinds of people" who pose a threat. How might stereotypes about risk and threat (e.g., taking into account ethnicity, gender, or class) be designed into risk technologies and categorizations, or how might "objective" determinations about risk be used to legitimate biased enforcement? Addressing these issues is part of the project of "un-black-boxing" technology and examining its use in practice.

CALCULABILITY AND INCALCULABILITY OF RISKS

There is an increasing reliance on risk calculation, as demonstrated by some of the measures explored here, such as Sanders et al.'s (chapter 4) examination of community safety initiatives' assessments of people and situations deemed to be at "acutely elevated risk" of crime and/or victimization; traffic safety cameras examined by O'Malley (chapter 1), which are deployed using risk calculations based on speed and accident rates; or the promises of predictive policing linked to big data, explored by Chan and Bennett Moses (chapter 2). Historically, and theoretically, the language of risk is one that points to the ability in the present to calculate the probability that hazards (or dangers) will come to pass in the future (Doron 2016; Porter 1995). Indeed, as Burgess (2016, 3) suggests, "increasingly refined calculation of likely future outcomes based on statistical analysis of what has happened in the past is a defining characteristic of our age." Although government and public confidence in data science, actuarial tools, and risk profiling technologies is growing, there remain profound limits to our predictive capacity (Harcourt 2007). For example, the Chicago Police Department's attempt to use big data to predict gun violence appears to have failed insofar as increased surveillance and arrests had no perceptible impact on homicide rates (Saunders 2016). Yet "many preventive measures are justified by implicit or explicit claims that it is possible to determine in advance who poses a risk and in what degree" (Zedner 2010, 24).

Subjecting particular individuals or groups, locations or neighbourhoods to increased levels of surveillance or censure due to predictions of risk poses a concern for the possibility of false positive determinations and the generation of further risk data to justify continued scrutiny and intervention. In this way, risk prediction and the resulting risk management strategies can form self-fulfilling prophecies, directing intensive criminal justice attention to particular groups or spaces, resulting in the increased detection of crime and deviance among those groups or spaces (Ratcliffe 2002; Sanders and Sheptycki 2017). Conversely, those groups or places designated as low risk receive less attention, and incidents of harm or danger may not come to the attention of criminal justice agents; risk data about these places or groups is not collected, and they continue to be the subject of less scrutiny or concern. These types of risk judgment are prone to bias and, as with the example of "carding" (or the police practice of stopping members of ethnic groups deemed high risk for criminal activity), may lead to increased scrutiny of groups that already experience social disadvantage and discrimination without any corresponding empirical evidence of risk reduction. Ethical engagement with risk technology requires that we create a space for evidence-based discussion to avoid the application of risk technologies in ways that unduly label and discriminate against marginalized persons (Mythen and Walklate 2010).

As Hannah-Moffat (2016, 245) puts it, "Regardless of their flaws, risk instruments foster confidence in the system because they *appear to be* objective, rational and empirical" (emphasis added). Underlying processes of discretion, self-selection, and bias are rendered invisible by the theatre of technological risk management (see Sanders and Hannem 2012), and, as Sanders et al. (chapter 4) show, the "success" of risk prediction is often measured by its resulting interventions, rather than any empirical evidence of harm prevention. In this sense, while risk prediction and management are widely used in the name of security and crime prevention, it is not clear that the proliferation of and investment in these technologies affords any appreciable decrease in harm. They may merely justify an increase in targeting the usual suspects. As critics have pointed out, it is incredibly difficult to empirically verify that preventive interventions have actually prevented harm—you cannot measure something that does not happen, only statistical decreases in events. In the case of a statistically rare phenomenon, there is no way to empirically demonstrate that risk prediction and intervention in fact prevented any given event, hence the reliance on calculating how often risk prediction results in intervention as "evidence" of its effectiveness.

RHETORIC AND REALITIES OF COST SAVINGS

Cost-consciousness by government and the potential of new technologies and approaches to produce "justice on a budget" is also a connecting theme of a number of the chapters that follow, although some developments, such as the massive increase in pretrial detention, are actually very expensive (see Doyle and McKendy, chapter 7). In 2013, the Canadian minister of public safety, on behalf of all federal, provincial, and territorial ministers responsible for justice and public safety, hosted the Summit on the Economics of Policing. The summit focused on increasing efficiency and effectiveness in the Canadian criminal justice system and was organized around three pillars for public safety: (1) efficiencies within police services, (2) new models of community safety, and (3) efficiencies within the justice system. The summit emphasized the importance of investing in "smart," "proactive," evidence-based initiatives (Public Safety Canada 2013). Governments and criminal justice or security agencies may see shifts toward predictive technologies and practices as a means of targeting human resources and interventions to maximize effect and minimize ongoing justice system costs. In some cases, technologies may actually be used as a means of income generation for the state, as when traffic cameras yield fines for speeding or red-light violations, and operate on a cost-recovery or profit model. In other cases, significant financial investments in technologies and data collection yield no financial returns, and possibly no tangible impact in terms of increasing security or decreasing risk of injustice, but instead provide performance measures and indicators for organizations to demonstrate accountability (see Sanders et al., chapter 4). Further, and more importantly, some technologies may actually exacerbate the possibility of false accusations of criminal behaviour, as with the ion scanners discussed by Hannem (chapter 3) or the police use of social media to collect purported "evidence" of criminal activity, as described in part by Schneider (chapter 6).

Taken together, these four themes, as explored in the following chapters, suggest a complex and uneasy relationship between ideas of risk, prediction, prevention, and pre-emptive intervention, and the leveraging of technology for identifying and managing risks. The analyses in this volume grapple with the ongoing need to balance the costs and benefits of the use of risk technologies and to better understand their socio-political implications and effects on the everyday lives of citizens.

OVERVIEW OF THE VOLUME

The chapters in this volume cover a vast terrain of practices and technologies for assessing, preventing, and ultimately controlling risk. Each of the chapters in *Security and Risk Technologies in Criminal Justice* carefully illuminates and grapples conceptually with some of the important questions underlying many contemporary risk management strategies and practices; collectively, the authors highlight the ways in which risk security is currently evolving. Here we provide a brief overview of each chapter.

In chapter 1, Pat O'Malley explores the development and spread of what he calls "mass preventive justice" located, O'Malley contends, "in risk's objective calculability." This new risk-based phenomenon, we learn, can be traced to the middle of the last century with the rise of road traffic and a corresponding statistical spike in related deaths, injuries, and property loss. The emergence of these statistical data created the conditions necessary for objective risk assessment on a massive scale, in particular with speeding and drunk driving. From these data emerges a "jurisprudence of risk" in which related risk calculations associated with these offences become embedded in the law itself. The result was the widespread implementation of new enforcement technologies to detect traffic offences and issue monetary penalties. O'Malley illustrates how political resistance to forms of mass preventive justice like red-light cameras reveal that its key strength—financial sanctions—is also its principal source of vulnerability.

The next chapter takes up the topic of prediction. Janet Chan and Lyria Bennett Moses investigate "predictive policing," an issue that has developed in relation to the advent of "social transactional data," now commonly referred to as "big data"—a phrase that gained more widespread usage in 2008 (Boellstorff 2013). As noted by Boellstorff (2013) in a special issue of *First Monday* on big data, "we live in a time when big data will transform society. Or so the hype goes." The authors in some ways seem to take this view, but with a skeptical eye directed at contemporary policing practices. Chan and Bennett Moses ask: Will predictive policing fundamentally change police practice? They develop a framework to illustrate the *uptake* and *impact* of "a new orthodoxy of policing" or "predictive policing." The term *predictive policing*, they tell us, is "applied to a range of tools and law enforcement practices" that now seemingly enable police to predict the specific locations and times of crimes in advance of any crime actually occurring. In their systematic review of the literature, coupled with their own empirical research, Chan and Bennett Moses, while not entirely convinced of the benefits of predictive policing, do find that a range of factors—technical, practical, and cultural—nevertheless point in the direction of the adoption of this technology, while concluding that it is difficult to predict its impact with any certainty.

In chapter 3, Stacey Hannem focuses on the use of ion mobility spectrometry, or IonScan, technology by Correctional Service Canada (CSC). The device, familiar to many, is sometimes referred to as the *trace portal machine* and is the same as those used in airports to identify trace particles of explosives. The technology, which first emerged in the 1970s and was introduced to federal prisons by CSC in the mid-1990s, has quickly become the front line of drug interception in Canadian correctional institutions. Despite the promise of the technology, implementation of these devices has not stemmed the flow of illegal drugs into prisons. Hannem argues that the IonScan technology does not act as an objective determination of risk, but rather, that the "technology enables the performance of security." Drawing from extensive interview data and an array of key documents, Hannem carefully illustrates how the devices are subjectively employed on visitors and not on correctional staff as a seemingly innocuous safety measure, albeit a largely ineffective one due to a variety of recurrent documented false positives. Nevertheless, avoiding pitfalls associated with critiques of ineffectiveness that would demand improvements of the technology (a matter addressed in chapter 1), Hannem concludes that the discretionary use of this technology under the auspices of objectivity can have damaging and lasting consequences on family relationships, "which are most beneficial to released inmates."

The next chapter continues with the topic of policing (discussed in chapter 2). In chapter 4, Carrie B. Sanders, Debra Langan, Katy Cain, and Taylor Knipe investigate new security networks that emerge as a consequence of issues related to the economics of policing. They focus their attention on the growing provision of security networks, specifically "situation tables" occurring across Ontario. A situation table consists of a face-to-face meeting of networked professionals who together seek to identify people at "acutely elevated risk" of crime and/or victimization with the goal of mitigating said risks. Drawing on a review of the literature, more than 100 hours of field observations, and in-depth interviews with key police and community agency representatives from one situation table operating in a mid-size urban centre in Ontario, Sanders et al. detail the political and economic shaping of the development of the implementation of situation tables. The chapter shows how these groups are governed, with police taking leadership due to their ascribed "economic, political, cultural, social and symbolic capital" (Dupont 2004, 76). This reveals the power that police wield in this risk mitigation initiative. The authors' analysis demonstrates the consequence of this state steering by showing how it expands and formalizes state control in a way that reinforces traditional policing practices targeted at the "usual suspects" (Gill 2000) under the auspices of collaborative approaches to community safety.

In chapter 5, Martin Dufresne, Dominique Robert, and Silvian Roy investigate the science that precedes risk assessment. Their concern in this chapter is the shift toward brain imaging in the field of psychopathy. The authors raise concerns about the strength of the psychopathy construct and its impact on the justice system, despite numerous criticisms levied against psychopathy from within the scientific community. To illustrate these concerns, Dufresne, Robert, and Roy direct their focus toward a critical examination of a single article. The selected article is significant insofar as the paper was instrumental in solidifying the construct of psychopathy and its related tools as key risk predictors, particularly in corrections. Their examination reveals that while psychopathy is unstable in theory, its power nevertheless continues to expand as it works in practice. Dufresne, Robert, and Roy conclude that while the idea of psychopathy draws strength and support externally (from the public), its usefulness as a calculation of risk continues to remain ontologically uncertain.

In the next chapter, we return again to policing. At the heart of chapter 6, Christopher J. Schneider considers social media as a "new type of risk media," where the police management of risk information now increasingly occurs in online public spaces. This chapter explores how police agencies respond in news reports to those perceived risks associated with social media. Schneider contends that these spaces in news media provide what Ericson and Haggerty (1997, 9) refer to as "focal points" for the "selection and definition of risks." In his examination of selected focal points, Schneider shows how police concern and response to social media risks shifts from *reactive* (specific risks) to *proactive* (unspecific risks). Schneider concludes the chapter by suggesting that social media as risk media formats contribute to the wider expansion of police social control efforts. In the next chapter, we return to an analysis of correction and risk, an issue only briefly mentioned in chapter 5.

In chapter 7, Aaron Doyle and Laura McKendy consider the factors that have led to the most overcrowded jails that Ontario—Canada's most populated province—has ever witnessed. This is an alarming and unusual predicament given that the sentenced population and crime are both steadily *decreasing*. In this chapter, Doyle and McKendy contend that this observation can be attributed to "a culture of risk aversion" that wields a powerful influence on the bail and remand process. The logic is that risk of additional crime can be minimized both through pretrial detention and excessive bail conditions; however, the expensive use of pretrial detention has not been empirically linked to decreased risk of recidivism or improved criminal justice functioning. The factors that shape the "bail crisis," argue Doyle and McKendy, do not lend themselves to any one particular theory of punishment. Rather, they conclude, understanding the forces that have given rise to the current bail crisis remains an imperative endeavour in order to develop necessary strategies for change.

In the final chapter, Karine Côté-Boucher, drawing inspiration from the sociology of policing (see also Chan and Bennett Moses, chapter 2, and Schneider, chapter 6), explores the "empirical complexity" of so-called "smart borders." Chapter 8 details how technological developments in border security alter its practice and, in doing so, inadvertently renew various power struggles within border agencies. Furthermore, Côté-Boucher's analysis reveals a more insidious consequence of "smart" technologies at the border. When implemented as "reforms to customs work," these technologies facilitate internal tensions among everyday border control practices, in essence complicating and "restructur[ing] what the border does." Côté-Boucher shows how these dynamics contribute to changes in how border guards work and also how they interact with other security agencies. Côté-Boucher concludes that all is not lost, however, as the removal of decision-making power from border officers in lieu of risk management technologies opens a space to critically question claims of the efficiency and neutrality of "smart borders."

As a volume, these chapters encourage the reader to engage critically with recent developments in technology and security that are shaping the practice of criminal justice. Where media and political rhetoric often present the intended and positive effects of technology, scholars of critical criminology and criminal justice are increasingly pointing out the need to carefully consider the less obvious implications and possible iatrogenic consequences of the wholesale adoption of security technologies and risk management. Each chapter will direct the reader to consider the complexities of understanding the roles and integration of risk technologies in our society from a slightly different theoretical perspective. This multi-faceted approach highlights the contested nature of these technologies and the multiplicity of angles that a social scientist might engage to critically consider the effect of risk technology on the justice system and, more broadly, on our social order. The challenges of examining the social implications of risk technologies in a fulsome and holistic way are made clear through these varied lenses. Taken as a collection, *Security and Risk Technologies in Criminal Justice* poses important questions and considerations about the role of risk technologies in the pursuit of justice and security, and the injustices that can result.

NOTE

1.   The term was coined by science fiction author Philip K. Dick in his 1956 short story, "The Minority Report" (McCulloch and Wilson 2016). A film of the same name, loosely based on Dick's story, directed by Steven Spielberg and starring Tom Cruise, was released to critical acclaim in 2002.

REFERENCES

Amicelle, Anthony, Claudia Aradau, and Julien Jeandesboz. 2015. "Questioning Security Devices: Performativity, Resistance, Politics." *Security Dialogue* 46 (4): 293–306.

Bijker, Wiebe E. 2010. "How Is Technology Made?—That Is the Question!" *Cambridge Journal of Economics* 34 (1): 63–74.

Boellstorff, Tom. 2013. "Making Big Data, in Theory." *First Monday* 18 (10). http://firstmonday.org/ojs/index.php/fm/article/view/4869/3750.

Burgess, Adam. 2016. "Introduction." In *The Routledge Handbook of Risk Studies*, edited by Adam Burgess, Alberto Alemanno, and Jens Zinn, 1–14. New York: Routledge.

Doron, Claude-Olivier. 2016. "The Experience of 'Risk': Genealogy and Transformations." In *The Routledge Handbook of Risk Studies*, edited by Adam Burgess, Alberto Alemanno, and Jens Zinn, 17–27. New York: Routledge.

Dupont, Benoit. 2004. "Security in the Age of Networks." *Policing and Society* 14 (1): 76–91.

Ericson, Richard V., and Kevin Haggerty. 1997. *Policing the Risk Society*. New York: Oxford University Press.

Feeley, Malcolm M., and Jonathan Simon. 1992. "The New Penology: Notes on the Emerging Strategy of Corrections and Its Implications." *Criminology* 30 (4): 449–74.

Gill, Peter. 2000. *Rounding Up the Usual Suspects? Developments in Contemporary Law Enforcement Intelligence*. Aldershot, UK: Ashgate.

Griffiths, Curt Taylor. 2014. *Economics of Policing: Baseline for Policing Research in Canada*. Ottawa: Public Safety Canada. https://www.publicsafety.gc.ca/cnt/rsrcs/pblctns/bsln-plcng-rsrch/bsln-plcng-rsrch-en.pdf.

Grove, Nicole Sunday. 2015. "The Cartographic Ambiguities of HarassMap: Crowdmapping Security and Sexual Violence in Egypt." *Security Dialogue* 46 (4): 345–56.

Hannah-Moffat, Kelly. 2016. "Risk Knowledge(s), Crime and Law." In *The Routledge Handbook of Risk Studies*, edited by Adam Burgess, Alberto Alemanno, and Jens Zinn, 241–51. New York: Routledge.

Harcourt, Bernard E. 2007. *Against Prediction: Profiling, Policing and Punishing in an Actuarial Age*. Chicago: University of Chicago Press.

Lyon, David. 2007. *Surveillance Studies: An Overview*. Cambridge, UK: Polity.

———. 2015. *Surveillance after Snowden*. Cambridge, UK: Polity.

MacKenzie, Donald, and Judy Wajcman, eds. 1985. *The Social Shaping of Technology*. Philadelphia: Open University Press.

Manning, Peter K. 2008. *The Technology of Policing: Crime Mapping, Information Technology, and the Rationality of Crime Control*. New York: New York University Press.

McCulloch, Jude, and Sharon Pickering. 2009. "Pre-crime and Counter-Terrorism: Imagining Future Crime in the War on Terror." *British Journal of Criminology* 49 (5): 628–45.

McCulloch, Jude, and Dean Wilson. 2016. *Pre-crime: Pre-emption, Precaution and the Future*. New York: Routledge.

Mythen, Gabe, and Sandra Walklate. 2010. "Pre-crime, Regulation and Counter-Terrorism: Interrogating Anticipatory Risk." *Criminal Justice Matters* 81 (1): 34–46.

Orlikowski, Wanda J. 2000. "Using Technology and Constituting Structures: A Practical Lens for Studying Technology in Organizations." *Organization Science* 11 (4): 404–28.

Orlikowski, Wanda J., and Daniel Robey. 1991. "Information Technology and the Structuring of Organizations." *Information Systems Research* 2 (2): 143–69.

Orr, Julian E. 1996. *Talking about Machines: An Ethnography of a Modern Job*. Ithaca, NY: Cornell University Press.

Porter, Theodore M. 1995. *Trust in Numbers: The Pursuit of Objectivity in Science and Public Life*. Princeton, NJ: Princeton University Press.

Prus, Robert, and Richard G. Mitchell. 2009. "Engaging Technology: A Missing Link in the Sociological Study of Human Knowing and Acting." *Qualitative Sociology Review* 5 (2): 17–53.

Public Safety Canada. 2013. *Summit on the Economics of Policing: Strengthening Canada's Policing Advantage*. Ottawa: Public Safety Canada.

Ratcliffe, Jerry H. 2002. "Damned if You Don't, Damned if You Do: Crime Mapping and Its Implications in the Real World." *Policing and Society* 12 (3): 211–25.

Sanders, Carrie. 2014. "Need to Know vs. Need to Share: The Intersecting Work of Police, Fire and Paramedics." *Information, Communication and Society* 17 (4): 463–75.

Sanders, Carrie B., and Camie Condon. 2017. "Crime Analysis and Cognitive Effects: The Practice of Policing through Flows of Data." *Global Crime* 18 (3): 237–55.

Sanders, Carrie B., and Stacey Hannem. 2012. "Policing 'the Risky': Technology and Surveillance in Everyday Patrol Work." *Canadian Review of Sociology* 49 (4): 389–410.

Sanders, Carrie B., and Samantha Henderson. 2013. "Police 'Empires' and Information Technologies: Uncovering Material and Organizational Barriers to Information Sharing in Canadian Police Services." *Policing and Society* 23 (2): 243–60.

Sanders, Carrie B., and James Sheptycki. 2017. "Policing, Crime, 'Big Data': Towards a Critique of the Moral Economy of Stochastic Governance." *Crime, Law and Social Change* 68 (1–2): 1–15. https://doi.org/10.1007/s10611-016-9678-7.

Saunders, Jessica. 2016. "Pitfalls of Predictive Policing." *The RAND Blog*. October 11, 2016. https://www.rand.org/blog/2016/10/pitfalls-of-predictive-policing.html.

Sheptycki, James. 2004. "Organizational Pathologies in Police Intelligence Systems: Some Contributions to the Lexicon of Intelligence-Led Policing." *European Journal of Criminology* 1 (3): 307–32.

Suchman, Lucy A. 1987. *Plans and Situated Actions: The Problem of Human-Machine Communication*. Cambridge, UK: Cambridge University Press.

Zedner, Lucia. 2007. "Pre-crime and Post Criminology?" *Theoretical Criminology* 11 (2): 261–81.

———. 2010. "Pre-crime and Pre-punishment: A Health Warning." *Criminal Justice Matters* 81 (1): 24–25.

SECTION I

BIG DATA AND CRIME RISKS

Everyday life is filled with numerous interactions with technologies that collect, store, and share our information. Through these interactions we are creating **"big data"** that documents our collective behaviour (Sanders, Christensen, and Weston 2015). The term *big data* is currently a buzzword both within and outside academia (Chan and Bennett Moses 2014). Scholars claim that big data has become an important resource that "will transform how we live, work and think" (Mayer-Schönberger and Cukier 2013, 12). To date, there is no clear or agreed upon definition of big data, but most definitions focus on the three Vs: volume (amount of data), velocity (speed by which it can be processed and analyzed), and variety (number and diversity of databases and sources used) (Chan and Bennett Moses 2014). Big data, by this definition, "refers to things one can do at a large scale that cannot be done at a smaller one, to extract new insights or create new forms of value, in ways that change markets, organizations, the relationship between citizens and governments and more" (Mayer-Schönberger and Cukier 2013, 6).

Yet, such definitions are **technologically determinist** in nature[1]—often focusing on the way big data impacts society, while ignoring how society "gets inside of" and serves to shape big data (Pinch and Bijker 1984; van den Scott,

Sanders, and Puddephatt 2017). boyd and Crawford (2012, 663), on the other hand, argue that big data rests on the interplay of:

(1) *Technology:* maximizing computation power and algorithmic accuracy to gather, analyze, link and compare large data sets.

(2) *Analysis:* drawing on large data sets to identify patterns in order to make economic, social, technical and legal claims.

(3) *Mythology:* the widespread belief that large data sets offer a higher form of intelligence and knowledge that can generate insights that were previously impossible, with the aura of truth, objectivity and accuracy.

By identifying the interplay of technology, analysis, and mythology, they provide a way for scholars to be attentive to the social shaping of big data.

There is considerable hype around the value of big data for predicting and controlling crime by providing public safety organizations with the tools to identify patterns of human behaviour that enable the prediction of future human behaviours. Presently, big data has been incorporated in policing for purposes of mass surveillance, DNA identification, and predictive policing (Babuta 2017). For example, at the 2015 Canadian Summit on the Economics of Policing, Ryan Prox, an intelligence analyst with the Vancouver Police Department, explained how his patrol car computer terminals can *direct* officers to the scenes of crime to "within 100 metres with 70 percent accuracy" *before* the crime occurs. In fact, a recent article in the *Police Chief* claims that predictive policing enables small police forces to work more effectively:

The strategic foundation for predictive policing is clear enough. A smaller, more agile force can effectively counter larger numbers by leveraging intelligence, including the element of surprise. A force that uses intelligence to guide information-based operations can penetrate an adversary's decision cycle and change outcomes, even in the face of a larger opposing force. This strategy underscores the idea that more is not necessarily better, a concept increasingly important today with growing budget pressures and limited resources. (Beck and McCue 2009, para. 10)

Such promises have made big data technologies attractive to government and other public safety organizations. For example, police services are looking to predictive policing software to guide resource allocation in an effort to enhance efficiencies while reducing costs, while corrections are looking toward predictive algorithms for predicting offender rehabilitation. However, available research on police use of big data suggests that the capability of policing agencies to take advantage of big data technologies is uneven (Bennett Moses and Chan 2016; Chan and Bennett Moses 2016a). For example, Babuta (2017) identified a number of "fundamental limitations" to the implementation and effective use of big data technologies, such as fragmented technological platforms and databases; lack of organizational access to, and training for, advanced analytic tools; and legal constraints governing data usage (see also Chan and Bennett Moses 2016a, 2016b; Ridgeway 2018). Further, the risks associated with the use of big data technologies are likely to be met with community concerns about privacy, surveillance, and profiling, while also raising a "myriad of practical and ethical concerns for the processes of criminal justice and society" (McCulloch and Pickering 2009, 628).

The chapters in this section provide important critical insight into various aspects of big data—development, integration, and utilization—for public safety initiatives and preventive justice. The chapters move beyond theoretical or philosophical discussions of the role of, and possible ethical implications associated with, big data to illustrate how big data is as much a social phenomenon as it is a technological one. Collectively, the following chapters reinforce the importance of analyses that are attentive to the ways in which big data technology shape, and are shaped by, economic, political, organizational, and cultural factors.

NOTE

1. Technological determinism consists of two parts: (1) that technological developments occur "outside society, independently of social, economic, and political forces," and (2) that "technological change causes or determines social change" (Wyatt, 2008, 168).

REFERENCES

Babuta, Alexander. 2017. "An Assessment of Law Enforcement Requirements, Expectations and Priorities." *RUSI Occasional Paper*. https://rusi.org/sites/default/files/201709_rusi_big_data_and_policing_babuta_web.pdf.

Beck, Charlie, and Colleen McCue. 2009. "Predictive Policing: What Can We Learn from Wal-Mart and Amazon about Fighting Crime in a Recession?" *Police Chief* 76 (11): 18–24.

Bennett Moses, Lyria, and Janet Chan. 2016. "Algorithmic Prediction in Policing: Assumption Evaluation, and Accountability." *Policing and Society.* http://doi.org/10.1080/10439463.2016.1253695.

boyd, danah, and Kate Crawford. 2012. "Critical Questions for Big Data." *Information, Communication and Society* 15 (5): 662–79.

Chan, Janet, and Lyria Bennett Moses. 2014. "Using Big Data for Legal and Law Enforcement Decisions: Testing the New Tools." *UNSW Law Journal* 37 (2): 643–78.

———. 2016a. "Making Sense of Big Data for Security." *British Journal of Criminology.* http://doi.org/10.1093/bjc/azw059.

———. 2016b. "Is Big Data Challenging Criminology?" *Theoretical Criminology* 20 (1): 21–39.

Mayer-Schönberger, Viktor, and Kenneth Cukier. 2013. *Big Data: A Revolution That Will Transform How We Live, Work and Think.* London: John Murray.

McCulloch, Jude, and Sharon Pickering. 2009. "Pre-crime and Counter-Terrorism: Imagining Future Crime in the War on Terror." *British Journal of Criminology* 49 (5): 628–64.

Pinch, Trevor, and Wiebe E. Bijker. 1984. "The Social Construction of Facts and Artefacts: Or How the Sociology of Science and the Sociology of Technology Might Benefit Each Other." *Social Studies of Science* 14 (3): 399–441.

Ridgeway, Greg. 2018. "Policing in the Era of Big Data." *Annual Review of Criminology* 1: 401–19.

Sanders, Carrie B., Tony Christensen, and Crystal Weston. 2015. "Discovering Crime in a Database: 'Big Data' and the Mangle of Social Problems Work." *Qualitative Sociology Review* 11 (2): 180–95.

van den Scott, Lisa-Jo K., Carrie B. Sanders, and Antony J. Puddephatt. 2017. "Reconceptualizing Users through Enriching Ethnography." In *The Handbook of Science and Technology Studies*, 4th ed., edited by Clark A. Miller et al., 501–27. Cambridge, MA: MIT Press.

Wyatt, Sally. 2008. "Technological Determinism Is Dead; Long Live Technological Determinism." In *The Handbook of Science and Technology Studies*, 3rd ed., edited by Edward J. Hackett, Olga Amsterdamska, Michael Lynch, and Judy Wajcman, 165–80. Cambridge, MA: MIT Press.

1

Technology and Resistance in Mass Preventive Justice[1]

Pat O'Malley

By the late 20th century, new surveillance and informatics technologies epitomized by traffic safety cameras—focused specifically on detecting and preventing risk-laden actions—had become widespread. This development is arguably as significant to the history of criminal justice as was the invention of permanent police forces in the 18th and 19th centuries. The emergence of professional police shifted crime prevention from a spasmodic and largely amateur activity backed up by erratic demonstrations of judicial force to a permanent, disciplined, pervasive, and constantly operating professional apparatus. The new technologies of detection and prevention magnify these preventive potentials of policing, making it possible to subject all "at-risk" spaces and actions to 24/7 panoptic surveillance. More significantly, they focus on prevention in novel ways: through the monitoring and processing of offences that themselves are *defined* by risk.

A shift toward risk-based preventive justice was first registered in relation to what became known as "**actuarial justice.**" Here a **jurisprudence of risk** emerged that justifies the long-term incapacitation or risk-neutralization of offenders (Feeley and Simon 1994). Alongside these changes, and more central to this chapter, increasing numbers of preventive offences have been created for which risk calculations are embedded in the law itself (Fox 1996; O'Malley 2009, 2010). Speeding and drunk driving, in particular, are subject to a jurisprudence of risk: both have become offences defined and justified by risk. That is, both sets of offences are justified by scientific data linking the offence to the statistical potential for future harm. These offences do not require that harm actually occurs—the harm itself is not being punished—rather, the offence is to create a risk of harm. In both cases, scientifically generated risk measures have become integral to the offence. Volumes of alcohol consumption (usually measured by blood alcohol content or BAC) and gradations of speed (especially as measured by remote detection devices) are correlated with rates of injury, death, and property damage, both to justify legal intervention and to calibrate the "seriousness" of the offence. In turn, these risk measures define the offence. In other words, the offence is simply to record a BAC or a speed above a certain defined level—in sum, to exhibit a risk factor. As well, this is risk calibrated: the higher the speed or BAC, the greater the risk, and thus the more severe the sanction.

At first sight, the technological advances in detection and prevention bring to bear a form of justice that is almost irresistible. Justified by a jurisprudence of safety, effected through sophisticated electronic technologies of detection, relatively cheap to operate (especially when contrasted with reliance on police and court labour), and largely sanctioned through revenue neutral or revenue positive sanctions such as fines, **"mass preventive justice"** could appear as infinitely expandable. However, in this chapter, I argue that the implied scientific determinism embedded in this vision of technologically driven risk-based justice fails to consider the possibilities for resistance created by every shift in governance. And, as is often the case, the very strengths of this new technology of risk prove, unexpectedly, to be key sources of vulnerability.

INVENTING MASS PREVENTIVE JUSTICE

Well into the 20th century, drunk driving was judged by individual (in)ability, registered by tests such as walking the white line. Failure to "toe the line" indicated an incapacity to drive and thus the driver could be considered dangerous. Three things should be noted about this. First, individual differences meant that some individuals could drink far more than others yet still pass the test. Second, the test was a matter of individual judgment, usually by a police officer, and thus open to legal challenge. Third, it was always open to dispute whether an individual's behaviour constituted a danger, and thus justified legal intervention (Castel 1991). Much the same was true for speeding. For many years, speeding offences were politically contested because speeding could not always be established as dangerous: it was argued that road conditions and the capacities of the driver and of the vehicle were key variables that made simple measures of speed invalid measures of dangerousness. Speeding was ridiculed as a "tax on progress." In addition, because judgments of speed routinely relied on subjective estimates made by police, only rarely backed up by the marginally more objective use of stopwatches, speeding charges were often challenged effectively and overturned.

As the volume of motorized road traffic increased exponentially after World War II, so too did the scale of death, injury, and property loss associated with it. By the early 1960s this had become a matter of national concern not simply in terms of the individual tragedy of accidents, which had existed from the start, but in the figure of the "road toll" as a threat to the well-being of the population. It was in this context that road deaths and injuries appeared as both a statistical phenomenon and one of national importance, and it was in this context over the ensuing decade or more that traffic safety appeared primarily in the form of aggregate risk rather than individual danger. Thus, risk assessments and legal measures that embraced and embodied these statistical realities proliferated around the road toll: drunk driving, road engineering, vehicle design and equipment and, of course, speeding were all transformed in a relatively short span of time around measures of aggregate risk.

Once speed became a precisely calculable risk factor for death and injury, it came to be associated with new enforcing technologies that operated in the name of a criminal law based on risk. New instruments in the form of speed and red-light cameras—dubbed "safety cameras"—could now measure crime "objectively" and, for that matter, remotely. They could "scientifically" detect *and* calibrate offending, courtesy of risk's objectification in the speed-harm nexus. The same shift emerged with respect to drunk driving with the use of BAC as a scientific measure of risk, and the use of Breathalyzers and random driver testing as a technology of mass detection. These apparatuses detected historically unprecedented volumes of offending (O'Malley 2009, 79–82). Almost unnoticed by criminology, a sea change without comparison in the history of criminal justice had occurred: the creation of "mass preventive justice"—a justice that was founded in risk's objective calculability.

It is possible to speculate why this is so. In part, of course, there is common sense perception that traffic issues are not *really* criminal, except in those cases where culpable loss of life or serious injury is concerned. This is despite the fact that so many "run of the mill" traffic issues do result in criminal prosecutions, and almost all drunk driving, red-light camera, and speeding offences are explicitly matters of criminal law. Many carry the potential for significant penalties, including imprisonment. It should be recognized that this failure of insight by criminologists is not altogether accidental. Much of the legal history of traffic offending has involved changes to procedural matters forced upon the state by the sheer volume of traffic offending. The development of on-the-spot fines was intended to remove traffic matters from the clogged courts, resulting in traffic offences being dropped from criminological agendas. Ironically, a more recent trend toward using penalty notices to deal with offences relating to public order, drunkenness, and the like has become the topic of considerable criminological concern, in large measure because of its net-widening potential and the consequent pressures on those issued with notices to accept (in effect, plead guilty), rather than challenge, the charge. Again, this has been a deliberate strategy: penalty notices very frequently offer a discounted sanction if paid in time, while the decision to proceed to court runs the risk of higher penalties (O'Malley 2013). Given the implications, it is critical for criminologists to consider the dimensions of these efficiency strategies for mass preventive justice.

TECHNOLOGIES OF MASS PREVENTION

As indicated, a key component of the development of risk-based mass preventive justice has been the appearance of an array of monitoring and recording apparatuses including red-light cameras, speed cameras, bus lane cameras, automatic number plate recognition technologies (ANPRs), and so on that are intended not only to detect but also, in important ways, to anticipate and prevent harms. Under a discourse of safety, they register and record offences and infringements, and transmit their data to central computers that, in turn, calculate and issue penalty notices according to simple algorithms. More rarely, they trigger pursuit and apprehension. All actively put into effect what are held to be preventive safety measures against risky offences and offenders.

In key ways this justice is digitized and **informatics**-based. The relevant enforcing technologies associated with such justice digitally register measurably "risky" behaviours. In the era of informatics, they attach these registrations to identifying codes: the digital images of registration plates, bar codes, driver's licences, and so on. These codes attach the action, calibrated as an offence, to a legal subject; however, for the most part, subjects remain electronically coded entities throughout preventive justice procedures, what Deleuze (1995) refers to as **"dividuals,"** corresponding to drivers, owners, operators, and so on. They are detected as codes, and judged and sentenced as codes; through coded informatics they expiate their sentence—overwhelmingly through electronic payment of a fine or cancellation of licence. For the most part, this electronically coded dividualization is what mass preventive justice relies on in order to work. In principle, the technology displaces expensive human labour and attracts fines that pay for its own endless expansion. The trajectory of technological expansion, thus funded, allows for the monitoring of all traffic, everywhere, and at all times.

RESISTANCE AND THE FANTASY OF CONTROL?

It is possible to imaginatively project this diagram of digital apparatuses and routines into a totally governed future, all in the name of risk and safety. This is even more so because, as only hinted at thus far, money is a critical feature of mass preventive justice. I have developed this argument elsewhere at length (O'Malley 2010). The predominance of the fine as the primary sanction in mass preventive justice makes *possible* the funding of its almost infinite expansion. In addition, the low political profile of fines, as merely money, as another price of modern life, can be regarded as minimizing opposition and resistance—especially when compared to the liberal fetish of liberty and corporal pain. The low-stakes nature of fines is likely enhanced when the entire process of such justice is publicly invisible and anonymous, as detection, judgment, and punishment may all be enacted electronically. In the vast majority of cases, there is no court ceremony or public identification and humiliation, and because money is involved, the law in practice cannot and does not investigate who actually pays. It may be the driver's employer, spouse, friend, or parent. What matters is only that money is paid, not who pays it. The principal sanction of criminal justice in this way appears literally rather than figuratively as a monetary price, fixed by a risk calibration and non-negotiable, payable by anyone, not only the wrongdoer. Fines seemingly appear as merely another annoying cost of everyday life in a consumer society.

In this light, mass preventive justice *could* be seen as expanding exponentially at the same time that it is disappearing into the monetized welter of commodified life. In his brief discussion of "control societies," however, Deleuze makes clear that he is presenting a *diagram* of power. That is, it is a model of an ideal knowledge or technology of governance and no more than this. The same needs to be recognized in relation to mass preventive justice. The danger with all such accounts is that they are projected forward into epochal visions in which a process already underway is made to appear as if it will inexorably unfold according to a technologically determined logic. It is a seduction not always resisted by some of Deleuze's most influential interpreters (Bogard 1996). For Deleuze, however, the response to identifying new diagrams of power should be neither to embrace them—for example, control could be seen simply as an escape from discipline's tyranny—nor to dread them as producing an even more perfect micro-management of all life. Rather, we should register the emergence of lines of flight associated with these emergent diagrams—the new and unanticipated directions that are created by, through, and around them—and identify and develop a politics that will locate and minimize the dangerous potentialities that appear.

Yet, if individuals disappear so completely from mass preventive justice, replaced by networked dividuals, then what politics can emerge? How could resistance form around isolated individuals identified mainly as codes, and justice that seemingly disappears into the virtual? How could opposition form against a jurisprudence that is scientifically constituted in terms of preventing or mitigating one of the most common causes of death and injury? What outrage is likely to be stimulated by a monetary sanction that appears little more than literally a mundane price of modern existence, rather than the violation of liberty?

In practice, however, political critiques and new political discourses and solidarities have emerged around such developments, facilitated by the very e-media and technologies upon which the new control technologies themselves depend. In many cases, these potentials for political resistance have been exploited and developed by individuals—or, more precisely, by anonymous individuals often writing under pseudonyms—whose solidarities are generated rather than destroyed by the disaggregation of identity. Separated from large-scale political movements, they form political groupings around single foci such as safety cameras that, as Agamben (1998, 86) expresses it, "form a community without affirming an identity." The politics that have opened up have challenged state-supportive evidence and expertise. In addition, they have directly challenged the money sanctions that the magnitude of perfect detection apparently renders an indispensable (and invisible) sanction for mass prevention. It is significant that the two foci of these "minor" politics have been exactly those—the jurisprudence of risk and safety, and the role of money sanctions—that theoretically driven analyses regard as key *resources* of government (O'Malley 2010). In some ways they have also proven Achilles heels. It is to the examination of these and related discussions concerning the procedures of mass preventive justice and its implied and actual threats to privacy that this analysis now turns.

CHALLENGING THE JURISPRUDENCE OF RISK

As well as being a medium for the expression of resistance, the Internet is a site where governments and their agencies promote mass preventive justice. Fairly typical is the New South Wales Road Transport Authority (RTA), which headlined its web page on mobile speed cameras with the caption, "Capturing speedsters. Anywhere. Anytime." This statement was immediately justified by reference to the road toll in terms of numbers killed and injured.[2] The RTA web page goes on to state that "mobile speed cameras have been introduced because they are recognized internationally as a best practice road safety countermeasure to reduce speeding, leading to a reduction of crashes. The introduction of mobile speed programs in Queensland and Victoria has reduced casualty rates in those states by at least 25 percent."[3] With respect to fixed safety cameras—which may be speed cameras, red-light cameras, or both—the RTA claims that "the use of cameras to enforce speeding has proven road safety benefits," and points out that "independent research found that where cameras have been installed there has been a 70 percent reduction in speeding resulting in a 90 percent decline in fatalities and a 23 percent reduction in injuries."[4] In turn, it claims that safety cameras are installed at sites determined by the number of crashes and the "cost to the community" of these crashes. Further, it is argued that evaluations of point-to-point enforcement—that is, speed cameras that check average speeds over long distances—have shown a 50 percent reduction in fatal and serious injury crashes.[5]

If these claims are taken at face value, then, as noted, they justify the rolling out of more blanket coverage and more sophisticated monitoring systems. But the Internet has proven a singularly effective medium for registering and circulating contradictory evidence. The most frequent challenges involve straightforward claims that data are far more varied and unclear than police and road safety authorities admit. In Britain, for example, a good deal of such critique has arisen around decisions by (largely conservative) local councils in 2010 to scrap the widespread use of speed cameras because of doubts about their effectiveness.[6] In many examples cited there was no increase in the rate of accidents after the removal of cameras (e.g., Tozer 2010). But what clearly triggered enduring and widespread concern was evidence on such activist sites as www.policespeedcameras.info that British government figures "showed for 32 speed camera sites there were an average of 48 *more* accidents involving death or serious injury" over the previous 12 months, while at 38 red-light camera sites there had been "an average of 62 *more* accidents" (Williams 2005; emphasis added). The reported increase in accidents clearly concerned most online contributors. Motoring association sites admitted being baffled and concerned, sometimes suggesting that there were "individual reasons" at each site. Sometimes speculations were put forward, such as that by the Royal Automobile Club, that "there could be a conflict between motorists who slow down for cameras and the growing underclass of unregistered drivers who do not" (Williams 2005). The most frequent claim was that drivers were distracted by cameras, although evidence was invariably anecdotal.[7]

In 2005, *Times Online* reported that the government was blocking the installation of nearly 500 new speed cameras "amid signs that many are beginning to doubt the effectiveness of the devices. The 38 camera partnerships which include police forces and local authorities have been ordered not to use cameras in any new sites" (Webster 2005). It is worthy of note that the Association of Chief Police Officers (ACPO) condemned the ban, saying "it could cost lives because dangerous roads were being left unprotected by cameras" (Webster 2005). But this argument was largely ignored except in corporate media sites. At the same time, it was reported that "the Department for Transport is reviewing the rules on deploying cameras after concerns that partnerships have failed to consider alternatives such as improving junctions or erecting warnings" (Webster 2005). Even the Parliamentary Advisory Council for Transport Safety admitted online that while it supported speed cameras, "in some cases partnerships may have chosen to install a camera when an engineering solution may have been better" (Webster 2005). Certainly this reflected long-held views expressed online from non-official sources. It was duly noticed by such opponents that cameras represent a considerably cheaper and easier option than engineering at locations where concerns had arisen about accident rates. Indeed, the UK Road Safety Minister was widely reported online as saying that the government would cut funding because local government bodies had relied too heavily on safety cameras for too long, and the focus needed to be on other safety measures. The lines between party politics and dividual politics converged.

As noted, a wide array of postings reported instances where the installation of speed cameras had *increased* accident rates. Bloggers have said that one study by a British insurance company in 2010 claimed that 28,000 road accidents have been triggered by speed cameras as drivers slowed down ahead of them and then sped up once they had passed them (Tozer 2010). It was also widely posted that the introduction of speed cameras and new speed limits in Australia's Northern Territory was associated with a 36 percent increase in road deaths, and in Cumbria, England, such deaths were reported to have risen by 40 percent after the introduction of speed cameras (Cavanagh 2008). In particular, one "secret" UK Ministry of Transport study (which online bloggers claimed could only be accessed after a Freedom of Information Act request) received huge Internet coverage because it showed a 55 percent increase in injury accidents when speed cameras were used at highway work zones, and a 31 percent increase when used on motorways where there were no road works.[8] Such data were associated with a mass demonstration on Britain's M4 motorway involving over 400 vehicles on the grounds that "safe driving is too complex to be measured in miles per hour" and that speed cameras had distracted government from more effective interventions because of their ease of installation and other revenue-related advantages. Individual voices added anecdotal evidence, a typical example (from hundreds) claiming that "speedcams make things more dangerous, not safer. You have to slow down really quickly from 70mph to 40mph and motorists slam on their brakes at the last moment."[9] One commentator went so far as to argue that "most accidents are caused because drivers are unable to concentrate on the road because they are looking for cameras."[10] In short, the online politics brought together competing and conflicting expert commentaries, and to these added the experiential politics of the discontented subjects of control.

Newspaper reports were also rebroadcast online when—for example, in Melbourne in 2004—predictions that accident rates would increase when speed cameras were withdrawn proved false. Thus

The Age newspaper was extensively quoted as arguing that this "raises questions about the Government's strong linking of speed camera enforcement to reductions in the road toll. The police figures compare Ring Road crash and injury statistics from 2002 and 2003 with data from the first 10 months of this year [2004]."[11] "Between January and the end of October, there were 60 crashes causing injury on the Ring Road. The year before there were 91 injury-causing crashes and 70 in 2002."[12]

Many online commentators highlighted the paradox that while speed cameras were attributed with reducing accidents in black spots, in practice it could often be found that overall accident rates at national or local government levels did not decline, and even that long-term declines had been turned around since the introduction of cameras. For example, the CEO of the British Institute of Advanced Motorists, self-proclaimed as "the largest road safety charity in the country," made the claim that speed cameras created feelings of resentment and victimization that led to a disrespect for speed limits. Thus, overall, many opponents concluded that while safety may or may not increase around cameras, crashes are driven elsewhere, and this accounts for the failure of road carnage to decline.[13] Most commonly aired were observations that cameras distracted drivers, with the president of the (US) National Motorists Association taking the view that an increase in speed limits in the United States contributed to declines in accident rates because "now motorists can coast at these faster speeds without being on the constant lookout for radar guns, speed traps and state troopers."[14] Such displacement arguments were common but rarely evidenced; however, this hardly halted strong opposition based on the assumption that it was fact. In one of the more extreme statements, Paul Smith, the founder of the British site SafeSpeed, proclaimed, "We must get these dangerous cameras off the roads right now. People are dying because of them. The term 'safety cameras' will go down in history as a sick joke."[15]

Red-light cameras have been the subject of a nearly equal amount of criticism. Overall, even government and other official research reports indicate that their benefits are mixed, with a tendency for right-angle crashes (which are more often fatal and injurious) to decrease, but for tail-end accidents to increase significantly—largely attributed to drivers braking suddenly at camera-controlled intersections.[16] However, other studies were cited, including a seven-year study of red-light cameras in the US District of Columbia that concluded there was no evidence of reductions in accidents or injuries, and there was evidence of significant increases in certain locales. As a result of such mixed findings, several US states that had installed red-light cameras abandoned the program, including Virginia and Hawaii, while an array of others have banned their future use (House Research Organization 2006).

Finally, claims of the success of speed cameras have been undermined by campaigns challenging them on various technical grounds. Specific conflicts have arisen around claims that individual speed cameras exaggerate recordings, resulting in unjustified prosecutions. In 2011, Alberta cancelled around 100,000 speeding tickets issued in the previous 14 months due to driver-led concerns with the accuracy of equipment (Wingrove 2011). The disabling of speed cameras on Melbourne's Ring Road system in 2004 was the direct consequence of an admission by the government that possibly thousands of drivers had been fined as a result of faulty cameras, a problem that also resulted in the 2009 disabling of the point-to-point cameras on that state's freeways.

It should be made clear that it is not my aim or interest to verify data or to arbitrate these disputes. Some have led to the withdrawal of cameras, while others are almost laughably inaccurate. The key points are two. First, it is by no means the case that we can witness an unresisted, technologically driven rollout of mass preventive justice in the largest field of such intervention. Second, the virtual environment has been a significant resource of opposition. While the politics of dispute flow back and forth between arenas of traditional politics and the Internet, as should be anticipated, resistance has been extensively mobilized by and between dividuals operating on single-issue politics. Contributors almost never reveal or raise class, education, gender, political party, or other traditional political solidarities. Their solidarity is formed around their dividuated status.

Their politics is challenging the technology of mass preventive justice, rather than its purported aims of producing increased safety. These challenges to the risk-based jurisprudence and apparatus on which mass preventive justice is founded were effected by various means: by valorizing conflicting conclusions of expert studies and experiential observations that conflicted with developing preventive practices and technologies, by proposing that risk reduction may be better achieved by other techniques, and by challenging universal explanations through reference to the impact of diverse local conditions (Wynne 1996). By challenging the scientific standing of the jurisprudence of risk in a key respect these online politics reveal that its strength—and thus a key strength of mass preventive justice—is also a major source of vulnerability.

CONTESTING MONEY SANCTIONS

It has already been suggested that money is one of the keys to understanding mass preventive justice. At least on the face of it, the fact that money sanctions are so cheap to administer compared to most other sanctions, linked with the fact that fines (and associated fees) produce revenues for the state, has made possible the sheer scale of traffic governance. As well, it has been suggested that the low political profile of money sanctions compared to the traditional penalties of liberal criminal law has made this expansion possible without raising insuperable barriers to the development of a form of criminal governance that governs populations not normally the target of punitive justice. Moreover, money may be directly connected to yet other facets of mass preventive justice. The (re)appearance of fines in the early 20th century was associated with the development of streamlined procedures in summary justice. The "it's only money" effect facilitated such stripping away of procedure precisely because liberty was not directly at stake (O'Malley 2009).

Yet money has proven to be a vulnerable preventive strategy. The reliance on fines was potentially a money-spinner for governments at all levels—and this was the ticking time bomb. Reflecting trends in the United States, Canada, and Australia, in 2010 the Conservative-led government in Britain began to respond to an enormous volume of complaints that despite official guidelines that prioritize accident prevention, speed cameras were not placed in areas of high accident risk but rather were placed where they could earn the most revenue. Such claims were commonplace on the Internet for a decade and were amplified when translated into party politics. In the United States, in particular, campaigns around this issue were prominent among factors leading to cameras being turned off in Texas as early as the 1980s, and later in Arizona, Illinois, and Alaska (House Research Organization 2006). In 2011, the New South Wales government banned the further rollout of speed cameras until the results of an audit, triggered by claims that some of the highest-earning cameras were in areas where crashes had never been a significant problem, were published. The government promised that where it could be shown that cameras were not proven to produce a measurable effect in increasing safety, they would be removed. Eventually 38 of 141 cameras were removed on these grounds (Smith 2011). In Britain, the 2005 rollout ban imposed by the government led to a multitude of posts repeating a *Times Online* claim that "[traffic safety] partnership staff may favour cameras over other solutions (because) they need to ensure a steady flow of income to pay their salaries" (Webster 2005). No doubt it is significant that while this report was widely aired, counterclaims from ACPO at the time, stating that all sites submitted for approval had met official guidelines, were generally marginalized or ignored (Webster 2005).

While the volume of money generated was not the only factor that raised opposition, this was the most frequently mentioned issue and generated high-profile cases. In Britain, one camera became the target of a political campaign because it was reported to have earned £1.3 million over the previous decade on a strip of dual carriageway, while in New South Wales another was reported to have earned AU$2.2 million in the 2010–11 financial year.[17] Some governments, such as that in the UK until 2007, dedicated the income generated to improvements in road safety, but more commonly—argued on the basis of budgetary rationality—treated fines simply as part of consolidated revenue. This, of course, makes governments vulnerable, especially as it leads to income from fines appearing in forward-planning estimates in state budgets.

Elsewhere forms of guerrilla action emerged. Some deployed humour—for example, where signs advertising speed cameras were altered to read "greed cameras," provoking online sympathetic responses, such as,

"Every time I see one of these signs has been altered I have got to laugh. The government and police are making a tidy sum from these cameras" (Levy 2006). More extreme saboteurs began destroying cameras. In Britain, in Essex alone, six cameras were set on fire (with each unit costing an estimated £24,000). In one instance, websites created a social bandit out of a figure named Captain Gatso (Gatsometer is the name of a brand of speed camera), who grandly announced a struggle "against an unjust form of taxation" and threatened "increased operations across the country" (Khan 2003). A group called MAD (Motorists Against Detection), which reported itself as having a core of 200 members, claimed responsibility for having destroyed 1,000 cameras since the year 2000. The group claimed to use "Internet chat forums, encrypted email and pay as you go phones to keep in touch and plan campaigns" (Khan 2003). In practice, this group—referred to insightfully in *The Guardian* newspaper as "a gang of web-surfing outlaws"—may have involved only a handful of isolated individuals, although the press estimated that some 700 cameras had been destroyed across the nation, with particularly active cells in Essex, Wales, and London (Khan 2003). The importance of such accounts is not so much the reality of the threats they posed; it was, rather, the symbolic role they appeared to occupy in an active online opposition movement mobilized primarily by the perception that money fines were an index of government agencies using the jurisprudence of risk as a cover for revenue-raising.

CONCLUSIONS

Central to the overall argument of this chapter is that technological determinism is a dangerous tendency when analyzing changes in governance, and that every advance in technology creates new and unanticipated potentials for resistance. However, a series of cautions is essential to forestall expectations that resistance will always be effective, that resistance is always progressive (whatever we mean by that term), or that resistance can be read in blanket terms as opposition *tout court*.

To begin with, it should be noted that much opposition is not to safety regulation as such, nor, largely at least, to risk-based justice. Claims that equipment is faulty, that accident statistics are not accurate, that cameras are not placed in high-risk traffic sites, and even that the state is more interested in revenue collection than safety are all readily soluble within the existing assemblage of mass preventive justice. Indeed, in most respects such critiques simply demand improvements in technology or its application that would refine the system in ways perfectly consistent with the jurisprudence of safety. In the medium to long term, far from implying a winding back or cessation of mass preventive justice, much of this opposition likely contributes to the future practical efficacy and ideological legitimacy of the system.

In the more radical forms of critique, certainly there is a potential for challenge to fundamentals. This is possible where, for example, opponents argue that local knowledge of roads and conditions is superior to that of abstract experts and their technologies. Likewise, such challenges could be seen where it is argued that technologies have unanticipated adverse effects—such as distracting drivers—that increase rather than decrease rates of accident. However, even these matters do not strike at the heart of this form of regulation. In almost all cases, dispute could be resolved one way or the other by further research on traffic behaviour. Is driver distraction a factor, and to what extent? Do drivers speed up after leaving monitored zones and thus cause accidents elsewhere? Do drivers with local knowledge make better judgments of risk than abstract expertise? Do decelerating drivers approaching speed cameras cause accidents? Not only are these empirically soluble questions, but even were the answers counter to the assumptions of system planners, the result is more likely to be further refinement and distribution of the assemblage, and subsequent improvement of its risk-reduction.

It should also be considered that even the most ferocious opponents of cameras claim to support road safety, and some of the most critical among these support the idea of cracking down on those hard cases who grossly exceed speed limits rather than "accidentally" straying. Likewise, there is no significant opposition to the system of demerit points, presumably for reasons consistent with the above; that is, only persistent and egregious offenders have their licences cancelled through this means. Furthermore, there is little or no resistance to the technological justice aimed at detecting and sanctioning drunk driving—for which the penalty is usually both disqualification and a fine. In many respects, the apparently radical politics of mass preventive justice is surprisingly conventional and socially wholesome in its defence of a "proper" regime of safety. Thus, while the critical politics of mass preventive justice is often fierce, even if all its claims prove justified, they would not necessarily result in significant winding back, and almost certainly not the dismantling, of mass preventive justice. Rather, the source of a possible demise of mass preventive justice lies elsewhere altogether.

It is a characteristic of the oppositional discourses examined in this chapter that where they do argue for alternatives to speed cameras and fines, they do not argue for other systems of justice and punishment but for better road engineering and increased vehicle safety. That is, they call for a different diagram of risk-based "control." It is easy to forget that road engineering immanently modulates risk, and governs circulations and distributions anonymously. Its archetype, perhaps, is the speed hump; its future may be driverless vehicles and/or systems of remote electronic vehicle control. Both are more or less on the doorstep and, if rolled out on a mass scale, conceivably would render the apparatus of mass preventive justice redundant. The dream of perfect prevention could thus be realized—or at least we could say that the governance of drivers would wither away. For this reason alone it should not be assumed that mass preventive justice and its assemblage of remote surveillance technologies, coupled with electronically issued and expiated fines and licence cancellations, is the future. Other risk-based technologies of governance are emerging but, as ever, other forms of resistance will emerge along with them.

DISCUSSION QUESTIONS

1. What is mass preventive justice?
2. Can you think of a few other examples where fines are merely "another annoying cost of everyday life in consumer society"? Does it matter who actually pays? What does this say about how fines are meant to govern risks in the examples that you have provided?

3. Are speed cameras actually effective? Would improvements to existing technologies help refine and justify the "jurisprudence of safety"? Why or why not?

4. How is the move toward mass preventive justice an example of broader changes in society—for example, the monitoring of credit card transactions, web-surfing activity, and smartphone usage—that use electronic tracking to govern risks in everyday life?

NOTES

1. This chapter draws on and develops arguments made in an earlier paper dealing with the issue of the politics of mass preventive justice (O'Malley 2013).

2. "Mobile Speed Cameras" at http://www.rta.nsw.gov.au/roadsafety/speedand speedcameras/avespeedsafetycameras/index.html (accessed May 16, 2016; link no longer available).

3. "Mobile Speed Cameras."

4. "Mobile Speed Cameras."

5. "Mobile Speed Cameras."

6. For an overview of this local politics and the data generated, see http://en.wikipedia .org/wiki/Traffic_enforcement_camera (accessed May 16, 2016).

7. "England and Scotland Speed Camera News" at http://www.policespeedcameras .info/Speed_Camera_News_United_Kingdom/uk_news (accessed May 16, 2016; link no longer available).

8. Available at http://www.roadsense.com.au/latest.html (accessed May 16, 2016; link no longer available).

9. "Speedcam Doubles Smashes on UK M-Way" at http://www.policespeedcameras .info/Speed_Camera_News_United_Kingdom/uk_news (accessed May 16, 2016; link no longer available).

10. Brian Gregory, spokesperson for the Association of British Drivers, quoted in Penny Stretton, "More Councils Poised to Scrap Speed Cameras" (2008, October 24), *Daily Express*. It is typical to see an anti-speed-camera advocate quoted in the printed media and then to have that quote placed online by another anti-speed-camera organization—in this case by http://www.roadsense.com.

11. Available at http://www.roadsense.com.au/latest.html (accessed May 16, 2016).

12. *The Age* (2004, December 2).

13. Available at http://www.policespeedcameras.info/Speed_Camera_News_United _Kingdom/uk_news (accessed May 16, 2016).

14. "With Higher Speed Limits American Highways Are Getting Safer" at http:// www.roadsense.com.au/latest.html (accessed May 16, 2016).

15. Quoted by the Australian site Roadsense.au: "Roads Fatalities Leap 39 Percent at Camera Sites" at http://www.roadsense.org.au/latest (accessed May 16, 2016).

16. See "Red Light Camera" at http://en.wikipedia.org/wiki/Red_light_camera (accessed May 16, 2016).

17. "Cash Cow Speed Cameras Raise $350m" (2011, June 2), *Sydney Morning Herald*.

REFERENCES

Agamben, Giorgio. 1998. *Homo Sacer: Sovereign Power and Bare Life*. Stanford, CA: Stanford University Press.

Bogard, William. 1996. *The Simulation of Surveillance: Hypercontrol in Telematic Societies*. Cambridge, UK: Cambridge University Press.

Castel, Robert. 1991. "From Dangerousness to Risk." In *The Foucault Effect*, edited by Graham Burchell, Colin Gordon, and Peter Miller, 281–98. Chicago: University of Chicago Press.

Cavanagh, Rebekah. 2008. "Northern Territory Road Toll Soars as Speed Cameras Take Their Toll." *Northern Territory News*, September 20, 2008.

Deleuze, Gilles. 1995. "Postscript on Control Societies." In *Negotiations, 1972–1990*, edited by Gilles Deleuze, 177–82. New York: Columbia University Press.

Feeley, Malcolm, and Jonathan Simon. 1994. "Actuarial Justice: The Emerging New Criminal Law." In *The Futures of Criminology*, edited by David Nelken, 173–201. London: Sage.

Fox, Richard G. 1996. *Criminal Justice on the Spot: Infringement Penalties in Victoria*. Canberra: Australian Institute of Criminology.

House Research Organization. 2006. *Red Light Cameras in Texas: A Status Report*. Austin: Texas House of Representatives. https://hro.house.texas.gov/focus/ redlight79-15.pdf.

Khan, Stephen. 2003. "Saboteurs Take Out 700 Speed Cameras." *The Guardian*, September 7, 2003. https://www.theguardian.com/uk/2003/sep/07/transport.ukcrime.

Levy, Andrew. 2006. "Flash of Wit (But Police Don't Think It's Funny)." *Daily Mail*, August 25, 2006. https://www.pressreader.com/uk/daily-mail/20060825/282209416330581.

O'Malley, Pat. 2009. *The Currency of Justice*. London: Routledge.

———. 2010. "Simulated Justice: Risk, Money and Telemetric Policing." *British Journal of Criminology* 50 (5): 795–807.

———. 2013. "Mass Preventive Justice." In *Prevention and the Limits of Criminal Law*, edited by Andrew Ashworth, Lucia Zedner, and Patrick Tomlin, 273–95. Oxford: Hart Publishing.

Smith, Alexandra. 2011. "Top Speed Cameras Still Make a Fast Buck." *Sydney Morning Herald*, July 28, 2011. http://www.walk.com.au/pedestriancouncil/page.asp?pageid=5436.

Tozer, James. 2010. "Town that Scrapped 'Motorist Tax' Speed Cameras Sees No Increase in Accidents." *Daily Mail*, April 24, 2010. http://www.dailymail.co.uk/news/article-1268392/Town-scrapped-speed-cameras-sees-increase-accidents.html.

Webster, Ben. 2005. "Speed Camera U Turn as 500 Sites Rejected." *The Times*, July 15, 2005. https://www.thetimes.co.uk/article/speed-camera-u-turn-as-500-sites-rejected-hctvj935n2m.

Williams, David. 2005. "Speed Cameras May Cause Accidents." *Evening Standard*, June 24, 2005. https://www.standard.co.uk/news/speed-cameras-may-cause-accidents-7208550.html.

Wingrove, Josh. 2011. "Alberta to Refund $13M in Speeding Fines; Photo Radar Network in Doubt." *Globe and Mail*, January 24, 2011. https://beta.theglobeandmail.com/news/national/alberta-to-refund-13m-in-speeding-fines-photo-radar-network-in-doubt/article563318.

Wynne, Brian. 1996. "May the Sheep Safely Graze? A Reflexive View of the Expert-Lay Knowledge Divide." In *Risk, Environment and Modernity*, edited by Scott Lash, Bronislaw Szerszynski, and Brian Wynne, 44–83. London: Routledge.

2 Can "Big Data" Analytics Predict Policing Practice?

Janet Chan and Lyria Bennett Moses[1]

In *Policing the Risk Society*, Ericson and Haggerty (1997, 3) have offered a "fundamental reassessment of how we think about police." Writing in the late 1990s, Ericson and Haggerty conceptualized police as "knowledge workers" in the "risk society" (Beck 1992). Rather than seeing policing only as "what the public police do," the authors argue that "policing consists of the public police coordinating their activities with policing agents in all other institutions to provide a society-wide basis for risk management (governance) and security (guarantee against loss)" (Ericson and Haggerty 1997, 3). Police mobilization is therefore "not only a matter of intervention in the lives of individual citizens but also a response to institutional demands for knowledge of risk" (1997, 5). Ericson and Haggerty (1997, 114) have identified two technological inventions that "have made a profound contribution to the constituting of risk society"—statistical thinking and communication technology:

> Statistics and probability theory, constituted in computer formats, structure truth. They present risk data as the basis of an objective standard that people *must* accept as objective reality and therefore use to form their identities and behaviour. Although the risk classifications and categories, and the resultant identities and behaviour,

are socially constructed, once in place they are "relative to nothing"; and become *the* standard (Hacking 1992, 135). They become truly rational and drive social change by routinizing it in institutional procedures. (Ericson and Haggerty 1997, 115)

The authors suggest that computers "allow the development of new formats of risk communication, as well as instant dispersal of knowledge of risk to interested institutions" (1997, 13).

The advent of big data analytics appears to be a continuation or even an escalation of this trend to combine statistical thinking and communication technology to present "risk data." As we have previously pointed out (Chan and Bennett Moses 2016, 23), the term *big data* is defined in a variety of ways: "by reference to the size and type of data sets being employed, the capabilities of a data storage, processing and/or analytic system, as a set of marketing claims about what is enabled by particular technologies or as a social and cultural phenomenon." While there are many potential uses of big data technology to policing (e.g., the automation of intelligence gathering through social media analysis), an important application of data analytics is the use of computer modelling or algorithms as predictive tools for risk analysis or crime prevention.

The rise of **predictive policing** goes beyond hot spot analysis, problem-oriented policing, and crime mapping to use data and analytics to "forecast where and when the next crime or series of crimes will take place" (Uchida 2014, 3871). These predictions can be about identifying "places and times with an increased risk of crime" or "individuals at risk of offending in the future," creating "profiles that accurately match likely offenders with specific past crimes" or identifying groups or individuals at risk of becoming victims of crime (Perry et al. 2013, 8–9). In addition to forecasting, predictive policing involves taking a proactive response to crime where the goal is to change outcomes (Beck and McCue 2009) through the identification of crime prevention tactics/strategies—mostly changes to police deployments—and the evaluation of police programs (Wilson et al. 2009). The apparently enthusiastic uptake of predictive policing software in the United States and elsewhere (see Bennett Moses and Chan 2018), together with the hype of big data, has created a new orthodoxy that technology can make policing "smarter" and information-based, rather than subject to human bias and occupational habits.

This chapter will focus on the following research question: What factors are likely to influence the adoption and impact of big data analytics for predictive policing?[2] Given the limited availability of independent evaluations of predictive policing, this chapter reviews past and current research on the use of technology or innovation by police and develops a framework for conceptualizing factors that affect the uptake of predictive policing and the processes that influence its impact on policing practice.[3]

The argument of the chapter will unfold as follows. The first section describes the attractions of data analytics for policing, the state of current development, and the extent to which it has been taken up by police organizations. In order to answer the research question posed, the next section develops a conceptual framework for analyzing the diffusion, uptake, and impact of policing technology. This framework draws on organization and policy studies, and empirical research on past instances of policing innovations. The section that follows assesses the likely uptake and impact on policing practice of predictive policing using current knowledge about predictive policing, and empirical research in Australia. The final section summarizes the analysis and discusses its theoretical and practical implications.

PREDICTIVE POLICING TECHNOLOGY

Predictive policing is a term applied to a range of analytic tools and law enforcement practices linked by the claimed ability to "forecast where and when the next crime or series of crimes will take place" (Uchida 2014, 3871), combined with changes in law enforcement decision making, particularly deployment of officers, based on those forecasts. As practised, mostly within the United States but also elsewhere, the analytic element typically involves an off-the-shelf or adapted software tool that analyzes historic crime data (and sometimes other data such as social media, weather, and mortgage defaults) to predict most commonly where, but sometimes by whom or to whom, crime will take place in the future.

Software used for predictive policing can range from simple spreadsheet programs to complex algorithms. It can be open source or very expensive (Olesker 2012), purchased off the shelf or specially tailored. Information on the tools themselves is often limited, and source code is often a trade secret. This makes it difficult to evaluate products provided by organizations such as IBM, Information Builders (Law Enforcement Analytics), SPADAC (Signature Analyst), Accenture, Palantir, Motorola (CommandCentral Predictive), LexisNexis (BAIR Analytics ATACRAIDS), Esri (GIS Crime Analysis Toolbox), Intrado (Beware), and Hitachi. There are some products about which more is known. For example, Hardyns and Rummens (2017) note some specific differences among PredPol, HunchLab, PreCobs, and Amsterdam's Crime Anticipation System, including the number of variables used by different products, method of data collection, crime types targeted, and special and temporal resolution. There is some information about PredPol because it is based on published research work centred at UCLA and Santa Clara University using an earthquake prediction model involving a self-excited point process (Mohler et al. 2011). Essentially, predicted rates of crime at a particular location were based on background factors as well as the "near repeat" (or aftershock) events related to historic events nearby in time and space. Outputs are 500-square-foot areas where it is predicted crime is more likely to occur. Police are then assigned to focus patrols on those areas. HunchLab has published a citizen's guide (Heffner 2017) that explains its methodology, also pointing out some advantages and limitations of its approach and assumptions. Rutgers Center on Public Security offers risk terrain modelling (RTM) through a product called RTMDx, with extensive material available on its website.

As a phenomenon, predictive policing is more than a set of tools or the ways in which they are used within particular police departments; it also relies on a belief that the use of these tools in particular ways is effective in reducing crime. More specifically, predictive policing is premised on the assumptions that it is possible to use technology to predict the likelihood of crime before it happens (Van Brakel and De Hert 2011), that forecasting tools can predict accurately, and that police will use this knowledge effectively.

An increasing number of police organizations report using predictive policing tools, mostly to identify areas where the likely frequency of future crime is higher. Focusing solely on tools that are explicitly forward-looking or predictive, non-exhaustive media searches and literature (including grey literature such as Robinson and Koepke [2016]) revealed the adoption of predictive policing software and approaches in the following jurisdictions:

Asia: Delhi, India (Enterprise Information Integration Solution), China (Situation-Aware Public Security Evaluation [SAPE] platform)

Europe: Amsterdam (Crime Anticipation System), Birmingham UK (Accenture), Germany (Oberhausen, München, Nürnberg, Ansbach, Stuttgart, and Karlsruhe) (PreCobs), Kent UK (PredPol), London UK (Accenture, PredPol), Manchester UK (PredPol, SPSS/IBM), Milan, Italy (KeyCrime), Northern Ireland UK (IBM), Switzerland (Zürich, Basel, and Aargau) (PreCobs)

North America: Albuquerque NM, Alhambra CA (PredPol), Atlanta GA (PredPol), Bellingham WA (ATACRAIDS), Baltimore MD (IBM, discontinued), Baltimore County MD (IBM), Boston area MA (Smart Policing Initiative), Burbank CA (discontinued), Charleston SC (SPSS/IBM), Charlotte-Mecklenburg NC (Information Builders Law Enforcement Analytics), Chicago IL (Strategic Subject List, RTM, Predictive Analytics Group), Cocoa FL (PredPol), Dallas TX (for financial crimes), Detroit MI (Datameer), Fort Lauderdale FL (IBM), Fresno CA (Beware, PredPol), Illinois State Police (Riverglass), Indio CA (Smart Policing Initiative[4]), Kansas City KS (Information Builders Law Enforcement Analytics, Smart Policing Initiative, RTM), Lincoln NE (HunchLab), Los Angeles CA (PredPol, Smart Policing Initiative, Palantir), Macon GA (SPSS/IBM gun crime only), Memphis TN (IBM Blue CRUSH), Miami FL (IBM Blue

PALMS, HunchLab), Milpitas CA (PredPol, contract terminated), Minneapolis MN (IBM, MPD Crime Analysis Unit), Modesto CA (PredPol), Nashville TN (arcGIS and bespoke), Nassau County NY (bespoke Nass-Stat), New Orleans LA (Palantir, PredPol), New York City NY (HunchLab), Newark NJ (RTM), Norcross GA (PredPol), Oklahoma City OK (ATACRAIDS), Philadelphia PA (HunchLab), Phoenix AZ (ATACRAIDS), Port George's County MD (Information Builders), Richmond VA (PredPol, discontinued), St. Louis County MO (HunchLab), Santa Cruz CA (PredPol, introduced July 1, 2011), San Diego CA (Department of Justice grant), San Jose CA (The Omega Group), Seattle WA (PredPol), Shreveport LA (funded by NIJ), Suffolk County NY (modelled on CompStat), Tacoma WA (PredPol, HunchLab), Toledo OH (HunchLab), Vancouver BC (bespoke)[5]
South America: Sao Paulo, Brazil (Microsoft Detecta rolled out in January 2015)

It is likely that the actual adoption of predictive policing is even more widespread, with the Police Executive Research Forum (2014, 3) citing a survey suggesting that 38 percent of responding US police departments were using predictive policing at the time.

The underlying model of predictive policing is described in Perry et al. (2013, 128). As they state, predictive policing is "not fundamentally about making crime-related predictions" but about implementing a prediction-led policing business *process*, which consists of a cycle of activities and decision points: data collection, analysis, police operations, criminal response, and back to data collection. Each stage of the cycle involves choices that are made under diverse organizational conditions. For example, choices must be made about what types of data to collect and how frequently to collect it, and data analysis may be carried out in-house (with greater or fewer human and financial resources) or using a standard software package (Perry et al. 2013).

The term *predictive policing* enters the fray amidst a variety of other related but distinct terms describing policing approaches and styles. For example, predictive policing is clearly a type of **intelligence-led**

policing (Maguire 2000, 315) and data-driven policing. It is consistent with a temporal shift from post-crime to pre-crime and pre-emptive approaches in policing (Van Brakel and De Hert 2011; Zedner 2007), and shifts the focus of criminal justice apparatuses from punishment for moral failings to risk management and loss prevention (Ericson and Haggerty 1997; Zedner 2007). Particularly where predictive policing focuses on the locations of future crimes, it is closely related to "hot spot" policing (Sherman, Gartin, and Buerger 1989), except that it explicitly models the likely future locations of hot spots, often through evidence of the statistically broader geographical impact of a single crime event (e.g., Bowers, Johnson, and Pease 2004). Some police activities, such as monitoring social media feeds in real time during large events or automatically analyzing video feeds from closed-circuit television (CCTV) cameras to detect criminal activity, may be part of a predictive approach to policing, or may be used as a form of situational awareness as to the present.[6]

UNDERSTANDING THE DIFFUSION, UPTAKE, AND IMPACT OF TECHNOLOGY IN POLICING

While research on the diffusion, uptake, and impact of technology on policing is scarce (Manning 2014), there are a number of studies on the uptake and impact of policing *innovations* (see Willis and Mastrofski 2011) such as problem-oriented policing (Weisburd et al. 2010), hot spot policing (Braga, Papachristos, and Hureau 2014), intelligence-led policing (Darroch and Mazerolle 2012; Sanders, Weston, and Schott 2015), and community policing (Chan 1997; Graziano, Rosenbaum, and Schuck 2014). These studies can inform our development of a framework for understanding why certain technology is adopted and the technology's impact on policing practices. Predictive policing is in fact an innovation in *process* or, as Perry et al. (2013, 128) call it, a "prediction-led policing process."

We will continue to use the term *technology*, given the dependence of data analytics on technological advances such as the speed and capacity of data collection and data storage in relation to predictive policing processes. Nevertheless, technology needs to be conceptualized more broadly as consisting of three dimensions: (1) the *technical*, as already mentioned; (2) the *symbolic*—the ideological or discursive representation of how the technology is promoted, especially its narrative of being scientific and innovative; and (3) the *organizational*—the institutional or group interests that are at stake in the uptake of this technology.[7] For example, in predictive policing, the "marketing" or hype of this technology (the symbolic dimension) and the potential interests of policing agencies in enhancing efficiency and effectiveness (the organizational dimension) have been as important as, if not more important than, its actual technological capabilities.

UPTAKE AND IMPACT OF TECHNOLOGY

Two key elements in the framework we are developing in this section also require more discussion. The first is the *uptake* or adoption of technology and the second the *impact* of technology. As research in social studies of technology show, the uptake or adoption of technological innovations is never an all or nothing phenomenon. There are various degrees of uptake: acceptance of the ideas underlying the technology, decisions by leaders of organizations to invest in the technology, purchase of equipment or software associated with it, piloting of the technology in parts of the organization, or full-blown adoption of the technology throughout the organization.

Once taken up (to whatever degree), the technology has to be implemented before it can have an impact on practice. The importance of implementation cannot be overstated, and this will be discussed below. A more immediate concern is how evaluators define and detect impact. An important concept in this chapter is the notion of *practice*, which is central to our understanding of how technology makes an impact (see Chan 2003; Feldman and Orlikowski 2011; and, more generally, theorists of practice such as Piere Bourdieu, Anthony Giddens, and Theodore R. Schatzki). Assessing the impact of a new technology requires an appreciation that "technology is not valuable, meaningful, or consequential by itself; it only becomes so when people actually engage with it in practice" (Feldman and Orlikowski 2011, 1246). **Technology in practice** can be quite different from the "strategic design" and anticipated uses of managers and technologists; applications and their consequences may be unintended and unexpected (Feldman and Orlikowski 2011, 1246). Organizational outcomes, or the impacts of innovation, are shaped more by "the specific technologies in practice (enacted technology structures) that are recurrently produced in everyday action" than by the technological tools themselves or by hypothesized or general uses (Feldman and Orlikowski 2011, 1247). Technology in practice is recursive—over time, particular users draw on past experiences, including past uses (Feldman and Orlikowski 2011). Users learn to make sense of new technologies through a combination of organizational instruction and training, their own experimentation and encounters with a tool's possibilities and limits, and their own reading of the discourse surrounding the technology, both within and outside of their organization. Thus, institutional, interpretive, and technological conditions affect the extent and manner of use (Feldman and Orlikowski 2011), and hence its impact over time. The ultimate impact of predictive policing on police practice is thus not only linked to the number of police departments claiming to adopt this approach or purchasing specific software (diffusion), but also more importantly to the real effect on police practices, including policing strategies, police deployments, resource allocations, program evaluations, and modifications over time (impact).

A SOCIO-TECHNICAL FRAMEWORK FOR UPTAKE AND IMPACT OF TECHNOLOGY

Figure 2.1 provides a schematic overview of the framework we have developed for understanding factors affecting the uptake and impact of technology. The framework is indicative rather than predictive or deterministic. It captures the social and organizational dynamics at work in the processes of diffusion and implementation of technology.

Focusing on the upper half of the diagram (diffusion), it is hypothesized that conditions favourable to the uptake of a particular technology include the *symbolic* significance of using advanced science/innovation for leaders of organizations as a way of gaining prestige, as well as a way

DIFFUSION

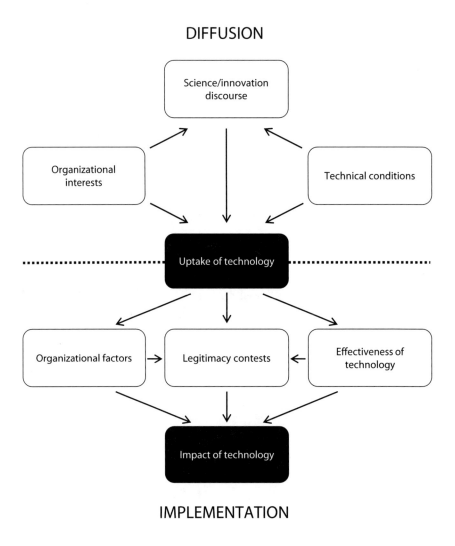

Figure 2.1: A Model of Uptake and Impact of Technology

of advancing *organizational interests* such as improving effectiveness and efficiency. However, the *technical conditions* have to be favourable for such an uptake—the technology has to be proven and have credibility for potential users. Here, the focus is the processes leading to a decision, at management level, to implement a predictive policing program, potentially through the purchase of particular software.

Moving to the lower half of the diagram (implementation), we hypothesize that once technology has been taken up by an organization (e.g., the decision is made by management to purchase the equipment/software for the technology), then the impact of technology on practice depends on how well the technology is accepted and implemented. Specifically, the impact depends on whether the *technology has proved to be effective* in meeting users' expectations, whether there are *administrative, political, or cultural obstacles within the organization* impeding the effective use of the adopted technology, and whether there are *contests about the legitimacy* of the use of this technology, especially from outside the organization (e.g., citizen groups, human rights organizations, court challenges).

Impact can be unpredictable; there can often be unintended consequences (Feldman and Orlikowski 2011). Conditions favourable to achieving the expected impact include the following: that the adopted technology is reliable and effective; that there is a well-managed process of implementation, including adequate training, support, and resources; that the adopted technology does not threaten established power structures; that the adopted technology does not require a marked change in users' standard operating procedures or work culture; and that the adopted technology is not politically controversial among citizens or not perceived to lead to undesirable outcomes for the community (or at least specific sections of the community). However, the absence of one or more of these does not imply zero impact. Positive factors may override negative ones, or practices may shift to accommodate the interests of users or citizens.

The distinction between uptake and implementation/impact can be blurred depending on which level of the organization we are discussing. For example, though written in terms of the uptake of **intelligence-led policing (ILP)**, Darroch and Mazerolle's (2012) research on New Zealand Police (NZP) can also be interpreted as a study of implementation/impact at the local level. This is because NZP "began experimenting with ILP from the late 1990s in a small number of areas" but the use of ILP was encouraged, not mandated (Darroch and Mazerolle 2012, 7). In one sense, the police organization has already adopted ILP but has left its implementation to local leaders.

SUPPORT FOR FRAMEWORK FROM PREVIOUS RESEARCH

While the literature is relatively sparse, the available empirical research on the uptake and implementation/impact of policing innovations (including technology) provides general support for the above framework. For both uptake and impact, the importance of the three dimensions of technology—organizational, symbolic, and technical—is highlighted. Note, however, that the three dimensions, though conceptually distinct, are often intertwined in practice. As can be seen in the following discussion, the same feature can impact along multiple dimensions. Further, an impact along one dimension can itself cause an impact along another.

Organizational Dimension

Organizational factors affecting uptake/implementation/impact of technology can take many forms, including leadership, management of the introduction of technology, organizational politics, and cultural resistance. Technological change can often destabilize the power balance within an organization, leading to forms of resistance among operational police (Ericson and Haggerty 1997; Koper, Lum, and Willis 2014). There are also studies, discussed below, demonstrating that there can be a low *fidelity* of implementation (Hassell and Lovell 2015) where users employ tools designed to change policing practice in fundamental ways for more traditional purposes (Braga and Weisburd 2007; Chan 2001; Koper, Lum, and Willis 2014; Sanders, Weston, and Schott 2015). However, this is contingent on management style and organizational culture (Darroch and Mazerolle 2012).

Hassell and Lovell (2015) have highlighted the importance of looking at fidelity of implementation when assessing policing innovations. Fidelity of implementation is "the extent to which a reform, as implemented, matches the way it was originally conceived" (Hassell and Lovell 2015, 507). Unless an innovation has been implemented according to the original concept, it is impossible to (a) attribute any success to the innovation, or (b) conclude that the innovation has failed. Fidelity of implementation can also help explain *why* a particular innovation fails or succeeds. In fact, the feasibility of an innovation/reform can be assessed by examining the fidelity of implementation (Hassell and Lovell 2015, 507). The five dimensions of fidelity are: "(1) *adherence* to the planned design, (2) *exposure* or *dose* (amount delivered), (3) *quality* of the delivery, (4) *participant responsiveness* and (5) *program differentiation* (presence or absence of the essential elements of the reform/program)" (Hasson 2010, in Hassell and Lovell 2015, 508). Hassell and Lovell's (2015, 516) case study in a small US Midwest police department found that "POP has not been institutionalized or implemented in a manner that is consistent with Herman Goldstein's conceptualization, although the department claimed to have done so." When looking at the impact of an innovation, it is thus important to ask, "impact *of what?*" There may be a change in practice that does not correspond to the innovation that was adopted.

In some instances, cultural issues and management of innovation issues are intertwined. For example, research in six Canadian police services found that the use of "crime science" and analytic technologies to support ILP was more rhetorical than real (Sanders, Weston, and Schott 2015, 711). More specifically, the "occupational culture of information hoarding . . . has shaped the use and functioning of police innovations" (Sanders, Weston, and Schott 2015, 718). In line with previous research on the "poorly understood and appreciated" role of crime analysts (Cope 2004), the lack of knowledge and training about crime analysis on the part of police managers and officers "has rendered many analysts to engage in simple crime counting and mapping instead of advanced analytics" so that instead of adopting a new approach to policing (ILP), new technologies are used to support "traditional modes of policing" (Sanders, Weston, and Schott 2015, 724).

Conversely, Darroch and Mazerolle's (2012) study of the uptake of ILP within NZP found that the high regard for local intelligence units was an important factor:

> For ILP to succeed, frontline officers needed to hold their local intelligence units in high regard. To ensure this, highly credible sworn officers were sought and trained for intelligence roles. Technical

proficiency was demonstrated through skill in the use of information technology tools and consistency in developing quality intelligence products that focused on achieving crime reduction goals. (Darroch and Mazerolle 2012, 24)

The use of sworn officers for intelligence roles is a strategy related to the *organizational* dimension of implementation, given the lack of trust demonstrated by police for civilian analysts.

Darroch and Mazerolle (2012) found leadership style (transformational rather than transactional) and the encouragement of leaders to be factors associated with "strong uptake" of ILP, although they did not find clarity of goals or manager commitment to ILP to be important factors. In terms of organizational culture, the researchers found an association between "strong uptake" and a "can-do" subculture:

> Our research shows the emergence of a distinctive subculture associated with the strong uptake of ILP innovation. The ILP subculture had the following characteristics: a broadly accepted focus on crime reduction as the overarching goal for local police, support for partnerships and problem solving as legitimate policing strategies, tolerance for experimentation and trial of novel approaches, support for ILP, a willingness to follow ILP leadership, openness to learning, and a willingness to participate and contribute to improvement and general innovation. (Darroch and Mazerolle 2012, 17–18)

Koper, Lum, and Willis (2014, 216) found that the impact of new technology on police could be "complex and contradictory": while technological advances could improve communication across the organization, they were also potentially detrimental to work relationships and organizational justice:

> Technology can also worsen perceptions of inequality for line-level staff, particularly patrol officers who may feel heavily burdened and scrutinized by the reporting demands and monitoring that often come with new information and surveillance technologies (in-car

and body-worn cameras provide examples of the latter). . . . All of these factors can foster resistance to technology and undermine its potentially positive effects. (2014, 216)

The authors concluded that new technology also did not appear to have led to improved management and accountability at the rank-and-file level:

Our observations suggest that while technology has fostered accountability at higher managerial levels in policing (e.g., through Compstat-type management processes), the innovative use of technology as a tool by middle- and lower-level supervisors to manage the performance of line-level officers still is neither institutionalized nor clearly understood. (2014, 217)

The limited impact of new technology on police use of technology for strategic purposes was a consistent finding across several studies (Braga and Weisburd 2007; Chan 2001; Koper, Lum, and Willis 2014). Chan's (2001) case study in Australia highlights the role of cultural factors in mediating the impact of technological change. She found a clash in "technological frames" (Orlikowski and Gash 1994) between the users and the architects of the information system: police expected IT to make their work easier without their having to change existing policing or management styles, while the architects had intended that police would use the system for tactical and strategic purposes. She found that even though new technology gave police an opportunity to follow a "smarter" or problem-oriented style of policing, traditional policing styles and values still dominated.

Koper, Lum, and Willis (2014, 216–17) similarly observed that police use of technology was affected by the way they "frame policing in terms of reactive response to calls for service, reactive arrest to crimes, and adherence to standard operating procedures," so that they were much more likely to "use IT to guide and assist them with traditional enforcement-oriented activities than for more strategic, proactive tasks."

In general, as Braga and Weisburd (2007, 17) observe:

> The police most easily adopt innovations that require the least radical departure from their hierarchical paramilitary organizational structures, continue incident-driven and reactive strategies, and maintain police sovereignty over crime issues.

Thus, innovations such as "hot spot" policing and "broken windows" policing "appeal to law enforcement practitioners primarily because they allow mostly traditional tactics to be deployed in new ways with the promise of considerably greater results," while the police have generally resisted the adoption of community policing and problem-oriented policing (Braga and Weisburd 2007, 17).

According to Koper, Lum, and Willis (2014), the inadequacy of training may have been one of the factors affecting the impact of technology. If the objective is to change the approach to policing, for example, it is not enough to demonstrate "the basics" as to how new software works technically. Training must also include guidance as to "how both the organization and individual officers can benefit from use of the technology" (Koper, Lum, and Willis 2014, 217).

Symbolic Dimension

The adoption of technology is not only driven by technological advancements but also by the symbolic significance of using new technology. The "scientification of police work," as Ericson and Shearing (1986, 134) point out, provides a "veil of legitimacy over police work." Technological innovations can also bring prestige to police organizations that adopt them. Adjectives associated with data-driven approaches to decision making (such as "smart" analytics) reflect positively on those who employ them.

Where technology presents broader risks to the community (or subsets thereof), this can change the discourse around that technology. Chan

(2003, 674) gives some examples of the kinds of risks that information technology can bring:

> Information technology can create new risks such as illegal or unauthorized use of information (Chan et al. 2001:112), the spreading of inaccurate or misleading information (HMIC 2000; Ericson and Shearing 1986:144), and the unfair targeting of specific groups based on "categorical suspicion" (Marx 1988; Meehan and Ponder 2002).

The use of new technology is also likely to raise concerns about surveillance, privacy, profiling, algorithmic accountability, and "function creep." Such concerns can escalate into contests about the technology's legitimacy.

Technical Dimension

The importance of the technological dimension itself to both adoption and impact is often taken for granted. Generally, technology will only be adopted if its function corresponds to a perceived organizational need or objective. Management will also need to be persuaded that it has been proven to be, or is at least likely to be, effective in performing its function. After adoption, effectiveness and ease of use are important in building user trust and confidence. Once adopted, technology can quickly lose its gloss if it fails to live up to its promise, either through technical problems or failure of implementation. Koper, Lum, and Willis (2014) found that technical problems during the implementation of new technology can complicate some of the cultural problems: "Implementation experiences and functionality problems with new technology have important ramifications for the acceptance, uses, and impacts of that technology" (2014, 215–16). In their study, difficulties experienced by one agency stemming from technical problems and user interfaces that officers found difficult and cumbersome to use and the need to learn new offence codes had subsequent negative effects on officer attitudes and performance.

Implementation issues may be minimized where there is greater consultation around requirements at the adoption stage and sufficient technical
assistance and training at the implementation stage (2014, 216).

LIKELY UPTAKE AND IMPACT OF PREDICTIVE POLICING TECHNOLOGY

The framework developed above can help us assess the likely uptake and
impact of predictive policing technology. A number of unique features
in predictive policing may set this innovation apart from previous technologies. In general, many conditions favourable to the uptake of this
technology by police organizations are present; however, its impact may
be less than anticipated.

In exploring the likely uptake and impact of predictive policing, we
rely on technical and policing studies literature as well as qualitative analysis of interviews conducted with law enforcement and security intelligence
officials as part of a broader project exploring the use of big data and data
analytics for national security.[8] The topic of predictive policing was not
specifically included as an interview question. The responses should thus
not be interpreted as confirming or denying the use of particular technologies or practices associated with predictive policing. Nevertheless, they
provide a broad gauge to perceive organizational understandings of and
approaches to data analytic tools more generally. A notable finding is that
the practices and technologies of predictive policing were not explicitly
mentioned by participants from operational organizations, even when
prompted about their uses of data and big data tools. In addition, specific
predictive policing software (as opposed to general analytic tools) was not
mentioned in the interviews when we asked participants to describe the
tools they used. However, there were references to related practices such
as identifying "hot spots," the capacity of big data to provide "a more
complete picture of exactly what's going on," and the use of data generally
for crime prevention and deployment. Some participants reported use
of geospatial or location-based analytical tools, including Geofeedia, a
location-based intelligence platform for social media analysis, and Esri,
a mapping platform. It remains possible that predictive policing is being

used in Australia; we did not conduct interviews with all law enforcement agencies, and sample sizes are small. There may be other local initiatives, such as the Suspect Targeting Management Plan program conducted by the New South Wales Police Force (Sentas and Pandolfini 2017), that rely on predictive methodologies to identify those at risk of offending. While predictive policing does not seem to be as widespread in Australia as in the United States, there are, nevertheless, uses of big data analytics, including the use of the Australian Criminal Intelligence Commission National Criminal Intelligence Fusion Capacity to identify "previously unknown criminal threats to the Australian community" (Australian Crime Commission 2013).

From the available literature and our research project described above, we identified a number of features of predictive policing that can affect its uptake and impact. These features are: effectiveness, cost, human resources, training, comprehensibility of outputs, complexity and transparency, infrastructure, focus on location, data requirements, centralization, discourse, and technological momentum. Table 2.1 analyzes these features of predictive policing and their likelihood of affecting the uptake of this technology and impact on policing practices. Each of the features can have positive (indicated by +), negative (–), mixed (+/–) or unknown (?) effect on uptake or impact. Note that each factor can relate to one or more dimensions (technical, organizational, and symbolic) discussed in the framework in figure 2.1. Where a feature is unlikely to have an impact within a particular dimension at a particular stage, the cell is left blank. For example, as discussed below, we do not believe that the issue of training will affect adoption, and its potentially negative influence on impact operates along the organizational and technical dimensions.

Effectiveness

Effectiveness is a factor that will affect both the uptake and impact of predictive policing. The media discourse around predictive policing suggests that it is highly effective. Percentage reductions in crime have been reported across the jurisdictions employing predictive policing

Table 2.1: Features of Predictive Policing Likely to Affect Uptake and Impact

Feature of predictive policing	Likely uptake			Likely impact		
	Organizational	Symbolic	Technical	Organizational	Symbolic	Technical
Effectiveness	+	+	–	?	?	?
Cost	+/–		–	+		
Human resources	?			+/– (*)		?
Training				?		?
Comprehensibility of outputs			+			+
Complexity and transparency			?	–	–	–
Infrastructure	–		+	+		+
Focus on location	+/–		+/–	+/–		+/–
Data requirements	+	–	–	–		–
Centralization	+			–		+
Discourse	+	+	+	+/–	+/–	–
Technological momentum	+					

* Generation may impact on whether the impact is positive or negative.

software tools (e.g., Ibrahim 2013; Mitchell 2013; Olesker 2012; Turner, Brantingham, and Mohler 2014); however, these are not backed up by evidence or references.

In Bennett Moses and Chan (2018), we have explored limitations of predictive policing software and approaches, and we point out that they are based on several assumptions that may not always hold. There are issues of data collection, in particular the limited extent to which "reality" is captured in police-held crime data, in part due to feedback loops as data collection is based on police activity, itself determined by the predictive policing process (see also Brayne 2017, 987, 997–1000). There are issues of data analysis including the presumption of continuity (which assumes no relevant intervention), choice of variables, technical bias in algorithms, and the frequent assumption that location is key to predicting crime. There are also assumptions about police operations, including the focus on police deployments as the primary intervention. Finally, there are questions of criminal response and the impact that police deployments have on preventing crime. While these are not analyzed here, they do combine to suggest that the effectiveness of predictive policing as a security strategy is not guaranteed and can thus only be measured through evaluation.

There are four evaluations of predictive policing programs of which we are aware. Hunt, Saunders, and Hollywood's (2014) evaluation of a 2011 predictive policing experiment in the Shreveport Police Department in Louisiana found that there was no statistical difference in crime rates between the experimental (predictive policing) and the control districts. Saunders, Hunt, and Hollywood (2016) evaluated Chicago's Strategic Subjects List, comprising individuals predicted to be at a high risk of gun violence who were targeted for preventive intervention. As a prediction tool, it suffered from the challenge of predicting low incidence events—those on the list were 233 times more likely to be a victim of homicide than other Chicago residents, but only experienced a 0.7 percent homicide rate. While the treated group was more likely to be arrested for a shooting, this could be attributable to the use of the list as an intelligence tool, so it is unclear whether it reflects an accurate prediction of likelihood of engaging in gun violence. In terms of effectiveness, the authors found that the pilot program had no significant impact on crime, and at-risk individuals were not more or less likely to become victims of a homicide or shooting as a result of being on the Strategic Subjects List. The third article evaluating predictive policing, Mohler et al. (2015), reached positive conclusions, both as to predictive accuracy and effectiveness; however, for reasons set out in Bennett Moses and Chan (2018), its results on effectiveness are inconclusive, and the study is further tainted by the fact that many of its authors were co-founders or stockholders in the company PredPol, whose product was being evaluated (a particular problem in the context of learning algorithms, where metrics of evaluation can be designed to match metrics deployed in training). A final evaluation, Ratcliffe et al. (2017), has only been reported briefly. This reported high percentage reductions in crime, but noted that the results were not statistically significant.

Overall, we believe that the effectiveness of predictive policing has yet to be sufficiently demonstrated. But these studies are not evidence that predictive policing is an ineffective strategy either. The "null effect" in Hunt, Saunders, and Hollywood (2014) was explained in terms of three factors: the low statistical power of the tests; a failure of program implementation, as there were variations in the extent to which the prevention model was implemented between districts and over time; or a failure of program theory (the program design was "insufficient to generate crime reduction" [Hunt, Saunders, and Hollywood 2014, xv]). The implementation issues point to a weakness in the management of the innovation:

> Treatment districts did not follow all aspects of the prevention model. Most important, the monthly planning meetings to set and maintain intervention strategies did not occur. These meetings were to be a key mechanism to ensure the prevention strategies were the same across police commands, and consequently to increase the statistical power needed for the impact analysis. Instead, the experimental districts made intervention-related decisions largely on their own . . . [and] the strategies and levels of effort employed varied widely by district and over time. (Hunt, Saunders, and Hollywood 2014, xiii)

Similar concerns about implementation were raised in Saunders, Hunt, and Hollywood (2016, 356), where the authors observe that little guidance was given on what interventions were appropriate for individuals on the Strategic Subjects List.

There are thus reasons to doubt that predictive policing will be effective in reducing crime, but until properly implemented and evaluated, it is difficult to tell. Where it is implemented but not found to be effective, police departments may terminate predictive policing programs, as has occurred in Richmond, Milpitas, and Baltimore (Robinson and Koepke 2016, 18).

Cost

Whichever software is deployed for predictive policing, there are financial costs involved. Money will need to be spent either on licensing specialist software or hiring data analysts to work with more basic tools. The financial cost itself is a potential barrier to the use of predictive policing. As one participant (with a joint operational/technical role) from a state police force said: "[Data analytics] is outside our role. We don't have the resources." However, tight budgets can also be used to justify innovation (to enhance efficiency) and can increase managerial support for use of a product once it is purchased in order to justify the initial investment.

Human Resources

Human resources are problematic even if the budget to hire staff exists. A research participant who is a manager in federal law enforcement referred to the short supply of analysts "across the national security space;" however, younger generations may be more willing to learn about and adopt computer-based approaches to understanding crime. Given the time it takes to gain the experience that is the foundation of instincts, computer tools may be seen as a way for younger police officers to advance. Their greater technological expertise can become a form of cultural capital. This depends on how crime analysts are viewed within organizations, and the extent to which data-driven approaches to policing come to dominate. Sanders, Weston, and Schott (2015) have explained how crime analysts often have a lower status within law enforcement agencies. However, the possibility of becoming "data scientists" in line with what has been described by *Harvard Business Review* as the "sexiest job of the 21st century" (Davenport and Patil 2012) may change attitudes of those considering such a career, and those working in law enforcement more generally. This may, on the other hand, leave older, more established police officers feeling left behind by technology.

Training

Training for new systems can raise issues at the implementation stage. One participant from a state police force pointed out general deficiencies in training, explaining that in the case of the general database intelligence system "very little time is dedicated to training members on how to use that system . . . you're just expected to use it." Training is a technical and organizational issue that may not be foreseen at the adoption stage. Where specialized software is used, technical training may be reduced, but there will still be a need for officers to understand how to implement police responses in practice. This point was also made by two research participants from the same team from the United Kingdom component of the study, who had experience evaluating a predictive policing program:

> To me it's you get out of the car and you talk to people. It's really simple, but the implementation issues are still there. Cops don't get it.

> Actually all of [the software tested] were pretty accurate. But what my evaluation was . . . it was a process evaluation, and then if it had been implemented properly, I would've looked at impact on crime. As it was, not many officers received information, there wasn't any clear guidance, clear information, [there] wasn't . . . an operational model as to why the officers needed this. It wasn't built in to the tasking process on the ground, so officers weren't getting it in the same way. . . . Why would you even expect to see reduction [in crime] when people aren't even using the maps they were given?

Comprehensibility of Outputs

If the analysis is to be outsourced, it is most likely that one of the predictive software products mentioned above (or a similar product) would be licensed. This requires financial resources, but relatively few additional human resources given that the analytics are contained within the software itself. The outputs from predictive policing software tools are easily understandable by non-technical experts. Predpol, for example, uses maps to show where crime is predicted as more likely to occur. Assuming the system itself is trusted, this reduces the human resource and training requirements. As one participant in a federal law enforcement agency noted, this can have significant resource implications:

> Because at the end of the day, I can have a great technical system that brings in all the data in the world and creates all these outputs but if . . . it doesn't work in with all the information that our investigators have in a way that they can understand, in a way they can draw the conclusions that they need, having all that data is of no use to them whatsoever.

Off-the-shelf predictive policing software can satisfy this need; police officers can understand what outputs mean (in particular, crime is more likely to happen in particular places) without opening the "black box" of the software itself. Further, the software resolves existing problems around information overload in managing and analyzing larger volumes of data, as the analysis is done within the software product itself. While this reduces *technical* training requirements, it does not reduce the need for training as to operational processes that will be adopted.

Complexity and Transparency

Law enforcement agencies can find it difficult to select appropriate software products that meet their needs. One research participant, a law enforcement officer from a state police force, was skeptical about decisions made within law enforcement agencies about appropriate information technology: "Traditionally and historically . . . [police have] not been very good at IT infrastructure . . . we're police officers realistically, we're not IT experts." This does not necessarily mean that the initial purchasing decision will not be made, but if an inappropriate product is purchased, this may lead to challenges in technical implementation.

Algorithms used in predictive policing are typically complex and, where specialist software is purchased, are often non-transparent due to commercial confidentiality. This may not be attractive, particularly to front-line police officers, who may feel that their understanding of the area and instinct is a better guide than computer software with opaque inner workings. Such skepticism about the ability of a computer to perform better than a human was discussed by one research participant who had worked in an intelligence organization:

> The best analytical tools will always be in the human brain and identifying patterns that computers couldn't see then and can't continue to see now. So there are always limitations around what computers can and can't do.

In addition, opacity raises issues for transparency and accountability of police decision making, potentially generating legitimacy concerns in the broader community (see Bennett Moses and Chan 2014; Robinson and Koepke 2016, 9–11). The negative impact of this factor is reduced where predictive policing software providers offer greater transparency, as in the case of Heffner (2017).

Infrastructure

In addition to a decision to purchase specific software, or to hire analysts able to conduct the analysis themselves, additional infrastructure is required. The hardware required will vary, depending on the product being used—for a simple spreadsheet program, most computers are sufficient, but other tools may require greater capacity. In some cases, outdated computers and storage facilities may need to be replaced with newer computers and more efficient data storage. While this increases the initial expense of adoption, it may enhance buy-in within the organization.

Focus on Location

Predictive policing software does not provide a complete tool for understanding crime. It focuses on one aspect of crime (mostly location) and attempts to predict that. It does not explain *why* crime may happen or, with few exceptions (such as Chicago's Strategic Subjects List), *who* will be the perpetrator or the victim. This limits the effectiveness of predictive policing tools to those crimes where location likelihoods are predictable; it excludes crimes, such as kidnapping, where historic location has only a weak correlation with future location (Hart and Zandbergen 2012, 58; Sherman, Gartin, and Buerger 1989, 47). The relevance of such limitations will depend on the alignment between agency priorities and crime types that are predictable.

Data Requirements

Predictive software tools require historic crime data, linked to particular locations, to make predictions. Two research participants in our study expressed concern about data accuracy and verification. Such issues are most likely to come to the forefront after the technology is deployed, depending on the extent to which leaders have insight into the limitations of data collection within their own agencies and, where relevant, beyond that. Predictive policing approaches rely on both accessibility of data currently held by law enforcement agencies and the accuracy or integrity of that data, which requires electronic recording of crime information, including relatively precise information about location. If accurate data is not used, this will negatively impact the technical implementation and effectiveness, the organizational culture (as inaccurate predictions lead to a loss of trust), and public legitimacy (if the public become concerned about wasted resources).

The precise data requirements of predictive policing software vary. As mentioned above, in addition to crime data, particular approaches may rely on demographic data, rates of home foreclosures, weather patterns, geographic features, and social media analysis. In some cases, there are practical challenges in procuring data, legal challenges restricting the availability of data, or technical challenges in obtaining data in a useable format. In interviews, 11 participants from operational organizations mentioned legal requirements (real or perceived) as a barrier to data sharing, 9 mentioned technical issues, and 6 mentioned cultural issues around data ownership and trust between data-holding agencies.

The extent to which each of these types of issues arises depends on the data required for the predictive model being deployed; however, many predictive models are based on crime data that is likely to be held locally by a particular law enforcement agency, including the type and location of recent crimes. This works in favour of the technology's adoption and implementation, at least where the data is analyzed by police themselves. Some jurisdictions, however, may be unwilling or unable to release data to a private commercial software provider such as PredPol (Hardyns and Rummens 2017). In addition, there may be public concern about public data being shared with private companies (Brauneis and Goodman 2018), as occurred in the media response to the use of Palantir in New Orleans (Winston 2018).

Where predictive models require access to other data sets, this only works against adoption and implementation from an organizational perspective if police cannot use the need for predictive policing to justify access to more data. If big data analytics can lead to the removal of traditional legal restrictions on the use of data, it is likely to be embraced by police. It is, however, an open question as to how issues of intragovernment data sharing will be resolved. The value of privacy has been discussed extensively within academia, and is an issue that has attracted some citizens' groups; however, the complacency with which personal and private data is made available online by citizens has strengthened law enforcement agencies' case for disregarding privacy issues (or so they claim).

A question of organizational focus is whether the organization is accustomed to analyzing trends or tracking individuals. Pre-crime disruption approaches can still be based on tracking and responding to the behaviour of individuals or networks of individuals rather than larger populations, as one research participant describes:

> One of the ideas around the National Disruption Group that we've set up is that everybody brings their data to the table *around a person of interest*. . . . In the disruption space we talk about . . . disruption plans where we bring that *assessment of an individual* together and put the options forward as to what the action might be. (emphasis added)

Understanding and acting on broader trends rather than assessment of individuals requires a different focus from that which currently dominates within law enforcement. One interesting finding from our empirical study was the very limited extent to which data *currently* shared among law enforcement agencies is de-identified data:

> Rarely is it de-identified, because the only reason we'd be sharing information is for investigative action or in support of an investigative outcome.

> It's no value if it's de-identified.

> It is possible that, in the future, police could use our data to predict trends.

Law enforcement agencies are more likely to communicate with each other about individual (or gang) threats than broader patterns and trends. While predictive policing can work on identified data, the lack of interest in de-identified data may signal a cultural wariness or unfamiliarity with trend analysis. This may ultimately affect the trust placed in predictive policing approaches.

Centralization

Predictive policing would need to be administered centrally, at least within a police patrol jurisdiction. This runs counter to the desire of some police officers to have systems that support rather than replace their decision making, and that are available during patrols rather than from a central location. One research participant, for example, described the desire of some police "to have data on device when out on the streets when doing their job." Predictive policing works differently than systems such as CrimTrac that provide access to the underlying data "to enable more informed and empowered decision making" by the police officers themselves. The system runs centrally and front-line police officers are sent to patrol particular locations. This is likely to be popular with police management as it provides managers with greater control over deployment decisions. It may lead to loss of morale for front-line officers, which is one of the reasons a predictive policing program was allegedly terminated in Burbank, California (Tchekmedyian 2016).

Alternatively, there may be some police officers or line-level supervisors who do not fully implement a predictive policing program, continuing to patrol (at least in part) based on instinct rather than computer outputs. This may itself depend on how well predictive policing tools are explained and justified, for example, through training programs. It may also depend on the extent to which the computer-generated outputs are consistent with police perceptions and intuitive strategy and thus perceived as a waste of time (Hunt, Saunders, and Hollywood 2014), or, alternatively, inconsistent with such perceptions and thus perceived as inaccurate. Some of the reactions of front-line police officers to being told where to patrol were observed by the two United Kingdom participants involved in the predictive policing evaluation:

> They don't necessarily like their roles pushed by evidence in that way.

> There was skepticism from officers, one of the maps that the police did looked like fishers. Just in terms of how they overlaid, and some officers found that funny.

However, implementation issues may be countered by the possibility of surveillance and monitoring of police to ensure that they patrol designated areas (Ericson and Haggerty 1997). Non-compliance with directions to patrol particular areas for particular lengths of time are easily noticed through geo-tagging police cars or tracking personal mobile devices. The ease with which compliance can be monitored and implementation measured likely works in favour of management interests, although it may lead to resentment among front-line officers (Koper, Lum, and Willis 2014). In particular, in Los Angeles, officers temporarily turned off automatic vehicle locators due to union resistance (Brayne 2017, 990).

Discourse

Predictive policing discourse works in line with many aspects of police culture, particularly for police management. Predictive policing promises information in the otherwise unpredictable environment of crime. As one research participant stated, "You can never be too well informed." Predictive policing builds on the broader mythology of big data to suggest that computers (with enough data) can be prescient and provide sufficient information for deployment decisions that themselves can "prevent" crime. Data analytics itself is "cutting edge," with strong scientific-technical credentials. Predictive policing thus frames a crime problem as something that can be solved *by police* (see Dixon 2005), particularly through "scientific" strategies of police management. The rhetoric of cutting edge, scientific, "smart" technologies for better policing outcomes, deploying advanced techniques that have yielded positive results in other sectors (Brayne 2017, 980), is likely to be attractive.

Such positive beliefs around predictive policing are often based on a mythological and unrealistic view of actual capabilities and practices. As an example, one article suggested that "this complex equation can in theory predict, with pinpoint accuracy, where criminal offences are most likely to happen on any given day" (Adams 2012). It is clear that this statement is flawed, even "in theory," since the complexity of software goes beyond solving a single equation; no tool offers "pinpoint accuracy" but rather larger blocks (such as 500-square-foot boxes or street sections), and not all "criminal offences" are equally suitable for forecasting. This may create issues at the implementation stage if the promises of the technology are not fulfilled.

The focus of predictive policing is crime prevention and disruption, rather than investigation of historic crimes. This is consistent with a temporal shift from post-crime to pre-crime approaches in policing (Zedner 2007) and a shift in focus from punishment for moral failings to risk management and loss prevention rather than punishment for moral failings (Ericson and Haggerty 1997; Zedner 2007). According to three research participants, this is a shift occurring at the moment in law enforcement in Australia from a prosecution focus to a disruption focus. While agency missions may be evolving, there was less agreement as to where they were along the path, as reflected in the views of three law enforcement managers from the same federal agency:

> We're very focused on prosecution. There's a real desire within parts of the agency to move away—certainly with some crime types, move away from prosecution and be more imaginative in terms of the strategies around disruption, deterrents, target hardening and the likes. . . . [I]f we weren't so focused in on prosecution all the time, I suggest that we would look for different data sources and we would ask different questions of the data, because we'd have a different mission if you like.

> We talk about a spectrum of activity. So we've got . . . traditional law enforcement so we always go for prosecution. If we can't prosecute we'll look for . . . an intervention like a control order or a preventive detention order and hey, we've had them for two years and we've only done two. But that indicates how the environment is changing. Then we'll go into the middle where we're looking at this sort of disruption thing.

> We had pretty much moved away from the prosecution being the main focus. Disruption now is the main focus.

Predictive policing hinges on disruption being an important part of the organizational mission of a law enforcement agency. Given the spectrum of views, it is difficult to work out precisely how far law enforcement has moved from a prosecution-focused mission to a disruption-focused mission; however, given that movement seems to be in that direction, this points in favour of the adoption of predictive policing software, at least over time.

Within the realm of pre-crime approaches, predictive policing is couched in the rhetoric of crime control rather than problem-solving policing. In particular, by focusing on "predicted" future crime locations, rather than the history of particular places (as occurs with traditional hot-spot policing), problem-solving approaches are made more difficult. The obvious approach to preventing future crime at a location (rather than understanding historic crime at a location) is police deployment to deter crime or catch criminals in the act. Police at all levels of the organization are likely to feel more at ease with this kind of rhetoric.

Not only does predictive policing offer the possibility of *informed* decision making, but it also creates an aura of neutrality. Because the patrol areas are determined "scientifically" rather than through human discretion, law enforcement agencies have a response to public accusations of bias as to where police patrol. The neutrality is illusory, for the reasons stated in Bennett Moses and Chan (2018) and evident in Brayne (2017) and in Sentas and Pandolfini (2017); however, the idea that decisions are made by a "neutral" machine can protect agencies against accusations of bias. The possibility of "neutral" decision making in law enforcement may also be attractive to traditionally marginalized communities. For such communities, which have not been well-served by traditional "craft-based" approaches to policing, the possibility of a neutral or scientific approach may be particularly appealing, provided, of course, that they are able to overcome any generalized suspicion of policing institutions brought on by long histories of negative experiences. For law enforcement agencies, data-driven approaches to policing can be used rhetorically to deflect accusations of bias (Brayne 2017).

The discourse around predictive policing can also have negative, dystopian overtones. Popular culture has an important impact on how new technologies are perceived, not only within user institutions, but also in society more broadly (Tranter 2011). Predictive policing is often associated with the book/movie *Minority Report*.[9] That story involves pre-crime police who stop and arrest "murderers" before an offence is committed. The intelligence base is not data analytics, but once-human Precogs who receive visions of the future. Further, predictive policing does not necessarily lead to arrests of those in the predicted crime locations (but see Ferguson 2012, explaining how predictive policing will have a significant effect on reasonable suspicion analysis in the United States). The potential negative impact of *Minority Report* on public perceptions of crime-control capabilities and misuse thereof was mentioned by one research participant in a federal law enforcement agency:

So we've got . . . *Enemy of the State, Minority Report* . . . these popular imaginings of technical capacities and the misuse.

This may have negative implications for how the community perceives predictive policing, even if the reality is a long way from dystopian fiction.

Finally, increased surveillance (either generally or targeted at specific groups) may create tensions within the broader community (Bennett Moses and Chan 2016). Where surveillance is broadened beyond those already having contact with law enforcement or to new data sources, this may also raise community concern (Brayne 2017). Where surveillance is targeted, there may be concerns about unfair selection, insufficient precision, flawed data, non-transparency, and/or stigmatization of marginalized groups (e.g., see Sentas and Pandolfini 2017). Where communities feel they are being unfairly targeted for surveillance (or ignored as victims) under a predictive policing program, this can affect the program's implementation and also, politically, its continued existence (see Thomas 2016). For example, there has been a negative reaction to the findings of racial bias described in Sentas and Pandolfini (2017).

Technological Momentum

The move to technology-driven solutions to policing problems has already begun. A great deal of police work is already being automated. Increasing use of telemetric policing (O'Malley 2013) is a good example of this. There may also be a belief that such changes are inevitable or required as part of maintaining security in today's world. This attitude was evident in some of the interviews with intelligence officials:

> There is no escaping [digital and computer technology], "it is here.". . . Big Data is something that happens to us, not something we are asking for.

> From a security perspective, can we afford not to be constantly traversing data for patterns, anomalies?

> As each new round of technology is rolled out we then look at it, utilize it, but then we start thinking about what additional features could be added or used to improve it. So it's a never-ending circle of improvement.

This does not imply any technological determinism, but rather suggests a kind of technological momentum as the use of these kinds of technologies becomes an increasingly accepted aspect of police practice (see generally Hughes 1994).

CONCLUSIONS

Koper, Lum, and Willis (2014, 215) found in their research on the impact of technology on policing in the United States that

> the effects of technology in policing are complex and . . . advances in technology do not always produce obvious or straightforward improvements in communication, cooperation, productivity, job satisfaction, or officers' effectiveness in reducing crime and serving citizens.

The effective implementation of technology can "depend on management practices, agency culture, and other contextual factors" (2014, 215). In this chapter, we considered a range of technical, practical, and cultural features of predictive policing and how these were likely to affect both the decision to use the technology and the impact and uptake of the technology in practice. We drew on interviews in Australian and UK agencies, as well as our own research on predictive policing and the broader literature. Ultimately, like Willis and Mastrofski (2012, 87), we find it hard to predict the likely impact of predictive policing; however, we have drawn out several strands that likely signal the features that will affect its successful implementation. Overall, most features point in favour of its adoption, while successful implementation sits on the edge, with many potential avenues to failure or infidelity in implementation. The challenge here is that without full compliance at the implementation stage, predictive policing tools are hard to evaluate—both as crime reduction devices and for broader social impacts. Although we are not convinced of the benefits of predictive policing approaches, adoption without successful implementation is likely the worst outcome. Thus, while not underestimating the importance of careful consideration of any decision to adopt predictive policing as an approach *at all*, we believe that any attempt to do so should not underestimate the importance of proper implementation and evaluation.

DISCUSSION QUESTIONS

1. What kinds of questions should a policing agency ask before considering the purchase of predictive policing software?
2. If deciding to adopt predictive policing strategies, what institutional structures will maximize the chance of a high fidelity of implementation?
3. As a member of the community, what concerns would you put to the leaders of your police service regarding the use of predictive policing?

NOTES

1. This research is partly funded by the Data to Decisions Cooperative Research Centre (D2D CRC). The views expressed in this chapter do not necessarily represent those of the D2D CRC. The authors are grateful for the research assistance of Elena Cama and Nicola Gollan, as well as the research of Cyberspace Law and Policy intern Jessica Lim.
2. This question is focused on the salient empirical factors that are likely to influence uptake and impact, rather than the normative principles that ought to be considered before adopting predictive policing. For an engaging discussion of the latter, see Ferguson (2017).
3. Note that the focus of this chapter, as with most research on policing innovation, is on public police rather than the private policing sector. While elements of our model, especially in relation to technical and discursive elements, are likely to be equally relevant in the private sector, the political/legitimacy issues will not necessarily be as influential.
4. A US program to provide federal funds to more than 30 local law enforcement agencies to support data driven policing (Brayne 2017, 981).
5. For Vancouver, see Sanders and Chan (forthcoming) and Meuse (2017).

6. Also known as *situation awareness*, this is a term often used in policing, military, and other emergency operations to refer to the state of being aware of relevant information about one's surroundings that is important for achieving a particular operational goal (see, for example, Endsley and Jones 2004).

7. This model is based on the trilogy of institutional context, discursive representation, and technical mechanism as proposed in Chan's (1992) theorizing of the formation and outcome of penal policy. Feldman and Orlikowski's (2011, 1247) use of practice theory similarly suggests that institutional, interpretive, and technological conditions both "shape the recursive enactment of different technologies in practice" and are shaped by these practices.

8. This project, Big Data Technology for National Security, was conducted in 2015–16, involving both an Australian and a comparative (with the United Kingdom and Canada) component. The Australian component includes 31 interviews with 38 stakeholders including law enforcement and intelligence officials, oversight agency officers, policy-makers, computer technologists, and officers in relevant civil society organizations. For further information on the project, see Chan and Bennett Moses (2017, 304). Interview excerpts used in this paper are drawn from both law enforcement and security intelligence sources, including some from UK interviews.

9. Philip K. Dick, "Minority Report," Leo Margulies (ed.), *Fantastic Universe* (January 1956); *Minority Report* (Dreamworks, Amblin Entertainment, 20th Century Fox, Cruise/Wagner Productions, Blue Tulip, 2002).

REFERENCES

Adams, Guy. 2012. "LAPD's Sci-Fi Solution to Real Crime." *Independent*, January 11, 2012, 32.

Australian Crime Commission. 2013. "CEO Keynote Address." International Serious and Organised Crime Conference, Brisbane, Australia, July 30, 2013. https://www.asiapacificsecuritymagazine.com/ceo-keynote-address-international-serious-and-organised-crime-conference-australian-crime-commission/.

Beck, Charlie, and Colleen McCue. 2009. "Predictive Policing: What Can We Learn from Wal-Mart and Amazon about Fighting Crime in a Recession?" *Police Chief* (November): 18–24.

Beck, Ulrich. 1992. *Risk Society: Towards a New Modernity*. London: Sage.

Bennett Moses, Lyria, and Janet Chan. 2014. "Using Big Data for Legal and Law Enforcement Decisions: Testing the New Tools." *University of New South Wales Law Journal* 37 (2): 643–78.

———. 2018. "Algorithmic Predictions in Policing: Assumptions, Evaluation and Accountability." *Policing and Society* 28 (7): 806–22. https://doi.org/10.1080/104 39463.2016.1253695.

Bowers, Kate J., Shane D. Johnson, and Ken Pease. 2004. "Prospective Hot-Spotting: The Future of Crime Mapping?" *British Journal of Criminology* 44 (5): 641–58.

Braga, Anthony A., Andrew V. Papachristos, and David M. Hureau. 2014. "The Effects of Hot Spots Policing on Crime: An Updated Systematic Review and Meta-Analysis." *Justice Quarterly* 31 (4): 633–63.

Braga, Anthony A., and David L. Weisburd. 2007. *Police Innovation and Crime Prevention: Lessons Learned from Police Research over the Past 20 Years.* No. 218585. Washington, DC: National Institute of Justice.

Brauneis, Robert, and Ellen P. Goodman. 2018. "Algorithmic Transparency for the Smart City." *Yale Journal of Law and Technology* 20: 103–76.

Brayne, Sarah. 2017. "Big Data Surveillance: The Case of Policing." *American Sociological Review* 82 (5): 977–1008. https://doi.org/10.1177/0003122417725865.

Chan, Janet. 1992. *Doing Less Time: Penal Reform in Crisis.* Sydney: Institute of Criminology.

———. 1997. *Changing Police Culture.* Melbourne: Cambridge University Press.

———. 2001. "The Technological Game: How Information Technology Is Transforming Police Practice." *Criminology and Criminal Justice* 1 (2): 139–60.

———. 2003. "Police and New Technologies." In *Handbook of Policing*, edited by Tim Newburn, 655–79. Cullompton, UK: Willan.

Chan, Janet, and Lyria Bennett Moses. 2016. "Is Big Data Challenging Criminology?" *Theoretical Criminology* 20 (1): 21–39.

———. 2017. "Making Sense of Big Data for Security." *British Journal of Criminology* 57 (2): 299–319.

Cope, Nina. 2004. "Intelligence Led Policing or Policing Led Intelligence? Integrating Volume Crime Analysis into Policing." *British Journal of Criminology* 44 (2): 188–203.

Darroch, Steve, and Lorraine Mazerolle. 2012. "Intelligence-Led Policing: A Comparative Analysis of Organizational Factors Influencing Innovation Uptake." *Police Quarterly* 16 (1): 3–37.

Davenport, Thomas H., and D. J. Patil. 2012. "Data Scientist: The Sexiest Job of the 21st Century." *Harvard Business Review* (October). https://hbr.org/2012/10/data-scientist-the-sexiest-job-of-the-21st-century/.

Dixon, David. 2005. "Why Don't the Police Stop Crime?" *Australian and New Zealand Journal of Criminology* 38 (1): 4–24.

Endsley, Mica R., and Debra G. Jones. 2004. *Designing for Situation Awareness.* 2nd ed. Boca Raton, FL: CRC Press.

Ericson, Richard V., and Kevin D. Haggerty. 1997. *Policing the Risk Society.* Toronto: University of Toronto Press.

Ericson, Richard V., and Clifford D. Shearing. 1986. "The Scientification of Police Work." In *The Knowledge Society: The Growing Impact of Scientific Knowledge on Social Relations*, edited by Gernot Böhme and Nico Stehr, 129–59. Dordrecht, Netherlands: D. Reidel Publishing Company.

Feldman, Martha S., and Wanda J. Orlikowski. 2011. "Theorizing Practice and Practicing Theory." *Organization Science* 22 (5): 1240–53.

Ferguson, Andrew G. 2012. "Predictive Policing and Reasonable Suspicion." *Emory Law Journal* 62 (2): 259–325.

———. 2017. *The Rise of Big Data Policing: Surveillance, Race, and the Future of Law Enforcement.* New York: NYU Press.

Graziano, Lisa M., Dennis P. Rosenbaum, and Amie M. Schuck. 2014. "Building Group Capacity for Problem Solving and Police–Community Partnerships through Survey Feedback and Training: A Randomized Control Trial within Chicago's Community Policing Program." *Journal of Experimental Criminology* 10 (1): 79–103.

Hardyns, Wimm, and Anneleen Rummens. 2017. "Predictive Policing as a Tool for Law Enforcement? Recent Developments and Challenges." *European Journal of Criminal Policy Research.* https://doi.org/10.1007/s10610-017-9361-2.

Hart, Timothy C., and Paul A. Zandbergen. 2012. *Effects of Data Quality on Predictive Hotspot Mapping; Final Technical Report.* Washington, DC: National Institute of Justice.

Hassell, Kimberly D., and Rickie D. Lovell. 2015. "Fidelity of Implementation: Important Considerations for Policing Scholars." *Policing and Society* 25 (5): 504–20.

Heffner, Jeremy. 2017. *A Citizen's Guide to HunchLab.* http://robertbrauneis.net/algorithms/HunchLabACitizensGuide.pdf.

Hughes, Thomas P. 1994. "Technological Momentum." In *Does Technology Drive History? The Dilemma of Technological Determinism*, edited by Merritt Roe Smith and Leo Marx, 101–13. Cambridge, MA: MIT Press.

Hunt, Priscilla, Jessica Saunders, and John S. Hollywood. 2014. *Evaluation of the Shreveport Predictive Policing Experiment*. Santa Monica, CA: RAND.

Ibrahim, Mariam. 2013. "Crunching Numbers to Catch Bad Guys; UCLA Researchers Develop Algorithm to Predict Crime." *Edmonton Journal*, May 11, 2013, C3.

Koper, Christopher S., Cynthia Lum, and James J. Willis. 2014. "Optimizing the Use of Technology in Policing: Results and Implications from a Multi-site Study of the Social, Organizational, and Behavioural Aspects of Implementing Police Technologies." *Policing* 8 (2): 212–21.

Maguire, Mike. 2000. "Policing by Risks and Targets: Some Dimensions and Implications of Intelligence-Led Crime Control." *Policing and Society* 9 (4): 315–36.

Manning, Peter. 2014. "Information Technology and Police Work." In *Encyclopedia of Criminology and Criminal Justice*, edited by Gerben Bruinsma and David Weisburd, 2501–13. New York: Springer-Verlag.

Meuse, Matt. 2017. "Vancouver Police Now Using Machine Learning to Prevent Property Crime." *CBC News*, July 22, 2017. http://www.cbc.ca/news/canada/british-columbia/vancouver-predictive-policing-1.4217111.

Mitchell, Robert L. 2013. "Predictive Policing Gets Personal." *Computerworld*, October 24, 2013. https://www.computerworld.com/article/2486424/government-it/predictive-policing-gets-personal.html.

Mohler, G. O., M. B. Short, P. J. Brantingham, F. P. Schoenberg, and G. E. Tita. 2011. "Self-Exciting Point Process Modeling of Crime." *Journal of the American Statistical Association* 106 (493): 100–8.

Mohler, G. O, M. B. Short, S. Malinowski, M. Johnson, G. E. Tita, A. L. Bertozzi, and P. J. Brantingham. 2015. "Randomized Controlled Field Trial of Predictive Policing." *Journal of the American Statistical Association* 110 (512): 1399–411.

Olesker, Alex. 2012. *White Paper: Big Data Solutions for Law Enforcement*. CTOlabs.com, https://core.ac.uk/download/pdf/30678906.pdf.

O'Malley, Pat. 2013. "Telemetric Policing." In *Encyclopedia of Criminology and Criminal Justice*, edited by Gerben Bruinsma and David Weisburd, 5135. New York: Springer-Verlag.

Orlikowski, Wanda J., and Debra C. Gash. 1994. "Technological Frames: Making Sense of Information Technology in Organizations." *ACM Transactions on Information Systems* 12 (2): 174–207.

Perry, Walter L., Brian McInnis, Carter C. Price, Susan C. Smith, and John S. Hollywood. 2013. *Predictive Policing: The Role of Crime Forecasting in Law Enforcement Operations*. Santa Monica, CA: RAND.

Police Executive Research Forum. 2014. *Future Trends in Policing*. Washington, DC: Police Executive Research Forum. http://www.policeforum.org/assets/docs/Free_Online_Documents/Leadership/future%20trends%20in%20policing%202014.pdf.

Ratcliffe, Jerry H., Ralph B. Taylor, Amber P. Askey, John Grasso, and Robert Fisher. 2017. *The Philadelphia Predictive Policing Experiment: Impacts of Police Cars Assigned to High Crime Grids*. http://www.cla.temple.edu/cj/center-for-security-and-crime-science/the-philadelphia-predictive-policing-experiment/.

Robinson, David, and Logan Koepke. 2016, August. "Stuck in a Pattern: Early Evidence on 'Predictive Policing' and Civil Rights." Washington, DC: Upturn. https://www.teamupturn.org/reports/2016/stuck-in-a-pattern.

Sanders, Carrie B., and Janet Chan. Forthcoming. "The Challenges Facing Canadian Police in Making Use of Big Data Analytics." In *Security and Intelligence Surveillance in a Big Data Age*, edited by D. Lyon. Vancouver: UBC Press.

Sanders, Carrie B., Crystal Weston, and Nicole Schott. 2015. "Police Innovations, 'Secret Squirrels,' and Accountability: Empirically Studying Intelligence-Led Policing in Canada." *British Journal of Criminology* 55 (4): 711–29.

Saunders, Jessica, Priscilla Hunt, and John S. Hollywood. 2016. "Predictions Put into Practice: A Quasi-experimental Evaluation of Chicago's Predictive Policing Pilot." *Journal of Experimental Criminology* 12 (3): 347–71.

Sentas, Vicki, and Camilla Pandolfini. 2017. *Policing Young People in New South Wales: A Study of the Suspect Targeting Management Plan*. Sydney: Youth Justice Coalition NSW.

Sherman, Lawrence W., Patrick R. Gartin, and Michael E. Buerger. 1989. "Hot Spots of Predatory Crime: Routine Activities and the Criminology of Place." *Criminology* 27 (1): 27–56.

Tchekmedyian, Alene. 2016. "Police Push Back against Using Crime-Prediction Technology to Deploy Officers." *LA Times*, October 4, 2016. http://www.latimes.com/local/lanow/la-me-police-predict-crime-20161002-snap-story.html.

Thomas, Emily. 2016. "Why Oakland Police Turned Down Predictive Policing."
    Motherboard 29 (December). https://motherboard.vice.com/en_us/article/
    ezp8zp/minority-retort-why-oakland-police-turned-down-predictive-policing.

Tranter, Kieran Mark. 2011. "The Speculative Jurisdiction: The Science Fictionality
    of Law and Technology." *Griffith Law Review* 20 (4): 817–50.

Turner, George, Jeff Brantingham, and George Mohler. 2014. "Predictive Policing in
    Action in Atlanta, Georgia" *Police Chief.* http://www.policechiefmagazine
    .org/predictive-policing-in-action-in-atlanta-georgia/.

Uchida, Craig D. 2014. "Predictive Policing." In *Encyclopedia of Criminology and
    Criminal Justice*, edited by Gerben Bruinsma and David Weisburd, 3871–79.
    New York: Springer-Verlag.

Van Brakel, Rosamunde, and Paul De Hert. 2011. "Policing, Surveillance and Law
    in a Pre-crime Society: Understanding the Consequences of Technology Based
    Strategies." *Journal of Police Studies* 20 (3): 163–92.

Weisburd, David, Cody W. Telep, Joshua C. Hinkle, and John E. Eck. 2010. "Is
    Problem-Oriented Policing Effective in Reducing Crime and Disorder? Findings
    from a Campbell Systematic Review." *Criminology and Public Policy* 9 (1): 139–72.

Willis, James J., and Stephen D. Mastrofski. 2011. "Innovations in Policing:
    Meanings, Structures and Processes." *Annual Review of Law and Social Sciences*
    7: 309–34.

———. 2012. "Compstat and the New Penology: A Paradigm Shift in Policing?"
    British Journal of Criminology 52: 73–92.

Wilson, Ronald E., Susan C. Smith, John D. Markovic, and James L. LeBeau.
    2009. *Geospatial Technology Working Group Meeting Report on Predictive Policing*.
    Scottsdale, AZ: US Department of Justice.

Winston, Ali. 2018. "Palantir Has Secretly Been Using New Orleans to Test Its
    Predictive Policing Technology." *The Verge*, February 27, 2018.

Zedner, Lucia. 2007. "Pre-crime and Post-criminology?" *Theoretical Criminology*
    11 (2): 261–81.

SECTION II

THE LIMITS AND IMPLICATIONS OF CRIMINAL JUSTICE RISK TECHNOLOGIES IN PRACTICE

The logic of risk technologies and predictive capability suggests that criminal justice actors should, in theory, be consistently applying the tools at their disposal to identify potential sites of threat or persons of interest, and responding to manage those risks accordingly. In a perfect world, the technologies would be rigorously tested, empirically validated through controlled experimental design, and employed objectively without bias or error. The result would be the ability to accurately predict and prevent crime or harm, thus drastically reducing insecurity; however, we don't live in a perfect world—the everyday use of risk tools and technologies is fraught with difficulties. The chapters in this section take up the challenge of examining the use of risk technologies and tools in everyday criminal justice practice, and consider the limitations of technologies and classifications for risk assessment, prediction, and management.

Technologies and tools for risk prediction and threat identification may appear, on the surface, to be objective insofar as they rely on counting the presence of risk factors and translating this into a measure of risk, independent of individual characteristics such as gender, race, and social class. Singular cases become reduced to their constituent classifications, which are assumed to be independently correlated to the threats or harms of interest; however, what these tools and assessments obscure is the process by which the classification systems and technologies *themselves* are socially constructed, relying on (at least somewhat) subjective determinations of risk and threat, and subject to interpretation as they are applied by individual actors in the criminal justice field. The three chapters in this section illustrate the ways and the moments in which subjectivity is introduced into the design and use of risk assessment tools and technologies, and the privileging of power and social capital that shapes their application. In this sense, the goal of this section is to turn a critical eye to the idea that technology and tools are "objective," to consider the limitations of such, and to consider the implications of these tools and technology being used by people in positions of power—often directed at people with comparatively less power in the situation.

First, it is important to be clear that when we speak of "technologies" of risk, we are not necessarily referring to material, electronic, or computational technologies. Rather, following Prus and Mitchell (2009, 17), we conceive of technology as "humanly engaged, conceptually achieved instances of enabling devices." In this case, risk technologies enable human actors to make decisions about how they will respond to or intervene with people and situations, by rendering assumptions of threat and insecurity as seemingly calculable and manageable. In this sense, technologies operate to mediate individuals' definition of the situation and to provide a kind of external reification of previously vague notions of risk and threat. Following this conceptualization of technology, the chapters in this volume and particularly in this section engage with an array of technologies, some of which are the kind of material, electronic devices that are commonly called "technology" by contemporary citizens (Hannem, chapter 3), and others that may take the form of a list of "risk factors" (Sanders et al., chapter 4) or a pencil-and-paper checklist (Dufresne, Robert, and Roy, chapter 5) but that nonetheless operate as "enabling devices" in determinations of risk and threat and serve to shape human action.

What ostensibly distinguishes risk technologies from other kinds of information that guide human decision making is the belief that these technologies compile information about factors that are calculably and significantly correlated to the likelihood of threat or harm. The assumption that underlies our reliance on these technologies is that the background science to identify the risk factors of importance has been conducted, the technologies have been tested, and human actors need only apply the technology to determine the "correct" level of risk or course of action; however, as will be shown in the chapters that follow, the ways in which so-called risk technologies are created do not always employ rigorous scientific methods, do not always compile the necessary big data to ascertain statistical correlation, and may not always accurately predict the likely outcome. These are fairly significant limitations.

The processes of constructing risk technologies are generally shrouded in mystery, and they operate in a "black box." It is not often that the development of risk assessment tools or the creation of detection devices is made transparent. The great strength of chapter 5 by Dufresne, Robert, and Roy is that it renders visible the ways in which power and cultural capital may shape the design and dissemination of risk technologies—Hare's Psychopathy Checklist being a prime example of a risk technology that has been fraught with conceptual difficulties. The academic context in which Hare's checklist was created is one in which transparency of method and peer review are both valued and expected. This offers a unique opportunity to consider the construction of a widely used risk technology—a process that would be more difficult to study in the context of the kind of private research and development being done by commercial creators and distributors of other risk technologies, like traffic cameras (O'Malley, chapter 1), predictive policing software (Chan and Bennett Moses, chapter 2), ion scanners (Hannem, chapter 3), body cameras, or social media (Schneider, chapter 6).

Once risk technologies are developed and put into place, another moment that may introduce bias and subjectivity in the determination of risk or threat is the point of implementation. Tools and technologies are employed by people in contexts that often place the individual using the technology in a position of power. Sometimes that power is very overt and direct, as when correctional officers who screen visitors to correctional institutions have the ability to deny entry (and thus, perhaps, deny access to an incarcerated loved one), or when police have the power to arrest and detain individuals who are believed to be a threat to others. In other cases, the power differential is seemingly more innocuous, as when those in the "helping professions" direct attention and intervention to individuals whom they judge to be "at risk"; however, the intervention and help itself may be unwanted and perceived as an intrusion on the individual client's autonomy, marking them as in need of control and as incompetent social citizens—a process described by Hannem (2012) as "structural stigma." In either case, the operation of power in determinations of risk and threat is often obscured by the facade of objectivity provided by technologies. The fact that these technologies are most often directed at "the usual suspects" (Gill 2000) raises questions about their broader usefulness in combatting insecurity: even the most accurate tool can't detect threat if it is not applied in a systematic and unbiased way. Directing the use of risk technologies toward individuals who are intuitively believed to be a threat provides opportunity for confirmation bias, and poses a significant limitation to detecting unforeseen threats.

The chapters that follow encourage the reader to think critically about the kinds of assumptions we make about risk technologies, and to more carefully consider the ways in which they are employed—to move toward taking technologies out of their "black boxes" and shedding light on the ways in which they affect the everyday lives of citizens.

REFERENCES

Gill, Peter. 2000. *Rounding Up the Usual Suspects? Developments in Contemporary Law Enforcement Intelligence*. Aldershot, UK: Ashgate.

Hannem, Stacey. 2012. "Theorizing Stigma and the Politics of Resistance: Symbolic and Structural Stigma in Everyday Life." In *Stigma Revisited: Implications of the Mark*, edited by Stacey Hannem and Chris Bruckert, 10–28. Ottawa: University of Ottawa Press.

Prus, Robert, and Richard G. Mitchell. 2009. "Engaging Technology: A Missing Link in the Sociological Study of Human Knowing and Acting." *Qualitative Sociology Review* 5 (2): 17–53.

3 The Ion Mobility Spectrometry Device and Risk Management in Canadian Federal Correctional Institutions

Stacey Hannem

The presence of illicit drugs in correctional institutions is a long-standing and ongoing concern for Correctional Service Canada (CSC). Linked to concerns about violence against staff and inmates, and the transmission of blood-borne illnesses (Office of the Correctional Investigator 2012), efforts to prevent the entrance of drugs into correctional institutions have increased over the past 15 years. Spurred by a five-year, $120-million investment in CSC's anti-drug strategy in 2008, increasingly technological devices have become the first line of defence for drug interdiction in Canadian prisons. The introduction of new technologies as tools for risk management in correctional institutions mirrors similar developments in other areas of crime control and security, as described in other chapters in this volume, including policing (Sanders et al., chapter 4), anti-terrorism, fraud detection, and border control. The proliferation of new security technologies opens up a new space of analysis for sociologists to examine the ways in which technology enables the performance of security and how devices shape the behaviours of those who are responsibilized to maintain security in specific realms, and their interactions with those who are defined as posing a risk to security. As suggested by Amicell, Aradau, and Jeandesboz (2015, 294), "An analytics of devices . . . makes possible the examination of the configuration and reconfiguration of security practices by attending to the equipment or instrumentation that makes these practices possible and temporarily stabilizes them."

In this chapter, I argue that **IonScan** technology masquerades as an objective determination of risk in a theatre of prison security; in fact, the IonScan is neither discriminatory enough to identify individuals who are actually carrying drugs, nor does it prevent drugs from entering prisons. Instead, the device offers an opportunity for CSC to focus on an external locus of threat to the institution (visitors) and to divert attention from the fact that they have never looked seriously at their own staff in the course of their interdiction efforts. In short, the technology functions as what Young (1999) would have called a kind of *cordon sanitaire* to exclude undesirable people. The technology presents a facade of objectivity but allows correctional officers to make their own subjective determinations about who poses a risk to institutional security and who does not.

While the IonScan itself does not determine outcomes for those to whom it is applied, assumptions made about the value and efficacy of the technology shape its users' actions and interpretations of the device's measurements in concert with their own pre-existing social judgments. Only recently have visitors to institutions and the family members of prisoners begun to speak out publicly about their perceptions of the injustices that may result from uncritical reliance on IonScan technology and the resulting collateral punishments for prisoners and their families (see, e.g., Harris 2016; MacAlpine 2016; Vivar 2014; White 2017). Drawing on an interactionist analysis, this chapter's findings emphasize that

> the internal characteristics (technical, logical and cognitive) of devices both constrain and enable the action of their users[;] . . . security devices are not static: their force of action also depends on processes of production, translation, circulation, appropriation, experimentation or resistance. The dynamic process of "dialogue" between a socio-technical device and a specific context of action can produce unexpected and unintended effects. (Amicell, Aradau, and Jeandesboz 2015, 294)

Correctional Service Canada first introduced the use of the IonScan ion mobility spectrometry device to select institutions as part of a pilot initiative for drug interdiction in December 1995 (Jackson 2002). The devices are used as part of CSC's "non-intrusive search" protocol to screen visitors to prisons.[1] The technology was integrated across Canadian federal prisons on a rolling basis in response to the 2000 CSC *Report of the Taskforce on Security*, which enthusiastically supported the effectiveness of the ion scanners (40), albeit without any explanation of their evaluation criteria. While CSC management, staff, and policy-makers strongly promoted the integration of the ion scanning technology as a key tool in the prison anti-drug strategy, there were early indications that the use of the scanners was not without controversy. The *2003–04 Annual Report of the Office of the Correctional Investigator* indicated that by early 2003, shortly following the full integration of ion scanning technology across the federal system, the Office of the Correctional Investigator (OCI) had already received many complaints from inmates and visitors about false positive test results on the ion scanners. Inmates and visitors complained that "**false positive**" readings had resulted in the removal of visiting privileges and that these determinations were made on the basis of the ion scan alone, without any other evidence that the visitor was carrying or attempting to traffic drugs. These complaints resulted in the OCI holding consultations in October 2003, attended by CSC officials, staff, managers, inmates, and a representative from the company that created the ion scan devices—Smiths Detection (CSC 2006; OCI 2004). As a result of these consultations, CSC agreed to institute new policy with respect to how positive readings on the ion scanner should be interpreted in the context of a holistic threat risk assessment. They also agreed to conduct an empirical evaluation of the ion scanners' efficacy (OCI 2004). The course of this research uncovered no such subsequent evaluation; however, as will be discussed, CSC's 2006 internal audit of drug interdiction activities raised some questions about the ways in which the ion scanners were being used, and a 2016 access to information request revealed that "CSC does not possess documentation concerning the reliability factor of the IonScan machines" (CSC Access to Information and Privacy Division, personal communication with the author).

For the purposes of this research, I drew on 60 interviews with the family members of incarcerated persons in Canada (conducted in 2005–07 and in 2014–15), and on the transcripts of the 2011 hearings conducted by the Parliamentary Standing Committee on Public Safety and National Security (SECU) to investigate the problem of drugs in Canada's prisons. I also analyzed existing documents from CSC pertaining to the ion scanners, including the technical requirements for ion mobility spectrometry devices, and Commissioner's Directives on searching of staff and visitors (CD 566-8), the use of non-intrusive search tools (CD 566-8-1), visits (CD 559), and control of entry to and exit from institutions (CD 566-1). An access to information request provided documentation on the denial of visits and revocations of security clearance attributable to IonScan readings. Discourse analysis reveals that front-line correctional officers' perceptions of the IonScan technology and its application are not necessarily aligned with official correctional policy or managers' understandings of the tools. Further, we see that the selective use of the ion scanner to target the families of prisoners and other visitors, and not correctional staff, operates on the presumption that the source of insecurity and drug trafficking in prisons is primarily outside of the correctional organization. Despite evidence that correctional officers may sometimes be involved in trafficking drugs, the IonScan technology is used in a way that ignores correctional officers and staff as potential threats to security, focusing concern and attention on families and visitors. I argue that this ignores actuarial risk in favour of a focus on constructing families and visitors as dangerous and symbolically "risky" people, due to their ties to convicted criminals.

ION MOBILITY SPECTROMETRY AS SECURITY TECHNOLOGY

The science underlying the IonScan technology, ion mobility spectrometry (IMS), first emerged in the early 1970s (Hill, Siems, and St. Louis 1990) and was originally conceived as a means of detecting trace particles of explosives. Familiar to many, the devices used in Canadian prisons are the same machines used at airport security when your luggage, laptop, or shoes are swabbed for trace particles of explosives. At Canadian prisons, the IonScan devices are calibrated to identify trace particles of illicit drugs, rather than explosives. The principle of the IMS device is very simple: a sample is first swabbed or vacuumed from an item that is likely to be in contact with the individual's hands—a zipper, ring, glasses, identification, belt, or shoes, for example. The trace particles that are collected from the item are heated to the point of vaporization and then ionized by either adding or removing an electron—applying a radioactive source to create positively or negatively charged ions. The ionization process breaks down the molecule into its constituent particles—these ions are of varying sizes and weights and they travel at different speeds.

The ionized particles then travel through a drift tube (a tube with a magnetized collector plate at the far end) and the IMS machine measures the amounts of time the various particles take to reach the collector at the other end—the drift time. The subject particles collide with the molecules of the inert gas in the drift tube, providing friction and displacement; this causes particles of different sizes and weights to reach the collector plate at different times. The device then generates a drift spectrum, which shows the drift times of the composite ions and compares the drift spectrum or ion mobility spectrum of the subject particles to the known calibrated ion mobility of the target substances (in this case, illicit drugs). The IMS machine will alarm if the ion mobility spectrum of the sample matches that of one of the substances in its database, with a sufficient threshold, as determined by the machine's settings and CSC's positive result thresholds, which are outlined in the Commissioner's Directives on the Technical Requirements for Ion Mobility Spectrometry Devices (CD 566-8-2). Notably, any alarm at all for hash/marijuana or opium is sufficient to trigger a subsequent risk assessment for a prison visitor.

The CSC policy indicates that when an alarm of sufficient threshold is raised, "a positive indication by any non-intrusive search tool does not automatically result in a refusal of entry or a visit" (CD 566-8-1, 18). The Commissioner's Directive requires staff to conduct a second test using the IMS and to subsequently perform a "threat risk assessment," which includes a private interview with the individual in the presence of a witness (presumably another CSC staff member), offering the individual the opportunity to "provide an explanation for the positive search result (including mention of any products or medications)" (CD 566-8-1, 16c). The staff member is then to "consider the results of the interview in combination with other applicable information that may be available (e.g., intelligence information, past inmate and/or visitor history, observed behaviour, and the search results of one or more means)" (CD 566-8-1, 16d), in order to determine if the individual will be granted access for a visit.

IONSCAN TECHNOLOGY AND FALSE POSITIVES

While the introduction of IMS technology to Canadian prisons was intended to increase security for prison staff by allowing them to identify visitors to the institution who may be carrying drugs, there is little evidence to suggest that the IonScan is an effective means of reliably identifying individuals in possession of illicit drugs. Indeed, CSC's own report on the use of ion scanners in correctional facilities found that "these devices are oversensitive and are limited in their ability to detect certain forms of drugs" (Johnson and Dastouri 2011). The use of IonScan to identify persons suspected of trafficking illicit drugs is complicated by the fact that the technology itself has several known (though often unacknowledged) shortcomings, which can lead to false positive readings.

First, unlike human fingerprints, the **ion mobility spectrums** (also called plasmagrams) generated and read by the IonScan machine are not unique identifiers. That is, the ion mobility spectrums of closely related or similar chemical compounds may be so nearly identical that the technology is unable to differentiate them. Thus, the machine can indicate the presence of a substance that may be an illicit drug, but may also be a legal substance with similar chemical properties. For example, according to the original patent documents submitted by Smiths Detection for the IonScan (US Patent US 20080101995 A1), ranitidine, a common antacid medication known better by its brand name, Zantac, is known to have the same mobility constants as cocaine when the machine is operated in positive ion mode. A second scan in negative mode would be required to identify this as a false positive for cocaine, as cocaine will not be detected in negative ion mode (but ranitidine will). In its patent application, Smiths Detection suggests operating two machines, one in positive and one in negative ion mode, to correct for this problem.

There are a number of legal pharmaceutical medications and other substances that are known to alarm the IonScan machines because they either have a similar chemical composition, or actually share some chemical compound with illicit drugs. Correctional staff admit to keeping a "short list" of medications and other substances known to set off the alarm: asthma inhalers, nitroglycerine (for heart problems), and Adderall (for ADHD) will all alarm as methamphetamines; antifungal creams (used to treat athlete's foot or thrush) and residue from poppy seeds in bagels or other baked goods will alarm as an opiate; chlorine baby wipes and some perfumes and lotions are also prone to alarming as various types of drugs. Dussy et al. (2008) found that several types of detergents will present a false alarm for heroin. These alarms may be viewed as "false positive" in that individuals are rendered suspect who have never used or been in contact with illicit drugs.

Secondly, there is a high potential for cross-contamination and for individuals to inadvertently come into contact with trace amounts of illicit substances. Sometimes an alarm is not false—the substance that is detected is in fact an illicit drug—but this does not necessarily mean that the individual came in contact with the drug on purpose, nor that the drug is present in significant quantities or that the individual is attempting to carry the drug into the prison. Many banknotes contain micrograms of illicit drugs—far more than the threshold required to alarm the IonScan; some studies have found that up to 90 percent of banknotes will test positive for cocaine (Armenta and de la Guardia 2008). Thus, for example, handling cash prior to entering the prison can cause individuals to ring positive on the IonScan. Individuals may also come into contact with trace amounts of drugs in other ways—through contact with other people, or through particle transfer on door handles or other objects. Sometimes the source of contamination can be a complete mystery to family members who visit an incarcerated loved one:

> I was very leery of the ion scanners and I got frustrated . . . because for the first few months I tested positive all the time. And I didn't, I've never used drugs. And because I just moved here and I didn't know anyone so I never went to anyone's house and no one came over to mine and I always showered right before I got in my car to go see him, I couldn't understand it! (Interview 02-06)

The issue of false positives on the IonScan was highlighted in 2008 when the US Federal Bureau of Prisons suspended the use of ion scanners in all federal prisons in response to a prisoner's lawsuit alleging that his family members had been unfairly denied visits due to false positive readings (Prison Legal News 2009). When the Bureau of Prisons resumed the use of ion scanners in 2009, they were no longer authorized for screening visitors and were only to be used for screening prisoner mail and belongings, lockers, work areas, and visitation rooms (Prison Legal News 2010). Notably, federal prisons in the United States resumed their use of the IonScan for screening visitors in 2011.

A third issue concerns the (often erroneous) assumption that the presence of trace particles of drugs indicates that the individual is attempting, or may attempt, to carry drugs into the prison. Even in cases where trace particles of illicit drugs are present due to the individual's previous recreational use (e.g., of marijuana), the IonScan itself does not determine that the drug is present in larger quantities; however, the application of the threat risk assessment by correctional staff begins with the presumption of risk or guilt due to the individual's association with an incarcerated person (see Hannem 2011, 2012). This is made clear when visitors to the institution who are present in a professional capacity are treated very differently than family of incarcerated persons. For example, Kim Pate, former executive director of the Canadian

Association for Elizabeth Fry Societies (appointed to the Senate of
Canada in 2016), testified in 2011 to SECU about her experiences with
the ion scanner:

> Of course, I know the policy, so I'll ask for the risk-threat assessment;
> I'll ask for all of the appropriate measures. Everybody will agree that
> they have no concern that after 30 years of coming in [to the prisons],
> I would actually ever introduce drugs to the institution. Yet I've rung
> off falsely positive, so much so that at one point we went through a
> whole little charade of what kind of medication I might have touched
> in the previous two weeks. In the end, it was assessed that a Dimetapp
> I had given my child two weeks earlier may have caused it. Now real-
> ly, I suggest to you, that is stretching it . . . don't think anybody was
> fooled into thinking that it was in fact what caused me to ring off.
> It may have been the gas pump I touched earlier. It may have been
> the money I touched. It may have been anything or it may have been
> nothing. We don't know. (SECU 2011b, 4)

Kim Pate, with her position as a respected lawyer, educator, advocate, and executive director of a national organization, is able to describe
this **theatre of security** as a "charade"—her position makes it highly
unlikely that she would be denied entrance and, indeed, in the incident
she described, it seems that correctional staff went out of their way in the
threat risk assessment to ensure that Pate would not be denied entrance;
however, this kind of benefit of the doubt is not so likely to be extended
to the family of offenders who do not have access to the same social and
political capital.[2] In this sense, the IonScan operates to legitimate the
scrutiny applied to those who are already perceived as risky, but offers
enough ambiguity to allow correctional officers to exercise discretion
when individuals who are deemed trustworthy set off the alarm.

Finally, the IonScan is also subject to the possibility of operator error. If the machine is not properly cleaned following a positive reading,
subsequent scans will also alarm due to contamination. According to
CSC procedures for operating the IonScan, the operator is supposed to
verify that their hands are not contaminated by swiping them as a test

(CD 566-8-2, Annex B, Procedure 4). If an alarm is activated, the operator is required to change their gloves, clean the countertop surfaces, and run clean swabs until the machine no longer alarms; however, when the visiting room is busy, procedures may not always be followed and operator error may lead to cross-contamination and subsequent (false) alarms. In 2006, when CSC conducted an internal audit of its drug interdiction activities, it was noted that in 5 of 11 audited institutions, the IMS devices policy and procedures were not being followed according to the manufacturer's instructions (CSC 2006). Catherine, whose husband was incarcerated, described her experience:

> One time a lady went before me and tested positive for cocaine and I went behind her and I tested positive for cocaine. Well, you know, they're supposed to change their gloves and they're supposed to change the insert that goes into the scanner and they're supposed to use a new swab every time, but you know what? These people [correctional officers] are human and they don't know enough about this machine anyway. So when they tested me the second time, they did all that and tested again and I came up clean. But, yeah, the ion scanner is—I don't think that they know enough about it. And I'm not sure. I mean, I know they need something to try and prevent the transfer of drugs into the institution because of security and many other factors . . . but I'm not sure that the ion scanner is the way to go. (Interview 03-06)

Further complicating the question of operator error is the fact that the operator can, at will, cause the machine to alarm. According to the manufacturer's instructions, the IonScan machine requires calibration with known samples of the target substances (i.e., illicit drugs), which means that these samples are available to the operators and could, presumably, be used to cause the machine to alarm. While perhaps unlikely, the deliberate alarming of the IonScan is not unheard of. In her 2016 memoir, author Diane Schoemperlen recounts her final visit to her (now ex-) partner at a medium-security institution. The correctional officer responsible for operating the IonScan deliberately caused the alarms to ring positive, apparently as a joke and a "goodbye present" for the inmate, who was to be released the following day. Schoemperlen vividly describes her immediate dismay and concern for the potential consequences of the alarm, including the revocation of visiting privileges, the cancellation of her partner's parole, and the permanent record of suspicion that could affect all future decisions about his correctional plan (Schoemperlen 2016, 96–97). This anecdote illustrates just one more aspect of the fallibility of IonScan technology as an objective determiner of risk.

Given the potential for error and issues of false positives surrounding the IonScan technology, it seems reasonable that the device should be used carefully and that any positive reading should be contextualized with other risk factors. In fact, CSC policy is to conduct a threat risk assessment, as described above, in the event of an alarm on the IonScan prior to denying a visit or taking any further punitive action; however, these threat risk assessments do not always happen, and family visitors report that even if there is no evidence that the individual has any illicit substances on their person, they may still be turned away and denied visiting privileges. Family members may also have their visitation privileges and security clearance revoked entirely, requiring them to reapply to visit their family member—a process that can take months and may not be successful. A 2016 access to information request to CSC revealed that from fiscal year 2011–12 until 2015–16, 153,303 visitor security clearance requests were made (an average of 30,660 each year) and just over 35 percent of these requests (54,177) were cancelled, denied, or suspended. Further data showed that the number of requests denied in the same period due to outstanding criminal charges was 718—just 0.5 percent of all clearance requests and 1.32 percent of negative clearance requests. Based on CSC policy, presumably the remaining negative clearance requests may be due to previous criminal convictions, an application to visit inmates in multiple institutions without adequate justification, or CSC's assessment that the individual poses some risk to the security of the institution or would plan or commit a criminal offence while visiting the institution (CD 559). A number of these revocations were due to suspicion resulting from a positive reading on the IonScan.

OBJECTIVITY AND RELIABILITY: CONSTRUCTING THE IONSCAN AS SECURITY TECHNOLOGY

The credibility that correctional officers give the IonScan as a security device, and the resulting treatment of visitors who alarm on the scanner, seems at odds with its predictive and detective capabilities. In a response to an access to information request, CSC staff indicated that the organization "does not possess documentation concerning the reliability factor of the IonScan machines. . . . CSC staff who have attended training with the manufacturer [Smiths Detection] have been advised that the false alarm rate is below 0.1% as indicated by the manufacturer" (CSC, personal correspondence with the author, June 27, 2016). It appears then that CSC has collected no independent data on the efficacy of the IonScan machines and accepts the claims made by the manufacturer of its reliability (presumably under strictly controlled laboratory conditions and not reflective of "real world" applications). Further, when asked about the number of false positive readings on the IonScan documented by CSC each year, the Access to Information and Privacy Division of CSC responded thusly:

> Considering that such an occurrence rarely occurs, "false positives" are not recorded by any institution within CSC. Therefore, it would be difficult to provide an actual figure. Please note that the false alarm rate is below 0.1% as indicated by the manufacturer. In the event there is an alarm that appears to be a "false positive" for a controlled substance, CSC consults with the manufacturer to determine if a prescribed medication can cause an alarm. (CSC, personal communication with the author, June 27, 2016)

In this statement, CSC both denies that false positive readings occur, drawing on manufacturer claims, while confirming that substances that are not illicit drugs may cause the IonScan to alarm and that the manufacturer is aware of this phenomenon. This seeming contradiction raises troubling questions about CSC's due diligence in examining the efficacy of the technology that it employs; most concerning is the failure of the Canadian government to ensure the rigorous, third-party evaluation of this technology.

In 2011, SECU conducted a study of drugs and alcohol in prisons. As part of those hearings, members of CSC management and staff provided testimony and many of them spoke about the IonScan technology. There appeared to sometimes be significant differences in the weight that was given to this technology. For example, management discussion of the technology and its efficacy was often cautious; Pierre Mallette, national president of the Union of Canadian Correctional Officers, made the following statement:

> Let me make a distinction. The IONSCAN does not necessarily go off because the person has drugs on them. It can go off because they were in contact with drugs or they were around drugs. It doesn't mean that you have to have drugs on you. We must be careful. (SECU 2011a, 11)

Similarly, CSC security intelligence officer Darcy Thompson was aware of the limitations of the IonScan:

> Our tools aren't foolproof, but they're very, very good tools. Our ion scanner for testing visitors entering our institution is an excellent tool, but that tool is not going to tell me if the individual has drugs on him or herself. It's just going to tell me if the person has been in recent contact with drugs. (SECU 2011d, 9)

On the other hand, some front-line staff appear to think that the technology is infallible, as it is described by William Normington, a veteran 35-year correctional officer:

> When the ion scanner is used, there's no doubt in my mind that *the machine doesn't make errors*. We can detect on the individuals who come in, on their wallets or their jewellery or their clothing, quantities of drugs. We can detain them until the authorities come and

arrest them with probable cause, or we can ask them to leave the institution. That has eliminated one problem. But what happens is that individuals come in for visits. They mule in their drugs, if you will. They are passed off. As soon as they get into V&C, the visitors and correspondence area, it's almost impossible to detect and recover them. So, yes, those tools are invaluable and make the environment a safer environment to work in. (SECU 2011c, 9; emphasis added)

Kevin Snedden, an acting assistant deputy commissioner at CSC, was markedly more guarded in his discussion of the technology:

The ion scanner is a machine. If it's operating properly and operated properly by the operator, it's a very reliable tool. *To guard against things like false positives*, we'll run second tests and things of that nature. It's a piece of information that we'll consider when we do our threat risk assessment. If we do get a high hit on an ion scanner or some hits over the threshold, we'll do a threat risk assessment and try to bring all of the information we have to bear to make a decision to safeguard against those false positives. But not having that machine in the first place or our detector dogs would be detrimental to our goal of trying to keep drugs out of the institution. As warden, I try to reinforce with staff that these are tools in our tool box. We have to apply them. We do so with dignity and respect toward those who are entering our institutions. We follow our policies that have been established to guard against things like false positives and things of that nature. *We don't just believe the box*, to the effect that "As the box says, I will do." No, it's a human business and we apply human judgment in a policy context to what those readings are. (SECU 2011c, 11; emphasis added)

Snedden's conviction that the IonScan technology is effective in drug interdiction when contexualized with other information falls in line with CSC policy, but flies in the face of claims that the technology does not result in "false positives"; however, CSC's reluctance to apply the technology to its own staff raises questions about CSC's awareness of false positives and the potential for the ion scanner to unduly hamper employees' entrance to the institution. Further, the failure to exercise all available forms of interdiction with staff, even in the face of evidence that staff may be implicated in drug trafficking, raises questions about the symbolic value of technology and policy in demarcating risky populations.

When Don Head, commissioner of CSC, was asked about staff involvement in drug trafficking, he acknowledged that 12 employees had been dismissed in 2011 and subsequently charged with drug trafficking offences (SECU 2011a, 7–8). At the time, in fall 2011, Kevin Snedden testified to the parliamentary committee that, "For staff, no, we don't use the ion scanners and [drug] dogs. When I walk into the institution in the morning, for example, I go through a similar process that visitors to this building would go through with metal detectors. All my baggage, my briefcase, and things of that nature are all scanned through an X-ray machine" (SECU 2011c, 11). The commissioner testified that "over the years the approach with [screening] staff has not necessarily been as rigid as it has been with visitors or contractors, MPs, or the commissioner. This is something we're working on right now, and there will be some changes in the very, very near future" (SECU 2011a, 8). Despite his assurances, at the time of this publication in 2018, no significant policy changes had been made with respect to staff screening, and front-line officers of CSC were still not subject to the IonScan upon entry to correctional institutions.

IONSCAN AS THEATRE OF SECURITY

Data from interviews with family of incarcerated persons suggest that the introduction of the IonScan technology presents a significant barrier and disincentive to prison visiting; family members report that they experience anxiety about the IonScan and that the possibility of being accused of trafficking due to a false positive IonScan looms large in their consciousness (see Hannem 2012; Hannem and Leonardi 2015). The technology's inability to accurately and consistently discern the presence and quantity of illicit drugs poses an ongoing concern for family members and raises questions about the ways in which correctional officers determine who will be denied visits or refused entry to the prison.

In his discussion of "technological dramas," Manning (1992) suggests that the introduction of technology into organizations results in various forms of adjustment to accommodate the technology into existent practices. One possible means of adjustment, technological reconstitution, occurs when "the apparent or surface features of the work change, but the underlying code, or rules and principles that determine when a message has meaning in a context, remains unchanged" (Manning 1992, 339). Following Manning, we might argue that the introduction of the IonScan technology has altered the means by which correctional officers make assumptions of risk visible and identify risky individuals for closer scrutiny, but has not fundamentally altered the symbolic and interactional processes by which correctional officers determine which risky subjects will be denied entry to the institution. While the positive reading on the IonScan serves as a seemingly "objective" confirmation of an officer's suspicions, subsequent threat risk assessment processes return discretion entirely to the individual officer, who decides the outcome for the family member or visitor. For example, Anne, whose husband was incarcerated, described that she had benefitted from the use of discretion, where others had not:

> They don't apply the rules to everybody the same way. I'm lucky because they've been positively flexible for me. I've seen people turned away for, because they tested positive on the drug scan, where I've never been turned away. Even though I tested [positive] a couple of times. Three or four. (Interview 01-06)

The convergence of the selective application of the IonScan, its questionable reliability and discernment, and the ultimate reliance on the individual judgment of correctional officers in permitting or disallowing entrance to the institution suggests that the IonScan operates within a technological drama to produce a theatre of security. As previously stated, and confirmed by CSC's own analysis, the IonScan cannot, in itself, conclusively identify and prevent drug trafficking; however, the investment in IonScan technology and its presence in the institution(s) allows CSC to claim that they engage high-tech drug interdiction strategies, alleviating political and public pressures around concern about drugs in prison, while maintaining a highly discretionary and individualized approach to visitor security. Further, the entire technological drama surrounding the IonScan obscures the underlying symbolic assumption that it is visitors, and not staff, who pose a security risk to the institution. The selective application of security technology suggests that it is not the neutral risk management tool that CSC constructs.

Although the rhetoric of objective technological responses to risk resonates with the general public, family of incarcerated persons who visit correctional institutions remain aware of the differential treatment of staff and visitors, and this perceived bias in scrutiny can be a source of discontent among family members who begin to question CSC priorities in screening for drugs:

> You know, we are searched [with the ion scanner] and my sister and brother have been out to visit my son and the [drug] dog goes over them with a fine-tooth comb and finds nothing. My brother insists there's no way any drugs could get into the institution and yet they have a drug problem in the institution but *they don't do the same kind of stuff for staff. I've seen their staff walk in and out all the time.* And that sort of stuff, let alone what they're doing for the people who are dropping off the food or whatever other supplies have to come into the place. *I doubt that the problem really is visitors.* (Interview 09-15; emphasis added)

The IonScan, and its selective application, becomes symbolic of the power differential between staff and family of incarcerated persons. Other interviewees echoed the sense that they are subject to suspicion just by virtue of visiting a loved one in prison. The **courtesy stigma** (Goffman 1963) of association with a convicted person becomes encoded in institutional policies that identify visitors to the institution as a security risk, resulting in the enactment of structural stigma (Hannem 2012):

> You go into that prison and they bring the drug dogs and they do an ion scan on you. They make you feel so belittled, as if you are hiding

something and they are going to catch you, when all you are trying to do is just have a visit for two hours, so you can try and keep your marriage going and so your child gets to see his father. (Interview 38-15)

Compounding the sense of indignity and suspicion that accompanies the selective use of the IonScan, family members state that their interactions with correctional officers are often negative and they resent the lack of recourse and sense of powerlessness that they experience:

The worst part of this whole situation is how I get treated by the prison staff and the traumatic events they have put me through when trying to pass through security. I have been accused several times of contraband when this is completely against my character and values and yet it is their word against mine. There needs to be more accountability there. The system is set up to make it very hard and discouraging for family members to visit their loved ones. (Interview 44-15)

The selective application of IonScan technology to family members (and not staff) raises questions about its efficacy as a form of drug interdiction while, at the same time, marking a symbolic distinction between those who are considered a risk to the security of the institution and those who are not. The IonScan becomes part of a theatre of security in which the locus of threat is constructed as external to the institutional structure, and institutional policy for the use of the IonScan ignores evidence that staff members and other individuals who are part of the carceral apparatus may use their trusted status to introduce contraband into prisons.

DISCUSSION

This chapter suggests that IonScan technology is plagued with issues of false positives and also employed in a way that disproportionately constructs visitors as a threat to the security of correctional institutions, while overlooking other obvious sites of insecurity. This is not to say that the introduction of IonScan screening for staff would be a panacea to concerns about drug interdiction in prisons, but rather that a non-selective approach to the use of the IonScan might make visible the problems with the technology. The application of IonScan technology to families of incarcerated persons stigmatizes individuals in a relative position of powerlessness, without recourse or appeal, and allows CSC to appear to be engaging in drug interdiction efforts, without highlighting the ongoing challenges and iatrogenic consequences of the technology in marking individuals who are not carrying drugs into the prison as suspicious, based on the presence of microscopic trace particles.

These positive readings can have serious consequences for family members who are denied visits and subject to revocation of security clearance, thereby preventing them from maintaining the family relationships that are most beneficial to released inmates. In 2016, an Ottawa-based advocacy group for families of incarcerated people, MOMS (Mothers Offering Mutual Support), started a petition to the federal government to protest the use of IonScan technology in Canadian federal prisons (White 2017). In June 2017, the minister of public safety (whose portfolio includes CSC) promised a full inquiry into the ion scanners and their use. While the scope and outcome of this investigation remains uncertain, families of incarcerated persons are beginning to demand that the use of technology for drug interdiction be contextualized with its efficacy, and that any technology considered accurate enough for use on visitors should also be applied to staff. In this sense, while the use of technology is never wholly objective nor absent of human discretion, its application in the context of prison drug interdiction might be made more transparent and less discriminatory.

DISCUSSION QUESTIONS

1. Consider the statement, "the machine doesn't make errors": how might this statement be understood as both true and false? What are the assumptions that underlie this argument?

2. What problems would Correctional Service Canada encounter in applying the use of IonScan technology to their staff? Do you think correctional staff should be subject to the same kinds of searches as visitors to the institution, whether with the IonScan or another technology? Why or why not? What are the benefits and drawbacks to a uniform drug screening protocol for *everyone* who enters the prison?

3. How does the use of electronic technology like the IonScan curtail or enhance individual human discretion and decision making in criminal justice settings?

4. If you were a policy-maker for Correctional Service Canada, weighing its financial costs and efficacy, would you recommend IonScan technology as a worthwhile investment for drug interdiction in Canadian prisons? Why or why not?

NOTES

1. Although the Commissioner's Directives on Non-Intrusive Search Tools state that "non-intrusive search tools will be utilized on all persons entering or exiting medium security, maximum security, and multi-level institutions" (CD 566-8-1), CSC's (2006) internal audit of drug interdiction activities and the 2011 parliamentary hearings on drugs and alcohol in prisons, along with current observations and interviews with prison visitors, confirm that the IonScan is not used on CSC staff entering the institutions.

2. While there is little discretion for correctional officers to use (or not use) the IonScan on visitors to the institution, they do have discretion in conducting the threat risk assessment and interpreting the results. While the IonScan itself is not necessarily used in a way that is discriminatory, interviews and observations suggest that factors such as gender, age, ethnicity, and class, as well as the index offence of the inmate who will be receiving the visitor, may factor into correctional officers' interpretations and treatment of individuals who ring positive on the IonScan. For example, if the incarcerated family member was convicted of a drug offence, his/her visitors will be subject to more scrutiny than those of an individual who was not involved with drugs.

REFERENCES

Amicell, Anthony, Claudia Aradau, and Julien Jeandesboz. 2015. "Questioning Security Devices: Performativity, Resistance, Politics." *Security Dialogue* 46 (4): 293–306.

Armenta, Sergio, and Miguel de la Guardia. 2008. "Analytical Methods to Determine Cocaine Contamination on Banknotes from Around the World." *Trends in Analytical Chemistry* 28 (4): 344–51.

Correctional Service Canada (CSC). 2000. *Report of the Taskforce on Security*. Ottawa: CSC.

———. 2006. *Audit of Drug Interdiction Activities*. Internal Audit Branch 378-1-209. Ottawa: Internal Audit Branch.

Dussy, Franz E., Christian Berchtold, Thomas A. Briellmann, Candid Lang, René Steiger, and Michael Bovens. 2008. "Validation of an Ion Mobility Spectrometry (IMS) Method for the Detection of Heroin and Cocaine on Incriminated Material." *Forensic Science International* 177 (2/3): 105–11.

Goffman, Erving. 1963. *Stigma: Notes on the Management of Spoiled Identity*. Englewood Cliffs, NJ: Prentice-Hall.

Hannem, Stacey. 2011. "Stigma, Marginality, Gender and the Families of Male Prisoners in Canada." In *Critical Criminology in Canada: New Voices, New Directions*, edited by Aaron Doyle and Dawn Moore, 183–217. Vancouver: University of British Columbia Press.

———. 2012. "The Mark of Association: Transferred Stigma, and the Families of Male Prisoners." In *Stigma Revisited: Implications of the Mark*, edited by Stacey Hannem and Chris Bruckert, 95–117. Ottawa: University of Ottawa Press.

Hannem, Stacey, and Louise Leonardi. 2015. *Forgotten Victims: The Mental Health and Well-Being of Families Affected by Incarceration in Canada*. Kingston: Canadian Families and Corrections Network. https://docs.wixstatic.com/ugd/540998_bf53cb6268de4f3bbff77c2ecf55c322.pdf.

Harris, Kathleen. 2016. "Inmate Families Say Prison Drug-Scanning Tool Finds False Positives at 'Alarming' Rate." *CBC News*, December 21, 2016. http://www.cbc.ca/news/politics/federal-prisons-drugs-ion-scanners-1.3905662.

Hill, Herbert H., William F. Siems, and Robert H. St. Louis. 1990. "Ion Mobility Spectrometry." *Analytical Chemistry* 62 (23): 1201–9.

House of Commons Standing Committee on Public Safety and National
  Security (SECU). 2011a. Evidence. SECU-04, 1st Session, 41st Parliament.
  September 29, 2011. Ottawa: Parliament of Canada.

———. 2011b. Evidence. SECU-05, 1st Session, 41st Parliament. October 4, 2011.
  Ottawa: Parliament of Canada.

———. 2011c. Evidence. SECU-06, 1st Session, 41st Parliament. October 6, 2011.
  Ottawa: Parliament of Canada.

———. 2011d. Evidence. SECU-09, 1st Session, 41st Parliament. October 27, 2011.
  Ottawa: Parliament of Canada.

Jackson, Michael. 2002. "Justice Behind the Walls." Online edition. http://www
  .justicebehindthewalls.net.

Johnson, Sara, and Serenna Dastouri. 2011. "Use of Ion Scanners in Correctional
  Facilities: An International Review." Ottawa: Correctional Service Canada.
  http://www.csc-scc.gc.ca/research/005008-rr11-01-eng.shtml.

MacAlpine, Ian. 2016. "Reliability of Drug Scanners Called into Question."
  Kingston Whig-Standard, June 6, 2016. http://www.thewhig.com/2016/06/06/
  reliability-of-drug-scanners-called-into-question.

Manning, Peter K. 1992. "Technological Dramas and the Police: Statement and
  Counterstatement in Organizational Analysis." *Criminology* 30 (3): 327–46.

Office of the Correctional Investigator (OCI). 2004. *Annual Report of the Office of the
  Correctional Investigator 2003–2004*. Ottawa: Government of Canada. http://
  www.oci-bec.gc.ca/cnt/rpt/annrpt/annrpt20032004-eng.aspx#IVR.

———. 2012. *Annual Report of the Office of the Correctional Investigator 2011–2012*.
  Ottawa: Government of Canada. http://www.oci-bec.gc.ca/cnt/rpt/annrpt/
  annrpt20112012-eng.aspx.

Prison Legal News. 2009. "BOP Suspends Use of Ion Spectrometry Drug Detection
  Devices." February 2009. https://www.prisonlegalnews.org/news/2009/feb/15/
  bop-suspends-use-of-ion-spectrometry-drug-detection-devices/.

———. 2010. "Ion Spectrometry Scans Resume at BOP Facilities." May 2010.
  https://www.prisonlegalnews.org/news/2010/may/15/ion-spectrometry-
  scans-resume-at-bop-facilities/.

Schoemperlen, Diane. 2016. *This Is Not My Life: A Memoir of Love, Prison, and Other
  Complications*. Toronto: Harper-Collins.

Vivar, Jose. 2014. "Drug Detectors Unfairly Target Visitors." *Kingston Whig-
  Standard*, July 2, 2014. http://www.thewhig.com/2014/07/02/drug-detectors-
  unfairly-target-visitors.

White, Patrick. 2017. "Prison Visitors Petition Ottawa to Scrap Sensitive Drug Scanners." *Globe and Mail*, February 2, 2017. https://www.theglobeandmail.com/news/national/prison-visitors-petition-ottawa-to-scrap-sensitive-drug-scanners/article33891061/.

Young, Jock. 1999. *The Exclusive Society: Social Exclusion, Crime, and Difference in Late Modernity*. Thousand Oaks, CA: Sage.

POLICIES REFERENCED

Commissioner's Directive, Visiting, No. 559, effective 2012-06-13.

Commissioner's Directive, Control of Entry to and Exit from Institutions, No. 566-1, effective 2015-07-02.

Commissioner's Directive, Use of Non-Intrusive Search Tools, No. 566-8-1, effective 2012-06-13.

Commissioner's Directive, Technical Requirements for Ion Mobility Spectrometry Devices, No. 566-8-2, effective 2012-06-13.

4

Nodal Governance and Technologies of Control: One Approach to Risk Mitigation in Ontario

Carrie B. Sanders, Debra Langan, Katy Cain, and Taylor Knipe

INTRODUCTION

In Canada and abroad there are new "collaborative" approaches to community safety that engage citizens, police, and stakeholders in developing and "investing in proactive, integrated community safety approaches [that] get at the roots of crime" (Public Safety Canada 2013). In Canada, these new collaborative approaches are a response to the rising concerns regarding the **economics of policing**. In 2013, the Canadian minister of public safety, on behalf of all federal, provincial, and territorial ministers responsible for justice and public safety, hosted the Summit on the Economics of Policing. The outcome of the summit was the development of the *Shared Forward Agenda*, whose key objective is to "develop a national implementation plan for the application of improved community safety models by all police services and in conjunction with other social agencies" (Steering Committee 2013, 4). In response to the *Shared Forward Agenda*, police services across Ontario, Canada, are creating partnerships with social services and community organizations to develop collaborative, risk-driven approaches to enhancing community safety and well-being (Kramp 2014). In Ontario, these initiatives and new security networks (Dupont 2004) are referred to as "**situation tables**" and have been informed by "the Hub" initiative in Saskatchewan. Similar collaborative approaches to community safety have emerged across the globe—for example, "hubs" in Glasgow, Scotland; Boston's "Operation Ceasefire" (Braga and Weisburd 2012); "safety houses" in the Netherlands (Jochoms et al. 2012; Terpstra 2008); and "crime and disorder reduction partnerships" in the United Kingdom (Crawford 2006).

The situation tables that we studied involve frequent in-person meetings among human service professionals from different agencies (e.g., police, social services, child welfare services, victim services, and mental health professionals, among others) "to detect acute elevations in complex client risk, share limited information necessary to identify client needs, and plan rapid interventions designed to mitigate those risks before harm occurs" (Nilson 2016, 58). Situation tables are a new community approach to the governance of security, which is future-oriented, strategic, and targeted based on an assessment of risk. Situation tables are described as enabling "human service providers from multiple sectors to collaborate around the improvement of client outcomes" (Nilson 2016, 58).

These situation tables, Sanders and Langan (2018) argue, are illustrative of a broader movement toward **nodal governance** and the creation of **security networks** (Dupont 2004). Dupont (2006a, 167) defines security networks as

> a set of institutional, organisational, communal, or individual agents or nodes that are directly or indirectly connected in order to authorize and/or provide security for the benefit of internal or external stakeholders.

Security networks consist of "recurrent interconnections and linkages" that bring these actors together on "a voluntary, contractual, or regulatory basis" for the purposes of delivering security through a range of services such as "the identification of needs and the resources available to respond to them . . . [and] the management of risks and the deployment of human and technological assets" (Dupont 2006a, 168).

Although security networks are becoming a central feature in the governance of security, little is empirically known about the relationship between risk and nodal governance. To date, much of what has been studied on security networks has provided a theoretical and descriptive mapping of the nodes. Yet, as Dupont (2006b, 87) explains,

> a study of the nodal governance of security . . . ought also to consider the more subjective relational sphere of each node, that is the perception of its own position in a larger organizational field, of the other nodes' roles, strengths and weaknesses, and of the resources that it can mobilize to achieve certain objectives derived from this reflective assessment.

In order to understand the "forms of linkages and power" situation tables generate, we engaged in a qualitative study of the development of one situation table operating in a mid-size urban centre in Ontario. Our research answers the following research questions: How do people from various organizations with different objectives and responsibilities perceive their role(s), and others' roles, within the security network? How is "acutely elevated risk" individually and collectively defined and understood across the security network? What are the intended and unintended implications of these new collaborative responses to community safety and well-being?

In what follows, we review the literature on nodal governance, security networks, and community safety. We then describe our qualitative study and our use of constructivist grounded theorizing (Charmaz 2006) for making sense of our data.

LITERATURE REVIEW

Governing through security networks is a result of the interconnectedness of insecurity and risks that proliferate the present "risk society" (O'Reilly and Ellison 2006). The push for community collaboration and enhanced efficiencies, coupled with the new risk mentality (Ericson and

Haggerty 1997; Garland 1996), has given rise to the development of security networks because "the creation of partnerships and networks ensure[s] a pooling of resources and a dilution of liability, making risk easier and more acceptable to handle" (Dupont 2004, 78; see also Fleming and Rhodes 2005). As a result, security within the contemporary environment is increasingly being provided by networks of public, private, and welfare organizations, resulting in communities and individuals being "expected to contribute to their own regulation, security, and safety" (Ransley and Mazerolle 2009, 366; Sanders and Langan 2018). Crawford (2006) argues in his research on crime and disorder reduction partnerships in the United Kingdom that these new security networks act as a "novel technology of control" that shapes the everyday practices of organizations and the individuals they serve—thereby rendering the community as both the agent and the object of security and community safety initiatives (for similar arguments, see Bania 2012; Dunbar 2010).

Within the growing literature base on security networks and **plural policing**, there are disagreements about the position and role the state holds within these networks. Cherney, O'Reilly, and Grabosky (2006), for example, describe a state-centred view of plural policing in which the police play a central role in creating networks and "brokering alliances" (379) by enlisting the co-operation of external partners with the objective of "enhancing the efficacy of state rule under "'multi-layered' conditions" (Shearing and Johnston 2010, 497). In this view, the police are the centre hub of the network—actively creating and structuring "the security network both in its presence and in its absence, both in its explicit directions and in its implicit permissions" (Loader and Walker 2004, 225). The primary function of the police is to be "brokers of public safety" by constructing, "harnessing," and "managing" external partners in the delivery of public safety (Cherney 2008). Such scholarship depicts a shifting police role wherein they engage in **"distanciated governance"** (Giddens 1990) by acting as a "social diagnostician and community mobilizer" tasked with "linking different service providers in a joint effort to address community safety issues" (Greene 2000, 314).

Osborne and Gaebler (1992) provide a nautical analogy for understanding the state-centred framework—the state maintains control, or what they call "steering" functions, while the external agencies become increasingly more responsible for "rowing." The nautical analogy is useful as it links the language of governance with the regulation state, because "regulation has become 'steering'; governing by setting the course, monitoring the direction and correcting deviations from the course set" (Crawford 2006, 453). Regulation, therefore, becomes redefined and focused on regulating self-regulation. As such, the state acts in an anchoring role in these networks, as well as in a symbolically distinct role that has led to the creation of novel technologies of control that both extend and supplement the formal authority of the state (Crawford 2006).

Other scholars, such as Johnston and Shearing (2003), perceive security networks as a form of **nodal governance** wherein relationships between and among actors (nodes) take different shapes and levels of coordination, competition, rivalry, and conflict (see also Brewer 2015). Nodes in security networks are conceptualized as sites of governance at which knowledge and resources are mobilized in order to "manage a course of events" (Burris, Drahos, and Shearing 2005, 33). Nodal governance does not recognize these new security networks to be hierarchical in nature. Instead, it adopts a perception of the networks as fluid and attentive to "temporary hubs of practice" and the "continuous, iterative and more or less temporary processes carried out by a range of . . . actors (nodes) according to different positions of power" (Wood and Dupont 2006, 4). Nodal governance consists of "complex of hybrid arrangements and practices in which different mentalities of governance as well (as) very different sets of institutional arrangements coexist" (Wood and Shearing 2007, 4). In this framework, official authority for the enactment of security practices can be dispersed across public and private agencies.

As demonstrated above, nodal governance rejects the state-centric framework and argues that governance is far more complex and requires the interplay of many agencies, with each able to "steer" and "row" at different times, thereby rendering the state as "one node among many"

(Johnston and Shearing 2003). Within this framework, power is "not a matter of imposing a sovereign will, but instead a process of enlisting the cooperation of chains of actors who 'translate' power from one locale to another" (Garland 1997, 182). Thus, to understand how security networks operate, it is essential to examine the internal dynamics and resources that establish and transcend boundaries within these security networks. Dupont (2004) argues that a node's **"capital"**—that is, its context-specific resources—are central for understanding how organizations acquire and yield power, and how they influence the operation of a network. He argues that an organization's access to different types of capital—such as economic, cultural, political, social, and symbolic—"determines to a significant degree the structure of the network" (Dupont 2004, 84).

Economic capital refers to access to financial resources, while *cultural capital* is associated with a unique level of knowledge and expertise that is acquired through such things as higher levels of selection and training and adoption of technology. *Political capital* is associated with proximity to, and sphere of influence over, the government. *Social capital* refers to the "whole set of social relations that allow the constitution, mainte-nance, and expansion of social networks" (Dupont 2004, 86). Economic, cultural, political, and social capital, Dupont (2004, 86) argues, are all mediated by *symbolic capital*, which, in turn, ascribes "legitimacy to an organization, and the power it holds to speak with authority to the other actor." Further, he argues that actors can use their capital (cultural and symbolic, specifically) to leverage their position as knowledge brokers with legitimacy within security networks. Burris (2004, 341) argues that adopting a nodal governance framework brings attention to the internal characteristics of nodes (such as access and use of capital) and enables an "analysis of how power is actually created and exercised within a social system."

Regardless of what position you take within the debate, both a state-centric framework and a nodal governance framework recognize a shift from government to **governance**, wherein the state governs at a distance (Garland 1996; Miller and Rose 1990; Terpstra 2004). This "distanciated governance" (Giddens 1990) facilitated by security

networks poses both promises—such as reduced costs and enhanced efficiencies and organizational interoperability—and threats to democratic
principles (Hughes 2002). In this chapter, we use one situation table as
an empirical site to interrogate this new networked landscape in order
to understand (1) what "forms of linkages and power" situation tables
generate, (2) how "acutely elevated risk" is individually and collectively
defined and understood across the network, and (3) what the intended
and unintended implications of these growing security networks are for
the people they serve. From this analysis we argue that the economic,
cultural, political, social, and symbolic capital afforded to police within
these security networks has led them to operate as a technology of social
control that extends the reach of the state. Further, we maintain that
the state-centric steering of these new collaborative security networks
has aligned them with traditional forms of policing that work to police
the "usual suspects."

METHODOLOGY: CONSTRUCTIVIST GROUNDED THEORIZING

We undertook a qualitative inquiry into the implementation of a situation
table in a mid-size urban centre in Ontario. After receiving institutional
ethics approval, we employed a triangulated methodology that included
field observations, in-depth qualitative interviews with members of the
situation table, and document analysis (Denzin 1978). We conducted
participant observation and took field notes at several Ontario Working
Group meetings that brought together police and community agencies
for the purpose of providing education on collaborative risk-driven interventions for community safety and wellness. We also gathered field
note data through more than 100 hours of observations at community
meetings and workshops for the implementation of the situation table
under study.

In combination, these data informed the development of a thematic, semi-structured interview schedule that guided 27 in-depth
qualitative interviews with police and community agency representatives from that situation table. We conducted interviews with the

managers/directors and supervisors of each node of the security net-work and "covered the formal and informal dimensions of existing partnerships" (Dupont 2006a, 170). We chose agency managers be-cause, while they may not be aware of all of the ties and relationships that their front-line workers have with other members of the security network, they are the ones who are always present at the regular sit-uation table meetings, and they also have the greatest influence over policy or practical changes (Dupont 2006a). The data for the document analysis are drawn from seven situation table program evaluations from across Canada, as well as policy and government reports on collaborative, risk-driven community safety initiatives. Specifically, we analyzed seven reports and resource papers from the Ontario Association of Chiefs of Police website (http://www.oacp.on.ca/news-events/resource-documents/ontario-working-group-owg).

Field notes, interview transcripts, and relevant documents were analyzed to identify and group together themes related to community safety and security networks, drawing on Charmaz's (2014) approach to constructivist grounded theorizing. We immersed ourselves in the data, mindful of our analytic interest in collaborative responses to communi-ty safety and attuned to a reflexive approach to data interpretation that prioritizes participants' experiences. We approached theorizing as an "on-going activity" (Charmaz 2014, 244)—"a practice . . . [that] entails practical activities of engaging the world and of constructing abstract understandings about and within it" (Charmaz 2014, 233). Through this process, we came to see the scholarship on security networks and nodal governance as relevant for guiding our understanding of the data, and for "guiding [our] interpretive theoretical practice" (Charmaz 2014, 233). In what follows, we begin by first describing the Ontario Working Group on Community Safety and Well-Being's directives on how situation tables should operate. We then explore the funding and development of situation tables in Ontario before looking at the process of defining and identifying people at acutely elevated risk. From this analysis we demonstrate how the political, economic, cultural, social, and symbolic capital afforded the police have shaped the table to operate as a traditional policing practice that targets the "usual suspects" (Gill 2000).

SITUATION TABLES: A COLLABORATIVE, RISK-DRIVEN, COMMUNITY SAFETY INITIATIVE

A situation table is portrayed as involving regular, frequent, in-person, "highly disciplined" discussions among multiple agencies in a community to provide "immediate coordinated and integrated responses through mobilization of resources to address situations facing individuals, families, or environments with risk factors" (Russell and Taylor 2014c, 17). At these discussions, agencies are directed to use a four-stage approach and share limited information about a case that "appears to extend beyond their own level of expertise" so that multiple services can swiftly be accessed to "reduce the possibility of the situation worsening" (Russell and Taylor 2014c, 17). In order to be "timely and effective" in taking action, the "qualified professionals" at the table do not have to obtain the explicit consent of the client to share information about the client (Russell and Taylor 2014c, 22).

For a client to receive "wraparound" service, they must first be identified as being at an acutely elevated risk of crime and/or victimization. Russell and Taylor (2014a, 3) define *acutely elevated risk* as "the threshold combining both the degree of probability of harm in any given situation and the degree to which the operating risk factors involved cut across human service disciplines." There are more than 100 pre-identified risk factors that the services work with, which are grouped within 26 risk categories.[1] Examples of risk factors include alcohol and drug use, diagnosed/suspected mental health problem(s), previous or current suicide risk, pregnancy, physical disability, terminal illness, self-harm, damage to property, parent-child conflict, isolation, and anti-social behaviour.

Once the situation table has identified the risk factors at play and determined that the individual is at an acutely elevated level of risk for crime or victimization, the agencies that deal with those risk factors become responsible for mitigating the risk and leading the interventions (Russell and Taylor 2014a, 22), with the police always in attendance. A representative from the lead agency (i.e., the agency assigned by the situation table to act as the leading organization for managing the client's case), accompanied by a uniformed officer and possibly another service

provider, will go to the person's and/or family's home, tell them that they have been identified as being at acutely elevated risk, and ask them if they will accept the assistance of the table. At that time, the individual(s) and/or family can choose to accept services—by either (a) listening to what services and options are available to them, or (b) listening and engaging with the services being offered—or they can refuse the assistance (see also Sanders and Langan 2018).

FUNDING AND DEVELOPING SITUATION TABLES

Situation tables gained traction in 2013 when four Ontario police services (Toronto Police Service, Greater Sudbury Police, Waterloo Regional Police, and Peel Regional Police) that had been individually engaging in new collaborative approaches to community safety came together to create the Ontario Working Group (OWG) on Collaborative, Risk-Driven Community Safety. This group put forth situation tables as the ideal model for community safety. At the same time, the Future of Policing Advisory Committee to the Ontario Ministry of Community Safety and Correctional Services developed an interest in collaborative, risk-driven approaches to community safety, and saw the OWG as an authoritative body on the subject (Russell and Taylor 2014c, 4):

> The confluence of all of these discussions and initiatives encouraged the Ministry to support the work of the OWG through the Proceeds of Crime (POC) Grant process. The four founding police services applied to the Ministry for financial support for their local initiatives; and donated a quarter of what they received to finance the work of the OWG.[2]

What resulted was the development and implementation of community situation tables—and protocols for their operation as outlined by the OWG—across Ontario and, more recently, across Canada.

The historical development of situation tables reveals the economic and political capital the police hold within these security networks.

Although the police frequently noted that situation tables are "not a police driven initiative" (field notes), the tables originated through the work of four police services. Further, representatives of these four police services, as well as a few private counterparts (some of whom were pursuing second careers after spending time in public policing), established the aforementioned OWG—through which they provided guidance on the processes for establishing, developing, and evaluating the security networks. This economic and political capital, we argue, enables the police to acquire and maintain a dominant position within these new security networks. This dominant position is further evidenced in the rhetoric surrounding the goals and objectives of the tables.

Situation tables, for example, are described as being "an excellent tactic in the new transformation from crime prevention to safety promotion because they: 1) [are] risk driven; 2) benefit from the value-added of interagency collaboration; and 3) result in a reduction in harm and victimization" (Russell and Taylor 2015, 11). Moving the focus away from "crime prevention"—a role largely managed by policing—and placing attention on "safety promotion" is, we argue, an important rhetorical strategy. It works to take the responsibility off of traditional policing and "its costs and effectiveness, to a consideration of the roles and responsibilities of virtually everyone else in the community" in order to proactively mitigate a spectrum of risk factors with the potential to cause harm (Russell and Taylor 2015, 10). As the OWG notes, while police still have to respond to any and all threats to personal and/or public safety, "they are not qualified to rectify more profound community problems" (Russell and Taylor 2015, 9). This is an interesting and important shift as it describes the primary role and responsibility of police to be fighting crime rather than fostering community safety more broadly—something they are described as "not qualified to rectify." It follows that safety promotion would, therefore, become the priority and responsibility of all people involved in the situation table. But do people working with different organizations—with different objectives and responsibilities—share a consensus on their understandings and definitions of acutely elevated risk, and, if so, how is that consensus reached?

ADOPTING A COMMON LANGUAGE: CONSTRUCTING AND APPLYING "ACUTELY ELEVATED RISK"

One way to interrogate these new security networks is to explore whether, how, and to what extent different understandings of risk are present at the table. Situation tables already have their own definition of risk and a process in place to determine the appropriateness of various types of risk. Through exploring interview data, it became evident that community partners attended the situation table with their own expertise regarding risk and its mitigation, yet drew upon the risk-tracking database (RTD) for identifying and classifying people at acutely elevated risk. The RTD is a tool that contains a "risk glossary" of 102 risk factors in 26 different risk categories. According to reports from the OWG, the risk database was first utilized in Prince Albert, Saskatchewan, for the purpose of "assist[ing] police in identifying and presenting high risk individuals and locations to the Situation Table" (Russell and Taylor 2014c, 8). As can be inferred by the description of the tool, it was created for police use. Although "many agencies, organizations, and individuals have invaluable information about local risks to safety and well-being," police occurrence data and the identification of provincial risk factors that are drawn from these data have been utilized to "steer" initiatives (Russell and Taylor 2014b, 29). This demonstrates one way in which police are believed to be "uniquely situated when it comes to identifying accumulating risk factors" because "by examining routine information flows, such as complaints, calls for service, witness accounts, by-law infractions, and street checks, patterns can be revealed that give early warning of situations that may be escalating towards disorder, crime, or harm" (Russell and Taylor 2014a, 3). Thus, the police, through their access to records management systems and information technologies, hold significant cultural capital within the network. As a result, they have adopted a central role in developing the mechanisms by which risk is to be identified, verified, and watched.

Interestingly, community partners often expressed ambiguity around the use of the risk glossary and its associated RTD. Community partners mostly spoke about using these tools to present cases of acutely elevated risk, rather than drawing on their expertise or tools utilized by their own organizations. As a result, the conversations often revolved around "fitting" situations into the constructions of risk provided. For instance, one service provider remarked,

> I'm okay with finding one that fits as best as it can . . . who really cares what you pick as long as the information's there? . . . From my glance at the glossary, they give you a reasonable number of options and you pick the one that seems the best fit. (I13)

As remarked by this interviewee, effort is made at the table to fit situations into the existing tools rather than altering the tool so that it reflects situations.

While participating services and community organizations worked with the tools provided, they critiqued the police's failure to include risk factor expertise in designing the tools. In referring to critiques of the development of the table's understanding of risk, two community partners made the following argument:

> **Social service provider 1:** It would have been a lot easier for me if we had been included in the initial planning and knowing that the police . . . made this application to do this, because all of us have to—must participate by virtue of our mandate.

> **Social service provider 2:** They [police] have the big title for risk factor and then subtitles and for mental health, mental health should be making up what's relevant [for mental health, but the police] make [it] up—"here's what's relevant." Not, "here's what I think is relevant for mental health when really I don't even work in this [field]." (I12)

As these comments from service providers demonstrate, community partners are mindful of the fact that they were not included in the development of the tools for the table, and they find this situation at least somewhat problematic. Further, given the expertise of each agency sitting at the table, they argue that the agency most directly associated with each risk factor should be the one defining the parameters of the risks linked to their field. Yet, as demonstrated by the willingness or necessity to fit understandings of risk into those conceptualized by the police-initiated glossary/risk matrix, standardized tools end up being valued over expertise in defining risk. The use of this tool and others like it, and their connection to police understandings of risk, represents one way in which police knowledge—and, by extension their symbolic capital—is prioritized and privileged at the table. This finding illuminates the way in which the police have been able to leverage their cultural and symbolic capital to establish their position as legitimate knowledge brokers within the security network.

Although participants stated that they could adequately fit their clients' situations into the risk categories provided by the RTD, there was significant ambiguity surrounding the translation of risk factors into a designation of acutely elevated risk. In other words, while community partners used the glossary of risk factors to identify which risks were present in particular situations, there was substantial misunderstanding about how many risk factors had to be present for a case to be representative of acutely elevated risk. This confusion demonstrates the lack of a shared definition of what constitutes acutely elevated risk. For example, when a participant was asked if a specific number of risks was required for an acutely elevated risk designation, they commented,

> In terms of a hard number, no . . . even though we try and say . . . one or more of these risk factors must be present in order to advance, you ignore that sort of spidey-sense to your detriment[;] . . . if one or more person that has a connection to a case at the table has a sense that it's going to turn to crap and it's going to be soon, there's a very real possibility that's the case. . . . In addition to the presence of the formal filter system and that sort of screening criteria, you know, we always sort of like to encourage people to pay attention to those, just the bad feeling that you get . . . that something might go bad. (I9)

In fact, when we asked participants how decisions were made to determine if a situation was at acutely elevated risk, service providers would draw on their own experience and intuitive sense of what constituted acutely elevated risk. For instance, one community partner remarked, "once you've been in this work for a long time it's quite obvious when something's a risk and when you get 20 of those kinds of people around the Table it's incredibly efficient" (I1). Referring to the identification of risk as "obvious" or originating from a "spidey-sense" demonstrates community partners' use of an intuitive sense to decide whether acutely elevated risk is present in a situation. It further highlights the "lack of objective measures of risk and risk assessments" (field notes).

In spite of the inclusion of experiential knowledge in making decisions about the presence or absence of acutely elevated risk, there was recognition among participants about the lack of "widespread agreement on what constitutes risk . . . [because] partners coming to the Table don't always have [similar] experiences" (I9). As the following participant explained, it would be valuable for each service to track how many of their clients are being referred compared to how many they are referring themselves, because, in her organization, she sees clients "who are operating [successfully] at high risk . . . so it's definitely perspective" (I13). She further notes that they wouldn't refer some people because they "are just too used to the high level of risk [the person] operates at" (I13). In this way, situation table members' understandings of risk and a client's ability to "operate at high risk"—or not—appear to vary and are shaped by one's organizational work.

Looking at the way the collective definition of risk (as put forth by the police) and the individual definitions of risk (as perceived by service providers) merge at the table identifies the cultural, social, and symbolic capital police possess within the network, as the police are the ones who have constructed the risk glossary and RTD and it is recognized as being the official determinant of who is "at risk." The police are also the table participants who most frequently refer individuals (over 85 percent of cases) to the table (Babayan, Landry-Thompson, and Stevens 2015). Further, the way in which interviewees accorded the police authority when it came to how they provided rationales to support their definitions of situations of acutely elevated risk reinforced our analysis that the police hold a dominant role within the network. As such, the police are important "knowledge brokers" who bring to the table significant capital (Dupont 2004) in terms of knowledge, data, and technologies. As one participant explained,

> The police always include the number of interactions with police over a specific period of time . . . so they know and they'll tell us that over ten years, over five years, there's been interactions but in the last year that's increased and jumped up to whatever. So they're able to show there's been a significant change somewhere that's caused that individual to be now at imminent risk. (I17)

As described above, police narratives at the table suggest access to unique data—which are, at times, reported as longitudinal—and technologies to which others at the table do not have access. In fact, the police narratives and their supporting technologies are evidence of the cultural and symbolic capital they wield that provides legitimacy to their client referrals to the table and, subsequently, their classifications of acutely elevated risk. As the following police officer explained,

> Identifying what all of the risks are . . . I think is our key ability because . . . the sad part is police ultimately understand all of the risk factors whereas service agencies . . . will only necessarily see information from one [client] . . . but because the last resort always ends up being police, we're aware of the challenges that are facing the whole family. . . . We do have records management that notes every time an individual has dealt with the police and what type of call it was and using that information is where I'm able to couple it with the referral that's received to determine whether it's acutely elevated risk or not. (I18)

The quote above illustrates the privileged position the police hold in constructing risk at the table because of their professed access to data and sophisticated technologies. The capital police bring to the table, we argue, ascribes credibility to them while also reinforcing and legitimizing the central and powerful role they hold in the security network. Thus, given the use of the risk glossary/RTD that was largely created by the police, and the privileged position of the police in determining who is deemed to be at acutely elevated risk at the table, the "collaborative" nature of the table is questionable. Indeed, how situations of acutely elevated risk are determined and responded to operates under a police-centric vision of what constitutes risk and risky people. As a result, the situation table, we argue, not only reproduces traditional policing logistics but, interestingly, also extends the broader policing logic to organizations outside of policing. This practice, we maintain, has profound implications for not only the people who are making decisions at the table, but also the clients who are the focus of table interventions, as well as the broader practice of community safety.

REFERRING APPROPRIATE INDIVIDUALS AND/OR SITUATIONS

While situation tables have been designed purportedly to provide immediate wraparound services to people identified as being at acutely elevated risk, some interview participants raised concerns about bringing clients forward to a table that had police representatives in attendance. For example, in the early stages of the implementation of the situation table, a participant explained,

> I understand that it's not a police-led initiative, but police are at the Table and how do you prevent that from becoming a criminal justice issue when that's part of the framework?. . . For example, there was a couple conversations about, you know, we're not here to arrest anybody but if you go to a house and there's a gun on the [kitchen] table, we're the police, we're going to do something about that. Well absolutely . . . but, you know, that's not the kind of intervention that we would do as a social service agency. (I9)

The quote above illuminates the difficulties associated with these new responses to community safety that are framed as "collaborative," but that reflect police priorities.

One participant wondered if the police presence would shape who she referred to the table:

> Are the police going to enact their authority and deal with that? . . .
> I don't know what the police responsibility is and following up that
> information and I have to admit, I—that may influence how much
> I present[;] . . . philosophically I could see how that could be a real
> problem between some of the agencies and our own ideas about how
> do we protect clients' rights to their own, you know, privacy of infor-
> mation and . . . are we putting them at further risk by an outcome that
> they maybe didn't expect? (I14)

Interestingly, during a pre-launch workshop for the situation table, the police led a hypothetical table scenario in which social service
providers were encouraged to bring mock cases forward for the table to
discuss. During the mock scenario, a social service provider asked the table about what to do for her male client who had previously been charged
with child sexual abuse and had just moved to the city to live with his
new girlfriend and her daughter. The man did not have any connections
in the new city and, due to the lack of connections, the worker saw him
as being at acutely elevated risk, and wanted to know what to do. Below
is an excerpt from our field notes of this scenario:

> The next situation that was brought to the table involved an individu-
> al who had previously been charged with child sexual abuse and had
> just relocated and didn't have supports. He also had other factors that
> suggested he was a case of acutely elevated risk and could use services.
> The social service worker asked, "what can I do for this man?" Right
> away [a police sergeant] said, "I know what the cop in me wants to
> do" and then he brought up Section 810.01 of the Criminal Code
> regarding the ability to place restrictions on individuals because they
> are a danger to children. . . . The social service worker who brought
> the case forward then proceeds to ask, "but what can I do for this
> man?" The police sergeant, as well as the Table consultant [who was

also a retired police officer] said that the police need to be involved for the safety of others . . . and that situations like this introduce more traditional forms of justice, not necessarily suitable for Table discussion. They then discussed how the woman living with the man was at acutely elevated risk and what could be done for her.

These field notes show the power the police hold within these security networks. They draw attention to the potential unintended consequences of these tables—agency workers may be cautious and/or unwilling to bring clients forward out of concern for the type of punitive actions that may be forthcoming from a police response. Further, the discussion that transpired during the mock scenario above illustrates how the police presence at the table contributes implicitly to understanding what "risks"—and by default, which individuals—are acceptable and, alternatively, unacceptable (e.g., perpetrators of child sexual assault) for consideration by the table.

Through further interrogating which "types" of individuals were deemed appropriate for intervention at the situation table, it became evident that individuals identified as being at "chronic risk" did not qualify for table intervention. Often the ineligibility of those living with chronic risk was understood as being a result of their inability to change. For instance, when service providers were questioned about why chronic individuals were inappropriate for table intervention, they offered explanations such as, "this person and this family is going nowhere" (I7). These sentiments were echoed by a number of service providers who were concerned that these individuals could not be reached since "they'd been living this way x amount of time" (I1). In referring to those at acute risk, one service provider noted that "the success rate's just gonna be higher" than working with those at chronic risk (I4). Without a systematic evaluation and objective process for risk assessment, situation tables may become nothing more than subjectively driven initiatives that "skim the cream" by choosing only those individuals who will demonstrate success—specifically, success for the initiative.

FREQUENT FLYERS AND TARGET COMMUNITIES

As described earlier, at the situation table the police were seen as having qualities and data uniquely suited to assessing/defining acute risk. The central and steering role held by the police, we argue, has led the table to be aligned with traditional policing practices even though discursively the table is constructed as exemplary of a "new" collaborative approach to community safety that is "not a policing initiative, nor police driven" (field notes). For example, through an analysis of the OWG documents, as well as the interview data, the table repeatedly referenced working specifically with "frequent flyers" from "marginalized neighbourhoods where [police] are called to respond most often" (Russell and Taylor 2014d, 9). *Frequent flyers* in this context are described as "those individuals who repeatedly require emergency room assistance; frequently get apprehended by police; and continue to make decisions that put themselves and others at repeated risk of significant levels of harm" (Russell and Taylor 2014a, 7).

For many participants, there was a recognition that the police come into contact with people at elevated risk because risk that is left unmitigated presents as a form of social disorder. By appearing "on the radar" (I4) and making contact with police, at-risk individuals trigger the need for social control. As the following participant explains,

> if you provided services and then all of a sudden that person, like 6 months later, appears on the radar—the police bring it back saying—we have to, again, intervene. (I4)

The table process is therefore utilized to instill social control through "risk mitigation" on those where "there's a marked departure from normal behaviour" (I2).

When reflecting upon the objectives of the situation table, one participant explained, "it's community safety; it's crime prevention; it's also to eliminate some of those chronic users of policing" (I6). Although situation tables are presented by the OWG as a strategy to promote community safety and well-being, because the table serves to enhance the symbolic and social capital the police possess, we argue that it has been used as a technology of social control to police the "usual suspects" (I5). As described above, a main objective of the table is "to eliminate some of those chronic users of policing" and to reduce crime and disorder. Thus, the table, while designed to identify and mitigate acutely elevated risk, is used on the ground as a technology of social control on those who are visibly in crisis and in frequent contact with the police. It therefore works to reduce the economics of policing by redistributing responsibility for social order from police to other social services. In this way, the table is focused on preventing criminality and securing order through agencies, because by getting individuals "connected to services, so that the police aren't having to go . . . the community becomes safer because these individuals are being connected" (I1).

The emphasis on frequent flyers is further reinforced by the way tables are measured and evaluated. For example, the OWG recommends that "police might want to track changes in calls for service and types of occurrences in target neighbourhoods'" in order to measure the table's effectiveness (Russell and Taylor 2014e, 4). Our experience with the table revealed that "changes in calls" refers to quantitative measures of how many frequent flyers were responsible for calls for service pre- and post-table interventions. The emphasis by the OWG on the use of police calls for service for assessing "effectiveness" reinforces the "steering" role held by police within these initiatives. As described above, police data are proposed to both identify risk and evaluate whether risk mitigation is effective. By using police data to identify individuals "at risk," or frequent flyers from "target neighbourhoods," the table can be seen as being utilized to police the "usual suspects" (Gill 2000). Within the OWG documents, target neighbourhoods are framed as areas where "people [are] living in marginalized conditions where police are responding most often to anti-social behaviour, and sometimes crime" (Russell and Taylor 2015, 87). As such, situation tables appear to be focused on re-targeting those who are already known to police, and who have, therefore, historically been problematic.

DISCUSSION

The push toward collaborative responses to community safety and wellness, we argue, is a consequence of concerns surrounding the economics of policing and new forms of security networks. While at first glance these new arrangements suggest a co-operative form of partnerships, upon closer examination, they appear to "reveal more expansive forms of control" and accountability (Scoular and O'Neill 2007, 764). These initiatives no longer hold police as solely responsible for the control and regulation of crime and victimization, but instead responsibility is increasingly managed through networks and partnerships. By partnering with community agencies, police seek to share the responsibility for clients who historically have become the sole responsibility of police services because police are often the first ones to be called to emergency situations that involve complex individuals.

While an analysis of the interview data shows that the table does not possess an overall shared objective or value, it does identify a number of overlapping interests that have been brought together by formal, voluntary, and contractual ties that have been largely spearheaded or influenced by the police. Our analysis further illustrates how the economic, political, cultural, social, and symbolic capital held by the police has "determined to a significant degree the structure of the network" (Dupont 2004, 84). Further, it has led other organizations to be informed by, draw upon, and utilize police definitions and understandings of "risk"—which, for some organizations involved, are quite distinct from their own orientations. As a state-centric security network, the table is utilized to institutionalize social control via agencies that are traditionally responsible for providing care. In addition, the economic advantages to police services are clear, as others are enlisted to deal with frequent flyers who present a drain on policing resources.

While a situation table ostensibly operates as a network of services, the police are not situated as simply "one node among many" (Johnston and Shearing 2003), but instead, as demonstrated above, they maintain a central role in the network's development, implementation, and governance (Osborne and Gaebler 1992). The discursive portrayals of the benevolent intentions that drive situation tables—as evidenced, for example, in characterizations of the table as collaborative and community-safety driven, concerned first and foremost with a client's well-being—serve to mask the ways in which state control is increased. The focus of situation tables on those at "acutely elevated risk" and "frequent flyers," we argue, has extended and formalized social control "not directly connected to formal policing" (Jones and Newburn 2002, 139). Situation tables operate as if they are neutral entities; however, by interrogating how members at the table identify and classify someone at acutely elevated risk, we illuminate how these initiatives are influenced, and, in many respects, end up mirroring traditional policing practices.

DISCUSSION QUESTIONS

1. What has facilitated the movement toward security networks? How does the current emphasis on security networks compare to previous approaches to community safety?

2. What is the role of police in relation to other agencies in shaping constructions of risk in the situation table model? How is "acutely elevated risk" defined, and how—and to what extent—does this concept inform what happens at various stages of the table process?

3. How are different forms of capital (political, economic, cultural, social, and symbolic) evident in how the table operates?

4. Imagine that you are a person who is visited by representatives of the situation table, without being notified in advance, because you have been deemed by them to be at acutely elevated risk. How would you feel, and how might you respond?

5. What are the implications of situation tables? That is, what impact(s) do you think they will have, and why?

NOTES

1. Risk categories include: alcohol, drugs, gambling, mental health, suicide, physical health, self-harm, criminal involvement, crime victimization, physical violence, emotional violence, sexual violence, elderly abuse, supervision, basic needs,

missing school, parenting, housing, poverty, negative peers, anti-social/negative behaviour, unemployment, missing/runaway, threat to public safety, gangs, and social environment.

2. As word spread about the work being done by the OWG, the Ontario Association of Chiefs of Police invited the OWG to act as a virtual subcommittee for their Community Safety and Crime Prevention Standing Committee (Russell and Taylor 2014a).

REFERENCES

Babayan, Alexey, Tamara Landry-Thompson, and Adam Stevens. 2015. *Evaluation of the Brant Community Response Team Initiative: Six Month Report.* Brant County Health Unit. October.

Bania, Melanie L. 2012. *New Ways of Working? Crime Prevention and Community Safety Within Ottawa's Community Development Framework.* PhD dissertation, Department of Criminology, University of Ottawa, Ottawa, ON.

Braga, Anthony A., and David L. Weisburd. 2012. "The Effects of Focused Deterrence Strategies on Crime: A Systematic Review and Meta-analysis of the Empirical Evidence." *Journal of Research in Crime and Delinquency* 49 (3): 323–58.

Brewer, Russell. 2015. "The Malleable Character of Brokerage and Crime Control: A Study of Policing, Security and Network Entrepreneurialism on Melbourne's Waterfront." *Policing and Society: An International Journal of Research and Policy* 27 (7): 712–31.

Burris, Scott. 2004. "Governance, Microgovernance and Health." *Temple Law Review* 77 (2): 335–61.

Burris, Scott, Peter Drahos, and Clifford Shearing. 2005. "Nodal Governance." *Australian Journal of Legal Philosophy* 30 (1): 30–58.

Charmaz, Kathy. 2006. *Constructing Grounded Theory: A Practical Guide through Qualitative Analysis.* London: Sage Publications.

———. 2014. *Constructing Grounded Theory.* 2nd ed. London: Sage Publications.

Cherney, Adrian. 2008. "Harnessing the Crime Control Capacities of Third Parties." *Policing: An International Journal of Police Strategies and Management* 31 (4): 631–47.

Cherney, Adrian, Juani O'Reilly, and Peter Grabosky. 2006. "Networks and Meta-regulation: Strategies Aimed at Governing Illicit Synthetic Drugs." *Policing and Society: An International Journal of Research and Policy* 16 (4): 370–85.

Crawford, Adam. 2006. "Networked Governance and the Post-regulatory State?: Steering, Rowing and Anchoring the Provision of Policing and Security." *Theoretical Criminology* 10 (4): 449–79.

Denzin, Norman K. 1978. *The Research Act.* New York: McGraw-Hill.

Dunbar, Laura Kristen. 2010. *Crime Prevention and Community: Operationalizing the Concept of Community in the City of Ottawa's Community Development Framework.* PhD dissertation, Department of Criminology, University of Ottawa, Ottawa, ON.

Dupont, Benoit. 2004. "Security in the Age of Networks." *Policing and Society* 14 (1): 76–91.

———. 2006a. "Delivering Security through Networks: Surveying the Relational Landscape of Security Managers in an Urban Setting." *Crime, Law and Social Change* 45 (3): 165–84.

———. 2006b. "Power Struggles in the Field of Security: Implications for Democratic Transformation." In *Democracy, Society and the Governance of Security,* edited by Jennifer Wood and Benoit Dupont, 86–110. Cambridge, UK: Cambridge University Press.

Ericson, Richard V., and Kevin D. Haggerty. 1997. *Policing the Risk Society.* Toronto: University of Toronto Press.

Fleming, Jenny, and Roderick Rhodes. 2005. "Bureaucracy, Contract and Networks: The Unholy Trinity and the Police." *Australian and New Zealand Journal of Criminology* 38 (2): 192–205.

Garland, David. 1996. "The Limits of the Sovereign State: Strategies of Crime Control in Contemporary Society." *British Journal of Criminology* 36 (4): 445–71.

———. 1997. "'Governmentality' and the Problem of Crime: Foucault, Criminology, Sociology." *Theoretical Criminology* 1 (2): 173–214.

Giddens, Anthony. 1990. *The Consequences of Modernity.* Stanford, CA: Stanford University Press.

Gill, Peter. 2000. *Rounding Up the Usual Suspects? Developments in Contemporary Law Enforcement Intelligence.* Abingdon, UK: Routledge.

Greene, Jack R. 2000. *Community Policing in America: Changing the Nature, Structure and Function of the Police.* Rockville, MD: National Institute of Justice.

Hughes, Gordon. 2002. "The Shifting Sands of Crime Prevention and Community Safety." In *Crime Prevention and Community Safety: New Directions,* edited by

Gordon Hughes, Eugene McLaughlin, and John Muncie, 1–10. London: Sage Publications.

Jochoms, Theo, Hani Quint, Kate Horton, Gabriele Jacobs, and P. Saskia Bayerl. 2012. "United under One Roof: Safety Houses in the Netherlands." In *Best Practices in European Policing: A Selection of Case Studies*, edited by Leslie N. Graham, Kathryn A. Bettteridge, Rebecca Casey and Arjen van Witteloostuijn, 77–92. Durham, UK: Durham University.

Johnston, Les, and Clifford Shearing. 2003. *Governing Security: Explorations in Policing and Justice*. London: Routledge.

Jones, Trevor, and Tim Newburn. 2002. "The Transformation of Policing? Understanding Current Trends in Policing Systems." *British Journal of Criminology* 42 (1): 129–46.

Kramp, Daryl. 2014. *Economics of Policing: Report of the Standing Committee on Public Safety and National Security*. 41st Parliament, Second Session. Ottawa: House of Commons, Canada.

Loader, Ian, and Neil Walker. 2004. "State of Denial? Rethinking the Governance of Security." *Punishment and Society* 6 (2): 221–28.

Miller, Peter, and Nikolas Rose. 1990. "Governing Economic Life." *Economy and Society* 19 (1): 1–31.

Nilson, Chad. 2016. "Canada's Hub Model: Calling for Perceptions and Feedback from those Clients at the Focus of Collaborative Risk-Driven Intervention." *Journal of Community Safety and Well-Being* 1 (3): 58–60.

O'Reilly, Conor, and Graham Ellison. 2006. "'Eye Spy Private High': Re-conceptualizing High Policing Theory." *British Journal of Criminology* 46 (4): 641–60.

Osborne, David, and Ted Gaebler. 1992. *Reinventing Government: How the Entrepreneurial Spirit Is Transforming the Public Sector*. Boston: Addison Wesley.

Public Safety Canada. 2013. *Summit on the Economics of Policing: Strengthening Canada's Policing Advantage*. Ottawa: Public Safety Canada.

Ransley, Janet, and Lorraine Mazerolle. 2009. "Policing in an Era of Uncertainty." *Police Practice and Research: An International Journal* 10 (4): 365–81.

Russell, Hugh C., and Norman E. Taylor. 2014a. *Consolidating Lessons Learned about Risk and Collaboration: Collaborative Analysis for Systemic Improvements*. Ontario Working Group on Collaborative Risk-Driven Community Safety, Ontario Association of Chiefs of Police. April.

———. 2014b. *Consolidating Lessons Learned about Risk and Collaboration: Framework for Planning . . . Community Safety and Well-Being*. Ontario Working Group on Collaborative Risk-Driven Community Safety, Ontario Association of Chiefs of Police. April.

———. 2014c. *Consolidating Lessons Learned about Risk and Collaboration: An Interpretive Guide to Information Sharing Practices in Ontario . . . Within the Context of Collaborative Risk-Drive Community Safety and Well-Being*. Ontario Working Group on Collaborative Risk-Driven Community Safety, Ontario Association of Chiefs of Police. April.

———. 2014d. *Consolidating Lessons Learned about Risk and Collaboration: Mitigating Acutely Elevated Risk of Harm Considerations in Adopting "The Situation Table."* Ontario Working Group on Collaborative Risk-Driven Community Safety, Ontario Association of Chiefs of Police. April.

———. 2014e. *Consolidating Lessons Learned about Risk and Collaboration: Performance Measures . . . for Community Safety and Well-Being*. Ontario Working Group on Collaborative Risk-Driven Community Safety, Ontario Association of Chiefs of Police. April.

———. 2015. *Gaining Momentum: Multi-sector Community Safety and Well-Being in Ontario*. Ontario Working Group on Collaborative Risk-Driven Community Safety, Ontario Association of Chiefs of Police. May.

Sanders, Carrie, and Debra Langan. 2018. "New Public Management and the Extension of State Control: Community Safety and Security Networks in Ontario." *Policing and Society*. https://doi.org/10.1080/10439463.2018.1427744.

Scoular, Jane, and Maggie O'Neill. 2007. "Regulating Prostitution, Social Inclusion, Responsibilization and the Politics of Prostitution Reform." *British Journal of Criminology* 47 (5): 764–78.

Shearing, Clifford, and Les Johnston. 2010. "Nodal Wards and Network Fallacies: A Genealogical Analysis of Global Insecurities." *Theoretical Criminology* 14 (4): 495–514.

Steering Committee. 2013. *Shared Forward Agenda*. Ottawa: Public Safety Canada.

Terpstra, Jan. 2004. "Police, Local Government and Citizens as Participants in Local Safety Networks." In *Policing in Central and Eastern Europe: Dilemmas in Contemporary Criminal Justice*, edited by Gorazd Mesko, Milan Pagon, and Bojan Dobovsek, 1–12. Maribor, Slovenia: University of Maribor, Faculty of Criminal Justice.

———. 2008. "Policing, Local Government, and Citizens as Participants in Local Security Networks." *Police Practice and Research: An International Journal* 9 (3): 213–25.

Wood, Jennifer, and Benoit Dupont. 2006. "Introduction: Understanding the Governance of Security." In *Democracy, Society and the Governance of Security*, edited by Jennifer Wood and Benoit Dupont, 1–10. Cambridge: Cambridge University Press.

Wood, Jennifer, and Clifford Shearing. 2007. *Imagining Security*. Cullompton, UK: Willan Publishing.

5 Enrolling Brain Imaging: How Psychopathy Becomes a "Neuro" Fact

Martin Dufresne, Dominique Robert, and Silvian Roy[1]

INTRODUCTION

Risk is a concept that we intuitively locate at the border of the known and the unknown, the full and the empty, the certain and the uncertain. From a realist perspective, risk is an inherent component of our late-modern society—a manifestation of the angst we feel about humans' place in the world and a result of our changing relationship with nature (Beck 1992). Risk calculation has been central to the administration of our society for decades, as the shift to pre-crime and preventive justice discussed in the introduction of this volume testifies. From this perspective, risk is conceived as an externality; it assumes there is a territory that science has not yet conquered. The modern narrative tells the story of an ever-developing knowledge that will eventually reduce, if not overcome, the great unknown. From a governance perspective, however, risk is a political technology. It is embodied, among others, in epidemiology, actuarial justice, and some political economy rationalities. Risk technology operates through the freedom of populations and subjects, subtly promoting values, allowing the constitution of hierarchies, and offering tools to actively design collective and personal biographies (Burchell 1996; Castel 1991; Ericson and Doyle 2003; Hannah-Moffat 1999; Lupton

1995, 2012; O'Malley 1992; Rose 1999, 2010). Risk technology assumes a series of conditions of possibilities, not a fixed set of determinants. Since it operates through incentives and deterrents, rather than sheer force, the ways social organizations and personal trajectories unfold through risk technology remain unknown until they crystallize in concrete instances.

In this chapter, our focus is on the science that precedes and feeds risk calculation (realist perspective) and risk technology (governance perspective). We are interested in **facticity**, the fabrication of facts. Risks, and the facts they rest upon, are materially and socially constructed. They are embedded within the tools we use daily. We want to open up the black box of risk; that is, we want to observe and make visible what serves as the basis for calculating risks and governing through them. We have elected to document the facticity of Robert Hare's (1980, 2000, 2004) concept of psychopathy. This controversial but well-entrenched clinical construct[2] and the instrument it is materialized in, the Psychopathy Checklist, are important components of the risk management strategies prevailing in various criminal justice systems. It is through constructs and technologies such as these that risk pervades the justice system. Because the psychopathy construct and the Psychopathy Checklist have a long history, we chose to focus on a recent episode in their trajectory: the first meeting between psychopathy and neuroimaging, more precisely, magnetic resonance imaging (MRI). This is a critical moment in the making and strengthening of the facticity of psychopathy.

Of course, looking for markers of psychopathy in the brain seems like re-animating the Italian Positivist School, raising fears and accusations of reductionism and determinism. In their very thorough and informative book, *Neuro*, Rose and Abi-Rached (2013) argue that the social sciences should not feel threatened by neurosciences. According to the authors, there are bridges to build between the two fields. For example, social sciences could help alleviate the pressures that neurosciences are subjected to:

> Neuroscientists might well be advised to be frank about the conceptual and empirical questions that translation entails, rather than suggesting that the outcome of a series of experiments with fruit flies or feral rats has something to tell us about human violence. . . . The

translational imperative under which all are now forced to work induces such reckless extrapolations. Perhaps one can have some sympathy for the researchers' dilemma, caught between the necessary simplification of the experimental design and the promises of rapid applicability demanded by those who fund the research. There is a role for the social sciences here in defending scientists from these demands. (228–29; emphasis in original)

We agree with the authors that the translational imperative might be more pronounced at times; however, scientific problems are never defined in a void. Crafting a scientific question also entails defining a social and political "problem." The idea of a scientist removed from society and its politics is part of what Latour (1993) calls the "modern constitution." Indeed, such a myth and its corresponding translational imperative rely on the premise that "hard" science can and should exist outside of society—that a firm border stands between the two and needs to be preserved for the good of all: nature and science in one corner, society and politics in the other. If "hard" scientists do their work protected from social pressures and constraints, the argument reasons, their research results will be purer, better, stronger.

Treading along the path laid out by Bruno Latour (2001) and his **actor-network theory** (ANT) colleagues Michel Callon and John Law, we wish to pursue the idea that scientific facts, namely risk scales and scores, are built and made stronger by the multiplication of alliances they create with other entities like demand, translation, partners, and so on—not by being isolated from them. By exploring the facticity of psychopathy, we follow the counterintuitive relational axiom, according to which the more a scientific statement is fabricated, the more robust it becomes. This model accurately describes the inherently heterogeneous threads from which science is woven. But, concretely, it means that we depart from the perspective adopted by our colleagues in some of the contributions in this volume that measure science and technology in terms of stability, validity, or objectivity. Instead, we choose to explore how facts embedded in and feeding technologies are made stronger by their social and material alliances.

Using the tools provided by the semiotic of scientific texts, we document the way psychopathy's turn towards brain imaging strengthens and renews its facticity—despite the controversies that it raises. After briefly describing Hare's construct of psychopathy and the Psychopathy Checklist and their criticisms, we outline Latour's model of science. We then shift our attention to Hare and his team's first key empirical article on psychopathy and MRI. By looking closely at the assertions it makes and the career this article has had in the world of research, we show that the facticity of the neurological basis of psychopathy is achieved through at least four processes: silencing the stated limits of the study, combining contrary results into broader assertions, the "zooming in and out of the brain" effect, and becoming relevant outside of the field of psychopathy. In conclusion, we reflect on ontological uncertainties at the basis of risk technologies and the democratization of science and technology. In our "uncertain world" (Callon, Lascoumes, and Barthe 2001), decision-makers and the public need to know not only what scientists know, but also what they debate and the extent to which science is permeated by uncertainties (Benbouzid 2015).

PSYCHOPATHY AND THE PCL-R: AN OBLIGATORY PASSAGE POINT AND A TARGET

In the 1930s, Hervey Cleckley developed the first contemporary conception of psychopathy while working with psychiatric in-patients. He observed that they did not display the usual signs and symptoms of mental illness and, after an initial assessment, seemed relatively normal (Babiak and Hare 2006; Cleckley 1976). Over time, the psychiatrist observed these patients charm, manipulate, and con other patients, family members, and hospital staff (Babiak and Hare 2006). He came to understand and classify these patients as psychopaths. His work marks the beginning of the contemporary clinical construct of psychopathy, which has maintained relative stability to the present day (Arrigo and Shipley 2001).

In 1980, Robert D. Hare published the Psychopathy Checklist (PCL). The PCL was an attempt to operationalize Cleckley's concept of psychopathy, moving beyond mere description into a scientifically verifiable, reliable, and valid diagnostic instrument. The PCL-R (revised) was published in 2004 after more than a decade of gathering data with the original PCL (Hare 2000, 2004). The PCL-R was viewed as a more valid and statistically sound revision comprising two factors: the first documents interpersonal and affective traits, and the second documents lifestyle, including instability and deviance. The scoring on the PCL-R is conducted using both a semi-structured interview and a review of secondary data (e.g., offender file information, including youth delinquency records) (Forth 2000; Hare 1996, 2004).

Today, the PCL-R is regarded by many as "the construct and measurement of psychopathy" (Seagrave and Grisso 2002) and the "standard of practice instrument" (Meloy 2000, 43). In this sense, it has become an obligatory passage point for any study on psychopathy.

The PCL-R was designed as a diagnostic tool, and was not intended "to predict criminal behaviour or to assess risk for violence" (Hare 2004, 145); however, there is a strong body of evidence that details a positive correlation between criminal behaviour and PCL-R scores (Cooke, Forth, and Hare 2012; Gacono 2016; Hare, Cooke, and Hart 1999; Hart 1998; Hart and Hare 1997; Hemphill, Hare, and Wong 1998; Hemphill and Hart 2003; Millon et al. 1998). Thus, the instrument has garnered credibility for its ability to predict criminal behaviour across a variety of criminal populations and contexts. The strong correlation between PCL-R scores and criminal behaviour has led criminal justice system practitioners throughout the world to employ it as a risk management tool (Hare 2004; Webster and Hucker 2007).[3]

This score has a serious impact on offenders' lives in the countries where it is used: "parole boards take into account an offender's PCL-R score in arriving at a release decision. Those with a high PCL-R score are less likely to receive conditional release than are other offenders" (Hare 2004, 147).[4] PCL-R scores that are part of more general risk profiles also play a role in imposing indeterminate sentences and the dangerous offender designation—an indeterminate life sentence without statutory parole review eligibility (Bonta and Motiuk 1996; John Howard Society of Alberta 2000).

The ample body of research and the extensive use of the PCL-R should not obscure the fact that Hare's psychopathy construct is also plagued by four types of controversies. First, the PCL-R has gained a reputation for being both the most valid diagnostic instrument for psychopathy and a definition of the construct itself. Researchers warn that this overreliance on the PCL-R causes a mono-operation bias that "may lead us into a conceptual cul-de-sac" (Cooke, Michie, and Hart 2006, 103), limiting the growth of knowledge about the topic.

Second, opponents affirm that research is more equivocal in its findings than is commonly perceived and that clinicians and researchers must be cautious about drawing overzealous and empirically questionable conclusions (Edens 2006). For example, Miller et al. (2011) observed 22 PCL-R certified clinical psychologists administer the assessment and found that some raters would assign consistently higher scores than others, due to their own personality biases. This study (and others like it) criticized the validity of the PCL-R, and since the definition of psychopathy is reliant on the PCL-R, the whole diagnosis is rendered controversial.

Third, in direct line with the previous set of controversies, the psychopathy construct has low validity amongst populations of women offenders (Vitale et al. 2002). It may also be used in a biased way to differentiate between racial groups and therefore reify racial biases as well as social class differences (Skeem et al. 2003).

Finally, the most widespread critique of psychopathy and the PCL-R takes issue with the tautological nature of the factor 2 traits (elements related to anti-social behaviours such as impulsivity, juvenile delinquency, etc.) and the prediction of future deviance. It is circular to use items detailing past deviance to predict future deviance (Cooke, Michie, and Skeem 2007). All this conceptualization is able to say with certainty is that a person with a history of deviance is at risk of committing future deviant acts. Because of this, "PCL-R recidivism research cannot answer the question whether psychopathy is a causal risk factor or whether its connection to future antisocial acts simply reflects the inclusion of items relating to past criminal behaviour" (Douglas, Vincent, and Edens 2006, 544).

Facing criticisms that undermine their certainty and validity, how could the concept of psychopathy and its measuring instrument become so widespread? This question can be answered using Latour's model of research.

THE FIVE HORIZONS OF RESEARCH

According to Latour's model of science (2001), it would be pointless to try and protect researchers from public demands or funding imperatives, since these are products of the research process itself. Research is a complex endeavour. It requires researchers to (a) mobilize the social and natural world through instruments, (b) convince colleagues of the truth of the statements they produce, (c) recruit symbolic and financial support, (d) capture the attention of the public and create a demand for the statements they produce, and (e) bring coherence to those disparate worlds through meaningful concepts. Building scientific facts requires acting on those five fronts simultaneously. That is why we can say that producing scientific facts requires building a socio-technical network—an aligned aggregate made up of heterogeneous composites: matter, equations and algorithms, laboratory equipment, other researchers working in areas that could benefit from one's assertions, highly rated scientific journals, funding agencies, real-life applications, and media recognition.

When one tries to describe how Hare's psychopathy construct forges alliances, one rapidly encounters numerous entities articulated to it. One is the Darkstone Research Group Ltd.,[5] a private company devoted to training health care and correctional professionals to use the PCL-R. Only accredited professionals are legally permitted to use this assessment tool and interpret its scores. It is noteworthy that carceral institutions all over North America rely on PCL-R scores to define the institutional trajectories of prisoners. The result is that carceral institutions must maintain personnel who are trained and accredited to use the PCL-R. Another entity connected to Hare's psychopathy construct is a non-profit organization called Aftermath: Surviving Psychopathy.[6] It is funded, in part, by Darkstone Research. Based in the United States, this group aims to provide education and support to researchers and therapists and, most specifically, to those whose lives have been impacted by psychopaths (criminalized or not). These are a few examples of the alliances that strengthen Hare's construct of psychopathy and sustain its pre-eminence. They also strengthen the demand for more research on psychopathy.

On another front, psychopathy is made possible through the management of public relations. One example is the threat of legal action Hare used in 2007 to prevent a scientific journal and two authors from publishing a positively evaluated article. Hare claimed that the paper's authors misrepresented his work. Only after multiple re-evaluations and corrections was the paper published three years later (Minkel 2010). Using mechanisms outside of academia, such as defamation law, to shape scientific publication is unorthodox, but shows the importance that Hare and his colleagues ascribe and the energy they devote to managing the public image of the construct and its creators.

While we could have investigated any of the five horizons that jointly contribute to the making of the scientific entity that is psychopathy, our analysis focuses on only one of them: the process of convincing one's colleagues of the veracity of one's scientific statement(s), otherwise known as the *autonomization of research*. We are especially puzzled by the capacity of psychopathy to shape the justice system's hunger for risk management despite the scientific criticisms levied on the construct and instrument. Thus, we are interested in documenting the different processes at play in the making of well-received papers for the specialized public—an academic public that is crucial to validating research results. Indeed, building a scientific fact is an inherently collective enterprise. It is only when other researchers accept, borrow, acknowledge, and cite an assertion that it becomes a scientific fact. Otherwise, it remains on the margins as an artefact (Latour 1987).

ENROLLING BRAIN IMAGING

Our empirical exploration of the facticity of the neuroscientific specificities of psychopathy is limited to one article published in 2001
by Hare and his team: K. A. Kiehl, A. M. Smith, A. Mendrek,
B. B. Forster, J. Brink, and P. F. Liddle, hereafter referred to as Kiehl
et al. The article published in *Biological Psychiatry* is titled "Limbic
Abnormalities in Affective Processing by Criminal Psychopaths as
Revealed by Functional Magnetic Resonance Imaging." This article
is Hare's team's most cited empirical paper about psychopathy and
brain imaging.[7]

Premised on the idea that psychopaths have difficulties or show abnormalities in processing emotions, the study aimed to examine criminal
psychopaths' brain activity during the performance of an affective memory task. The experimental study involved three comparable groups: eight
inmates who had a high PCL-R score[8] (criminal psychopaths), eight
inmates who had a low PCL-R score[9] (criminal non-psychopaths), and
eight people from the general population who did not meet the criteria
for psychopathy.

The experiment consisted of eight rounds of an affective memory
task. For each round, participants were asked to study a list of 12 words.
They were then exposed to 12 words, half of which were new, and were
asked whether they recognized those words from the list they had just
studied. In four of the eight rounds, the words listed were uniformly
neutral, whereas in the other four rounds, the words listed were uniformly negative.[10] These memory tasks were performed while the researchers
measured the subjects' brain activity through functional magnetic resonance imaging in 10 zones that were previously identified in a pilot
study with non-psychopaths as showing especially high activity during
a similar test.[11]

The criminal psychopaths showed *less* brain activity when processing affect-related words, compared to the neutral words, than did the
criminal non-psychopaths and the non-criminal participants in 6 of
the 10 brain zones studied. The criminal psychopaths also showed
less brain activity when processing affect-related words than did the

non-criminal participants in 4 of the 10 brain zones studied; however, the criminal psychopaths showed *more* brain activity when processing affect-related words compared to the neutral words, than did the criminal non-psychopaths and the non-criminal participants in two brain zones situated outside the limbic system. In brief, the researchers conclude: "We have shown that processing of affective stimuli is associated with less limbic activation in criminal psychopaths than in criminal non-psychopaths and non-criminal control participants. We have also shown that psychopathic offenders appear to use alternative neural systems to process affective stimuli" (Kiehl et al. 2001, 683).

How does this study lean on past knowledge? How were the results received? How were these results borrowed, built upon, or weakened by later studies? What is the career of these research results? The following two sections are devoted to answering these questions. By looking at how this research was taken up by the scientific community, we are able to identify the processes and strategies mobilized to turn research results into powerful facts and describe the network needed to solidify psychopathy and the PCL-R as key risk prediction tools in the criminal justice system.

Selecting Powerful Friends and Harnessing Nature Upstream

Any conventional empirical scientific article begins by laying out the groundwork that will support the statement it is about to put forth. Authors, or fact builders (Latour 1987), modalize statements from past studies to give weight to their own statements. In semiotics of scientific text, a sentence that modifies (or qualifies) another one is called a *modality*. A positive modality will reinforce a statement. A negative one will weaken it, usually by saying something about the methodology behind the statement (Latour 1987, 22–29). A succession of positive modalities will contribute to "black-boxing" an assertion—that is, to transforming it into a fact. The fate of the statement, Latour adds, is in the hands of the other researchers, highlighting the extent to which facticity is a social process.

In Kiehl et al. (2001), we find a self-referential process that high-lights and aligns the team's earlier publications over 40 years. This long self-referential loop results in the strengthening of their earlier statements. Indeed, it benefits their earlier published work by positively modalizing their results and black-boxing their global statement according to which psychopathy is a distinct and solid construct.

The text opens with a series of assertions it weaves together to form a coherent program—a program for which the present study will be a logical, if not necessary, development. The article begins by defining the criminal psychopath:

> Psychopathy is a personality disorder believed to affect approximately 1% of the general population and approximately 15%–25% of incarcerated offenders (Hare 1991). Compared with other inmates, psychopathic offenders commit a disproportionate amount of repetitive, often violent, criminal acts (Hare and McPherson 1984; Hart et al. 1994). Central to the disorder is a complex of features—glibness; superficiality; and lack of empathy, guilt, or remorse—that appear to be associated with difficulties or anomalies in the processing and production of affective material (Cleckley 1976; Hare 1993). Although the clinical symptomology of criminal psychopathy is well characterized (Hare 1991), relatively little is known regarding the neural systems mediating its affective abnormalities. (Kiehl et al. 2001, 677)

The next sentences reassert that psychopathy relates to affective abnormalities. Experiments using a negative emotional stimulation have shown the specificity of these deficits. Previous studies have tested whether psychopathy is "associated with abnormal processing of affective verbal material" (Williamson, Harpur, and Hare 1991) or with "abnormal processing of semantic and affective verbal information" (Kiehl et al. 1999). This association between deficits and negative emotional stimuli is further confirmed by three other studies.

However, in these first paragraphs, it is explained that we do not know the neural activity that corresponds to these deficits. The text refers to more than 10 studies that have suggested that "[brain] structures and systems may be implicated in psychopathic behaviour" (Kiehl et al.

2001, 678) but, as the authors remind us, "very little is known about the possible involvement of these structures in criminal psychopathy" (Kiehl et al. 2001, 678).

Based on these statements, the authors will articulate together the following entities: (a) criminal psychopaths, (b) affective processing of negative verbal material, and (c) neural structures. These entities mesh into a hypothesis that needs testing:

> In light of the substantial evidence indicating impaired processing of affect in psychopathy, we hypothesized that psychopaths would show less activation than healthy controls and criminal nonpsychopaths when processing affective words compared with neutral words, at those cerebral sites where healthy controls had exhibited significant activation for affective words compared with neutral words in the pilot study. (Kiehl et al. 2001, 678)

The team will produce the following results: "processing of affective stimuli is associated with less limbic activation in criminal psychopaths," and "psychopathic offenders appear to use alternative neural systems to process affective stimuli" (Kiehl et al. 2001, 683). What is the scientific career of the research results and how do they strengthen the existence of psychopathy, therefore lending legitimacy to the risk technologies that this construct supports?

Diversifying and Becoming Essential Downstream

To date, the Kiehl et al. paper has been referred to in hundreds of publications. From these, we identified at least four processes of fact building at work: silencing the stated limits of the study, combining contrary results into broader assertions, the "zooming in and out of the brain" effect, and becoming relevant outside of the field of psychopathy.

From Exploratory to Confirmatory: Silencing the Limits of an Experiment
The paper by Kiehl et al. is cautious, meticulous, and sober. It does not hint at or directly affirm any revolutionary discoveries. After describing the results, the authors explicitly state the limits of their

study: the sample size, the participants' comparability problem in generalizing fixed-effects analysis, the modest significance of the random-effects analysis at five brain sites, the unidimensional aspect of the stimuli used (only verbal stimuli), and so on. Moreover, when referring to the hyperactivation of the alternative neural system in psychopaths, the authors state the exploratory nature of their work: "It should be noted, however, that the analyses that revealed the excessive affective activation in the lateral frontal cortex in psychopaths were exploratory in nature and should be interpreted with caution" (Kiehl et al. 2001, 682).

Among the 418 papers that cite the Kiehl et al. 2001 study, some review papers mentioned these limits (Canli and Amin 2002); however, this is not the case for the bulk of these empirical studies. The vast majority of these papers positively modalize the study, simply reiterating its conclusion(s), and building on it for their own experiment. Some examples:

> In addition, they [psychopaths] showed reduced amygdala activation, relative to comparison individuals, during an emotional memory task (Kiehl et al. 2001). (Blair et al. 2002, 685)

> Interestingly, two recent neuroimaging studies have confirmed that amygdala dysfunction is associated with psychopathy (Tiihonen et al. 2000; Kiehl et al. 2001). (Blair 2003, 5)

> Corroborating this hypothesis, previous findings in pathologies associated with increased aggressive behaviour (e.g., borderline personality disorder, psychopathy) revealed decreased functional activity and recued [sic] anatomical volume in dACC (Kiehl et al. 2001; van Elst et al. 2003; Birbaumer et al. 2005; Whittle et al. 2006; Enzi et al. 2013). (Clemens et al. 2015, 1778)

Through the repetitive positive modalizations of the research by Kiehl et al., the exploratory quality of the results and the limits stated in the study are silenced. Therefore, when used to justify subsequent research, the Kiehl et al. (2001) paper comes across as a strong confirmatory study.

The Apologetic Character of Negative Modalizations:
Preventing the Growth of the Controversy
Negative modalizations that undermine the facticity of the research results are rather rare in the papers that refer to the Kiehl et al. study, but they do exist. One example of partial contradiction of the Kiehl et al. results is the Müller et al. paper (2003). While it concurs with the Kiehl et al. results on the over-activation of the frontotemporal brain area in criminal psychopaths when they are processing negative images, they arrive at different results when looking at the amygdala. In their experiment, Müller et al. (2003) found increased activation of psychopaths' amygdalae when processing negative images, while Kiehl et al. had found an under-activation of the whole limbic system, including the amygdala, when processing negative words. The Müller et al. paper acknowledges the inconsistency of its results as compared to the Kiehl et al. study, as well as the limits of their own research; however, Müller et al.'s paper points to some previous research that confirms their own results. Interestingly, Müller et al. dilute this contradiction in the conclusion of their article to such a degree that they embrace both their results and those of Kiehl et al.: "Significantly increased activation, as well as reduced activation, have been found in different parts of the emotion-related brain circuit compared with healthy control subjects" (Müller et al. 2003, 160). Three years later, in an article reviewing the cognitive neuroscience of psychopathy, Kiehl comments on what he considers to be the flaws in the Müller et al. study and, as in the prior paper, phrases his conclusion in such a way as to be inclusive regarding both over- and under-activation of the amygdala:

> In summary, cognitive neuroscience studies of affective processing have found that the neural circuits embracing the temporo-limbic system are either dysfunctional or hypofunctioning in psychopathy. (Kiehl 2006, 122)

Another example of negative modalization comes from psychobiologists interested in the ethical aspects of affective neurosciences, such as Canli and Amin (2002). On the one hand, they describe Kiehl et al.'s research procedures in detail. On the other hand, they explicitly call for replication of the few neuroimaging studies that they just reviewed, including the Kiehl et al. study: "The fact that the conclusions of any individual study can be softened by alternative interpretations or methodological concerns is a useful reminder that the knowledge-base in these domains is malleable and awaits replication and extension" (Canli and Amin 2002, 424). While they call for caution generally, Canli and Amin's negative modalization does not undermine Kiehl's study in particular, and it is likely that Kiehl's team itself would even agree with their assertion.

Others do not negatively modalize the results, as such, but rather Kiehl et al.'s interpretation. The following emphasizes the deficit model (lesser amygdala activation) that would characterize psychopaths rather than the over-activation noted outside of their limbic system:

> Given that research examining brain activity has concluded that psychopathic individuals use more cortical areas of the brain for processing affective stimuli (e.g., Kiehl et al. 2001; Munro et al. 2007), it may be that psychopaths are processing emotional stimuli in a more cognitive and rational manner as compared to nonpsychopathic individuals. In other words, rather than having a deficit, they may simply process the stimuli differently from nonpsychopaths. (Wheeler, Book, and Costello 2009, 639)

Based on a survey of the limited citations of the Wheeler et al. (2009) paper, thus far their alternative interpretation has not been taken up by Kiehl et al. or by any other well-known research team on psychopathy. The idea that psychopaths process information rationally rather than emotionally is a hypothesis that will remain an artefact and probably never develop into a scientific fact.

The literature referring to the Kiehl et al. study is not free of negative modalizations. Indeed, the three examples above show that the facticity of its research results is sometimes either directly questioned or at least presented as the outcome of a kind of bricolage, undermining the romanticism often associated with science as pure discovery. However, the effect of these negative modalizations is not so detrimental as to significantly undermine the facticity of the assertion according to which criminal psychopaths present an under-activation of the limbic system and an over-activation of the prefrontal cortex when processing affective content. Not all negative modalizations are lethal. Even if a scientific assertion is not black-boxed, or taken for granted, in an area of study, it does not mean that it is completely compromised. It can still be effective and operative.

Zooming In and Out of the Brain: Brain Borders' Fluidity and Potential Alliances

Borders between areas of the brain are subject to change and controversies. One just has to compare a few brain atlases to realize that the brain borders are as fluid as those of some Balkan countries over the last century. To add to the complexity, the brain can be divided along specific areas imbued with their own functions, but those areas can also gain function and significance by being part of an ensemble connected by neural pathways. In brief, the unit of analysis in neuro-imaging is not always easy to pinpoint. What is necessary to generate neuroscientific results? That an area is activated? That a few neighbouring areas are activated? That a specific circuit of non-contiguous areas is activated?

This brain mapping fluidity can be seen as a source of confusion, but it can also be a resource when it comes to producing facticity. The Kiehl et al. (2001) experiment tested 10 areas of the brain, and its first result was as follows:

> Compared with criminal nonpsychopaths and noncriminal control participants, criminal psychopaths showed significantly less affect-related activity in the amygdala/hippocampal formation, parahippocampal gyrus, ventral striatum, and in the anterior and posterior cingulate gyri. (Kiehl et al. 2001, 677)

However, in the conclusion of the paper, the result is framed more generically, encapsulating the areas named above under the term "limbic system."[12] Going from the areas mentioned in the result section to the limbic system in the conclusion can be seen as a partial translation. Indeed, "there is no universal agreement on the total list of structures that should be included in the term *limbic system*" (Vanderah and Gould 2016, ch. 23). Many papers that subsequently positively modalize the results of our study of interest state that Kiehl et al. have found an under-activation of the limbic system for psychopaths.

Around the same time the Kiehl et al. paper was published, prominent neuroscientists argued that the limbic system does not have a discrete unity in the brain nor a specific function. According to them, the limbic system is an idea that should be abandoned (LeDoux 2003). The position of those neuroscientists could have been devastating for all the empirical studies that affirmed the relationship between the limbic system and one trait, emotion, or defect, such as in our study of interest. It was not, for two reasons.

First, the limbic system was and still is believed by some neuroscientists to be a valid entity with its own dynamics and properties. Second, the limbic system, however fluid it was conceived to be, always comprised the amygdala. Over the years that followed the publication of the Kiehl et al. study, the amygdala has been reconfirmed in neuroscience as a key site for the processing of emotions. Hence, the Kiehl et al. paper was reframed in subsequent studies that referred to it as showing the under-activation of the amygdala, and not so much of the limbic system. The main author himself summarizes his paper as showing that in psychopaths, the amygdala is less activated than in control subjects when they process affective material (Kiehl, personal communication).

The fuzziness of brain borders and the possibility in neuroimaging of zooming in or out on the brain to focus on a brain system or one of its components allows a scientific statement to survive despite the controversy pertaining to one of its key elements: the questionable existence of the limbic system as a functional entity. Subsequent research that confirmed the importance of the amygdala as an emotion processing site helped to further legitimize the Kiehl et al. results. With the disappearance of the limbic system, the Kiehl et al. research result resisted becoming an artefact and rather gained in facticity.

The Flexible Relevance: Being Meaningful Outside of Psychopathy Studies
The brain imaging experiment conducted in the paper under study concerns criminal psychopaths—that is, adult prisoners who have scored higher than the average of a wide sample of prisoners on the PCL-R scale. It is therefore not surprising that the study is widely cited or referred to in the literature on criminal psychopathy and, more precisely, in the neuroscientific literature on criminal psychopathy. However, since its publication, the career of this paper has gone far beyond the borders of this topic. Indeed, it is cited or referred to in many neighbouring disciplines, in different health or justice topics, and with regard to diverse populations:

- forensic patients (Müller et al. 2003)
- community participants with different degrees of psychopathy, from none to severe (Glenn, Raine, and Schug 2009; Glenn et al. 2009)
- children with psychopathic tendencies (Budhani and Blair 2005)
- people identified as suffering from anti-social personality disorder (Del-Ben 2005)
- unmedicated patients with major depressive disorders marked by anger attacks (Dougherty et al. 2004)
- a delusional patient who killed her children (Kalbe et al. 2008)
- cocaine-dependent men and women (Li, Kosten, and Sinha 2006)
- aggressive or violent behaviours in general (Pérez Milán 2007; Siever 2008)
- untreated bipolar patients (Sassi et al. 2004)
- people with dementia (Cipriani et al. 2013)
- children and adolescents with behavioural problems (Sterzer and Stadler 2009; Viding and Jones 2008)

Despite the specificities of the sample that Kiehl et al. focused on (let's think, for example, about the effects of the prison environment on cognitive and emotional health), their results are mobilized by empirical studies on a wide array of topics and subjects.

It would be too strong to claim that the Kiehl et al. study has become an obligatory passage point for all those different bodies of research and that they have been enrolled into the Kiehl et al. team "empire" (Latour 2007, 120); however, all the fields that mobilize the Kiehl et al. study help to give it many other applications. The life of those research results grows, and so does their value. If colleagues in the field of psychopathy attempt to question their results, Kiehl et al. could easily show that they have allies in the fields of substance abuse, conduct disorders, and dementia. Moreover, those allies carry much more credibility in health and social policy circles and the public's mind than any prisoners, and prison researchers, can have: "Science is like Scrabble: the same word can generate two or three times the points if we can hook it to a white, pink or red tile" (Latour 2007, 124, our translation). The facticity of assertions is built by other researchers who cite and refer to them. It is lucrative and effective to diversify the portfolios of colleagues who participate in constructing a fact.

CONCLUSION

Calculating risks and governing through risks are made possible by extensive scientific work. In this chapter, we focused on a segment of the science behind psychopathy. The construct and the instrument it is embodied in, the Psychopathy Checklist, are important risk technologies in the criminal justice system.

According to one of actor-network theory's most provocative axioms, the more a scientific statement is fabricated, the more robust it is. Hence, in this model, scientists are not special human beings capable of observing some aspect of nature through a transparent window. Scientists are multi-taskers, busy building associations among heterogeneous entities from the laboratory (instruments, scores, experimental research designs), from the scientific world (research partners, funding agencies, previous scientific articles, research competitors), and from the community (knowledge transfer imperatives, marketing, and public image creation). Producing scientific assertions claiming that a phenomenon, such as psychopathy, is real means working on all those fronts simultaneously. A whole network of entities has to align for such an assertion to become concrete; however, in the end, facticity rests with those colleague scientists who continue to rely on one's assertions to the point that they are taken for granted. The assertions become part of common sense in the scientific milieu, the construct and technology are black-boxed, and, in the case of psychopathy, constructions of risk are hidden within the black-boxed technology.

Interestingly, psychopathy is certainly more black-boxed in the general domain than it is in the scientific milieu. As Pickersgill (2009, 668) reminds us, it is a "category in search of a referent . . . there has never been a clinical consensus regarding what causes psychopathy or what kinds of individuals should be classified with it." The mobilization of neuroscience and brain imaging is an attempt to find the missing referent, to locate psychopathy in the flesh, and to identify, after decades of research, the mechanisms behind the diagnostic. However, examining the facticity of the neurological basis of psychopathy in one key experiment shows that brain imaging does not resolve the existential crisis faced by this category. It is true that psychopathy reinforces existing relationships in the process of meeting neuroscience. It participates in reiterating and positively modalizing 40 years of research on the topic. It is also true that psychopathy makes powerful new allies through brain imaging (e.g., the fields of neurocognition, dementia, schizophrenia), therefore becoming stronger.

However, the turn towards high technology, such as functional magnetic resonance imaging (fMRI), adds other uncertainties to the psychopathy construct, such as contradicting studies and the controversy around the existence of some brain structures (e.g., the limbic system). We have shown that those added uncertainties are not fatal and are shaped in such a way as to contribute to solidifying the construct of psychopathy. But they certainly do not lead to the black-boxing of it in the scientific world.

And it does not seem to matter—the construct of psychopathy might not work in theory, but it certainly works in practice! Indeed, we have to wonder whether the ritual scientific quest for a referent is that important. Whenever there is a new technology in psychophysiology (e.g., skin conductance, the measurement of micro-facial expressions) or neuroscience (e.g., PET scan or fMRI), psychopathy researchers use it to conduct comparative studies aimed at differentiating the psychopaths from the non-psychopaths, therefore proving that psychopathy has ontological reality. Every time, they seem to confirm some difference between the two groups more or less persuasively, but there is still no rallying explanation for the differences. The construct of psychopathy has already made a life for itself; it is effective, it is operational, and it is widely used. In its own way, psychopathy offers an example of Alfred North Whitehead's reflection that "in the real world it is more important that a proposition be interesting than it be true. The importance of truth is, that it adds to interest" (cited in Latour 1994, 196).

Despite its ontological uncertainty, psychopathy keeps growing stronger by building new alliances. But since facts gain strength from the entities with which they are associated, they also depend on those associates. Hence, as psychopathy gains in strength, it also becomes externally determined. It is at the mercy of all the entities that lend it power, making its existence all the more unpredictable. From this perspective, facticity and uncertainties increase jointly. Taming risk, this race to convert the emptiness into fullness, necessarily entails the proliferation of uncertainties.

The contributions in this collection show us adeptly that we should remain skeptical of **technological determinism** and the infallibility of risk technology. They remind us that there are always human beings behind the design and the use of those technologies. We share with them the idea that technology is necessarily social; we would add that it is indistinctly social and material, and so is the scientific knowledge that supports it. Moreover, our empirical exploration of the facticity of psychopathy as a risk technology does not lead us to evaluate or denounce the flaws in the psychopathy construct, or the human biases and fallibilities associated with PCL-R use. As the controversies documented earlier in this paper attest, the specialists on psychopathy do that better than we can ever do. We are trying to document the persistence, biography, and effectivity of psychopathy, despite its uncertainties. This analysis invites us to embrace the idea that uncertainties populate science and technology without, to a certain extent, undermining them. We ought to work towards risk technologies that are more just, but it might be illusory to assess them, and the science they rest upon, according to their certainty.

Learning to develop relational accounts of risk and fact making is one of the intellectual tools we need to face an increasingly uncertain world—one that is ever more reliant on science. It not only teaches us what the scientists know, but also leads us to take stock of the doubts and debates that constitute the knowledge on a topic (Benbouzid 2015). A thorough description of risk facticity opens spaces for a more engaged discussion of the science and technologies behind policies and a more democratic practice of science itself. It is part of encouraging an ethic of complexity (Pickersgill 2014).

DISCUSSION QUESTIONS

1. What processes shaped the acceptance and use of the Psychopathy Checklist for calculating risk?

2. How is psychopathy a contested fact within the scientific realm, yet a relatively stable phenomenon outside the scientific milieu?

3. What does the history and development of the Psychopathy Checklist tell us about the construction of classification systems?

4. Beyond validity and objectivity, a scientific assertion or a technology gains strength as the scope of its connections grows (horizons of research). What does it mean to conceive of science and technology in this way?

5. What other examples of uncertain truths or uncertain realities come to mind?

6. Does the inherent uncertainty of science and technology mean that we have to rely instead on other means to guide our decisions (such as religion, habits, and authority)? What differentiates science and technology from other modes of knowing and organizing human collectivity?

NOTES

1. Authors are listed in alphabetical order.

2. *Construct* is the term psychologists and psychopathy researchers use themselves.

3. Moreover, the PCL-R has also been incorporated as an item into other risk assessment instruments that are employed internationally, including in Canada. The Violence Risk Appraisal Guide (VRAG) (Harris, Rice, and Quinsey 1993; Quinsey et al. 1998) and the HCR-20 (Webster et al. 1997) are two notable risk assessment instruments utilized by Correctional Service Canada that include the PCL-R as individual items.

4. In Canada, the federal correctional service supports Hare's (2004) assertion regarding the use of the PCL-R in corrections; the PCL-R is used to predict risks for recidivism (especially violent recidivism), and based on an offender's risk profile, which includes the offender's PCL-R score, the Parole Board of Canada may deny day or full parole, or the courts may even subject offenders to indeterminate sentencing, which overrides their statutory right to being released from prison after serving two-thirds of their sentence (Bonta and Motiuk 1996). Additionally, the PCL-R is often used in court hearings to determine if an offender should be assigned a dangerous offender designation, which also impacts offender sentencing and release decisions (John Howard Society of Alberta 2000).

5. Robert Hare is a key member of this company; see http://www.hare.org/welcome/darkstone.html.

6. See http://www.aftermath-surviving-psychopathy.org/.

7. Here is the rationale behind the selection of this article. Since our interest is Hare's psychopathy construct, using Scopus, we listed all the publications that he authored solo or with others. At the time, December 2015, that amounted to 187 publications. We then selected from the list those publications that contain the key words "psychopathy" AND "neuro*" OR "brain." This additional filter resulted in 54 publications. After reading the abstract of each for explicit and central reference to psychopathy and its relation to neuroscience or the brain, 20 publications that span more than 40 years were left. Among the 20 articles, the majority pertain to the brain activity (roughly from 1978 to 2004) of psychopaths, while the last few studies pertain to their brain morphology (roughly from 2008). In those later experiments, using optimized voxel-based morphometry (fMRI) technology, the studies quantify the grey matter found in psychopaths'

brains and attend to the location of the grey matter reduction zones in their brains. While not explicitly rejecting the information processing model of psychopathy, those morphology studies put forth the hypothesis of an alternative evolutionary brain development in psychopaths. Pertaining to the brain activity studies from the end of the 1970s, Hare conducted a study using measures of electrodermal activity of psychopaths as a proxy to trace the quantity of brain activity in the participants. Later on, with new generations of technology, namely EEG and PET scan, studies were conducted that identified the location of activity in the brains of psychopaths while conducting a task (usually being asked to categorize phonic or visual stimuli, often a concrete or abstract noun). The studies went on to refine the concept of location into patterns, neural pathways, or brain architecture that relates to the circuit of activity in the brain under certain conditions (usually categorizing stimuli). These studies were conducted using the fMRI technology. With one study explicitly testing and rejecting the hypothesis that psychopathy would be the result of cerebral damage, all the studies on brain activity of psychopaths support the information processing model of psychopathy. From those studies on brain activity of psychopaths, the most cited is a review: Hare (1996) "Psychopathy: A Clinical Construct Whose Time Has Come," cited 430 times. The next one is an empirical study: Kiehl et al. (2001) "Limbic Abnormalities in Affective Processing by Criminal Psychopaths as Revealed by Functional Magnetic Resonance Imaging," cited 418 times. Since our methodological apparatus is better suited to empirical studies, the latter article was chosen as our focus.

8. A high PCL-R score is defined as a score higher than the mean score for prison inmates.

9. A low PCL-R score is defined as a score lower than the mean score for prison inmates.

10. Rated using Toglia and Battig (1978).

11. Those zones are: rostral anterior cingulate, caudal anterior cingulate, left inferior frontal gyrus parietal lobe, posterior cingulate gyrus, right amygdala/hippocampus, left amygdala/hippocampus, left parahippocampus, right anterior superior temporal gyrus, left anterior superior temporal gyrus, and ventral striatum.

12. "In summary, we have shown that processing of affective stimuli is associated with less limbic activation in criminal psychopaths than in criminal nonpsychopaths and noncriminal control participants" (Kiehl et al. 2001, 683).

REFERENCES

Arrigo, Bruce A., and Stacey Shipley. 2001. "The Confusion over Psychopathy (I): Historical Considerations." *International Journal of Offender Therapy and Comparative Criminology* 45 (3): 325–44.

Babiak, Paul, and Robert D. Hare. 2006. *Snakes in Suits: When Psychopaths Go to Work.* New York, NY: Regan Books/Harper Collins.

Beck, Ulrich. 1992. *Risk Society: Towards a New Modernity.* London: Sage.

Benbouzid, Bilel. 2015. "De la prévention situationnelle au predictive policing." *Champ pénal/Penal Field* 12. http://champpenal.revues.org/9050.

Blair, R. James R. 2003. "Neurobiological Basis of Psychopathy." *British Journal of Psychiatry* 182 (1): 5–7.

Blair, R. James R., Derek G. V. Mitchell, Rebecca A. Richell, Steve Kelly, Alan Leonard, Chris Newman, and Sophie K. Scott. 2002. "Turning a Deaf Ear to Fear: Impaired Recognition of Vocal Affect in Psychopathic Individuals." *Journal of Abnormal Psychology* 111 (4): 682–86.

Bonta, James, and Larry L. Motiuk. 1996. *High-Risk Violent Offenders in Canada.* Correctional Service Canada. http://www.csc-scc.gc.ca/research/r50e-eng .shtml.

Budhani, Salima, and R. James R. Blair. 2005. "Response Reversal and Children with Psychopathic Tendencies: Success is a Function of Salience of Contingency Change." *Journal of Child Psychology and Psychiatry and Allied Disciplines* 46 (9): 972–81.

Burchell, Graham. 1996. "Liberal Government and Techniques of the Self." In *Foucault and Political Reason: Liberalism, Neo-Liberalism and Rationalities of Government*, edited by Andrew Barry, Thomas Osborne, and Nikolas Rose, 19–36. Chicago: University of Chicago Press.

Callon, Michelle, Pierre Lascoumes, and Yannick Barthe. 2001. *Agir dans un monde incertain. Essai sur la démocratie technique.* Paris: Éditions du Seuil.

Canli, Turhan, and Zenab Amin. 2002. "Neuroimaging of Emotion and Personality: Scientific Evidence and Ethical Considerations." *Brain and Cognition* 50 (3): 414–31.

Castel, Robert. 1991. "From Dangerousness to Risk." In *The Foucault Effect: Studies in Governmentality, with Two Lectures by and an Interview with Michel Foucault,* edited by Graham Burchell, Colin Gordon, and Peter Miller, 281–98. Chicago: University of Chicago Press.

Cipriani, Gabriele, Gemma Borin, Marcella Vedovello, Andrea Di Fiorino, and Angelo Nuti. 2013. "Sociopathic Behaviour and Dementia." *Acta Neurologica Belgica* 113 (2): 111–15.

Cleckley, Hervey. 1976. *The Mask of Sanity: An Attempt to Clarify Some Issues about the So-Called Psychopathic Personality.* 5th ed. St. Louis: Mosby.

Clemens, Benjamin, Bianca Voß, Christina Pawliczek, Gianluca Mingoia, David Weyer, Jonathan Repple, Thomas Eggermann, Klaus Zerres, Kathrin Reetz, and Ute Habel. 2015. "Effect of MAOA Genotype on Resting-State Networks in Healthy Participants." *Cerebral Cortex* 25 (7): 1771–81.

Cooke, David J., Adelle E. Forth, and Robert D. Hare, eds. 2012. *Psychopathy: Theory, Research and Implications for Society.* Dordrecht, Netherlands: Springer.

Cooke, David J., Christine Michie, and Stephen D. Hart. 2006. "Facets of Clinical Psychopathy: Toward Clearer Measurement." In *Handbook of Psychopathy*, edited by Christopher J. Patrick, 91–106. New York: Guilford Press.

Cooke, David. J., Christine Michie, and Jennifer Skeem. 2007. "Understanding the Structure of the Psychopathy Checklist-Revised: An Exploration of Methodological Confusion." *British Journal of Psychiatry* 190 (S49): 39–50.

Del-Ben, Cristina Marta. 2005. "Neurobiology of Anti-social Personality Disorder." *Revista de Psiquiatria Clinica* 32 (1): 27–36.

Dougherty, Darin D., Scott L. Rauch, Thilo Deckersbach, Carl Marci, Rebecca Loh, Lisa M. Shin, Nathaniel M. Alpert, Alan J. Fischman, and Maurizio Fava. 2004. "Ventromedial Prefrontal Cortex and Amygdala Dysfunction during an Anger Induction Positron Emission Tomography Study in Patients with Major Depressive Disorder with Anger Attacks." *Archives of General Psychiatry* 61 (8): 795–804.

Douglas, Kevin S., Gina M. Vincent, and John F. Edens. 2006. "Risk for Criminal Recidivism: The Role of Psychopathy." In *Handbook of Psychopathy*, edited by Christopher J. Patrick, 533–54. New York: Guilford Press.

Edens, John F. 2006. "Unresolved Controversies Concerning Psychopathy: Implications for Clinical and Forensic Decision Making." *Professional Psychology: Research and Practice* 37 (1): 59–65.

Ericson, Richard V., and Aaron Doyle, eds. 2003. *Risk and Morality.* Toronto: University of Toronto Press.

Forth, Adelle E. 2000. *Assessing Psychopathy with the PCL-R*. Paper presented at the Sinclair Seminars, San Diego, CA, January 2000.

Gacono, Carl B. 2016. *The Clinical and Forensic Assessment of Psychopathy: A Practitioner's Guide*. 2nd ed. New York: Routledge.

Glenn, Andrea L., Adrian Raine, and Robert A. Schug. 2009. "The Neural Correlates of Moral Decision-Making in Psychopathy." *Molecular Psychiatry* 14 (1): 5–6.

Glenn, Andrea L., Adrian Raine, Robert A. Schug, Liane Young, and Marc Hauser. 2009. "Increased DLPFC Activity during Moral Decision-Making in Psychopathy." *Molecular Psychiatry* 14 (10): 909–11.

Hannah-Moffat, Kelly. 1999. "Moral Agent or Actuarial Subject: Risk and Canadian Women's Imprisonment." *Theoretical Criminology* 3 (1): 71–94.

Hare, Robert D. 1980. "A Research Scale for the Assessment of Psychopathy in Criminal Populations." *Personality and Individual Differences* 1 (2): 111–19.

———. 1996. "Psychopathy: A Clinical Construct Whose Time Has Come." *Criminal Justice and Behaviour* 23 (1): 25–54.

———. 2000. *Assessing Psychopathy with the PCL-R*. Paper presented at the Sinclair Seminars, San Diego, CA, January 2000.

———. 2004. *Hare Psychopathy Checklist-Revised (PCL-R): Technical Manual*. Toronto: MHS.

Hare, Robert D., David J. Cooke, and Stephen D. Hart. 1999. "Psychopathy and Sadistic Personality Disorder." In *Oxford Textbook of Psychopathology*, edited by Theodore Millon, Paul Blaney, and Robert D. Davis, 5555–84. New York: Oxford University Press.

Harris, Grant T., Marnie E. Rice, and Vernon L. Quinsey. 1993. "Violent Recidivism of Mentally Disordered Offenders: The Development of a Statistical Prediction Instrument." *Criminal Justice and Behaviour* 20 (4): 315–35.

Hart, Stephen D. 1998. "The Role of Psychopathy in Assessing Risk for Violence: Conceptual and Methodological Issues." *Legal and Criminological Psychology* 3 (1): 121–37.

Hart, Stephen D., and Robert D. Hare. 1997. "Psychopathy: Assessment and Association with Criminal Conduct." In *Handbook of Antisocial Behaviour*, edited by David Stoff, James Breiling, and Jack Maser, 22–35. Hoboken, NJ: John Wiley and Sons.

Hemphill, James F., Robert D. Hare, and Stephen C. Wong. 1998. "Psychopathy and Recidivism: A Review." *Legal and Criminological Psychology* 3 (1): 139–70.

Hemphill, James F., and Stephen D. Hart. 2003. "Forensic and Clinical Issues in the Assessment of Psychopathy." In *Handbook of Psychology: Forensic Psychology*, edited by Alan M. Goldstein, 87–107. Hoboken, NJ: John Wiley and Sons.

John Howard Society of Alberta. 2000. *Offender Risk Assessment*. http://www .johnhoward.ab.ca/pub/old/C21.htm.

Kalbe, Elke, Matthias Brand, Alexander Thiel, Josef Kessler, and Hans J. Markowitsch. 2008. "Neuropsychological and Neural Correlates of Autobiographical Deficits in a Mother Who Killed Her Children." *Neurocase* 14 (1): 15–28.

Kiehl, Kent A. 2006. "A Cognitive Neuroscience Perspective on Psychopathy: Evidence for Paralimbic System Dysfunction." *Psychiatry Research* 142 (2/3): 107–28.

Kiehl, Kent A., Robert D. Hare, John J. McDonald, and Johann Brink. 1999. "Semantic and Affective Processing in Psychopaths: An Event-Related Potential (ERP) Study." *Psychophysiology* 36 (6): 765–74.

Kiehl, Kent A., Andra M. Smith, Robert D. Hare, Adrianna Mendrek, Bruce B. Forster, Johann Brink, and Peter F. Liddle. 2001. "Limbic Abnormalities in Affective Processing by Criminal Psychopaths as Revealed by Functional Magnetic Resonance Imaging." *Biological Psychiatry* 50 (9): 677–84.

Latour, Bruno. 1987. *Science in Action: How to Follow Scientists and Engineers through Society*. Cambridge, MA: Harvard University Press.

———. 1993. *We Have Never Been Modern*. Cambridge, MA: Harvard University Press.

———. 1994. "Les objets ont-ils une histoire? Rencontre entre Pasteur et Whitehead dans un bain d'acide lactique." In *L'effet Whitehead*, edited by Isabelle Stengers, 196–217. Paris: Vrin.

———. 2001. *Le métier de chercheur. Regard d'un anthropologue*. 2nd ed. Paris: Editions INRA.

———. 2007. "Portrait d'un biologiste en capitaliste sauvage." In *Petites leçons de sociologie des sciences*, edited by Bruno Latour, 100–29. Paris: La Découverte.

LeDoux, Joseph. 2003. *Synaptic Self*. New York: Penguin Books.

Li, Chiang-Shan R., Thomas R. Kosten, and Rajita Sinha. 2006. "Antisocial
     Personality and Stress-Induced Brain Activation in Cocaine-Dependent
     Patients." *NeuroReport* 17 (3): 243–47.

Lupton, Deborah. 1995. *The Imperative of Health: Public Health and the Regulated
     Body*. London: Sage Publications.

———. 2012. "M-Health and Health Promotion: The Digital Cyborg and
     Surveillance Society." *Social Theory and Health* 10 (3): 229–44.

Meloy, J. Reid. 2000. *Violence Risk and Threat Assessment*. San Diego, CA: Specialized
     Training Services.

Miller, Audrey K., Katrina A. Rufino, Marcus T. Boccaccini, Rebecca L. Jackson,
     and Daniel C. Murrie. 2011. "On Individual Differences in Person Perception:
     Raters' Personality Traits Relate to Their Psychopathy Checklist-Revised
     Scoring Tendencies." *Assessment* 18 (2): 253–60.

Millon, Theodore, Erik Simonsen, Morten Birket-Smith, and Roger D. Davis. 1998.
     Psychopathy: Antisocial, Criminal, and Violent Behaviour. New York: Guilford
     Press.

Minkel, J. R. 2010. "Fear Review: Critique of Forensic Psychopathy Scale Delayed
     3 Years by Threat of Lawsuit." *Scientific American*, June 17, 2010. https://www
     .scientificamerican.com/article/critique-of-forensic-psychopathy-scale-
     delayed-by-lawsuit/.

Müller, Jürgen L., Monika Sommer, Verena Wagner, Kirsten Lange, Heidrun
     Taschler, Christian H. Röder, Gerhardt Schuierer, Helmfried E. Klein, and
     Göran Hajak. 2003. "Abnormalities in Emotion Processing within Cortical
     and Subcortical Regions in Criminal Psychopaths: Evidence from a Functional
     Magnetic Resonance Imaging Study Using Pictures with Emotional Content."
     Biological Psychiatry 54 (2): 152–62.

O'Malley, Pat. 1992. "Risk, Power and Crime Prevention." *Economy and Society*
     21 (3): 252–75.

Pérez Milán, J. F. 2007. "Psycho-Social and Biological Aspects of Violent
     Behaviour." *Revista del Hospital Psiquiatrico de la Habana* 4 (2).

Pickersgill, Martyn D. 2009. "NICE Guidelines, Clinical Practice and Antisocial
     Personality Disorder: The Ethical Implications of Ontological Uncertainty."
     Journal of Medical Ethics 35 (11): 668–71.

———. 2014. "The Endurance of Uncertainty: Antisociality and Ontological
     Anarchy in British Psychiatry, 1950–2010." *Science in Context* 27 (1): 143–75.

Quinsey, Vernon L., Grant T. Harris, Marnie E. Rice, and Catherine A. Cormier. 1998. *Violent Offenders: Appraising and Managing Risk.* Washington, DC: American Psychological Association.

Rose, Nikolas. 1999. *Powers of Freedom: Reframing Political Thought.* Cambridge, UK: Cambridge University Press.

———. 2010. "'Screen and Intervene': Governing Risky Brains." *History of the Human Sciences* 23 (1): 79–105.

Rose, Nikolas, and Joelle M. Abi-Rached. 2013. *Neuro: The New Brain Sciences and the Management of the Mind.* Princeton, NJ: Princeton University Press.

Sassi, Roberto. B., Paolo Brambilla, John P. Hatch, Mark A. Nicoletti, Alan G. Mallinger, Ellen Frank, David J. Kupfer, Matcheri S. Keshavan, and Jair C. Soares. 2004. "Reduced Left Anterior Cingulate Volumes in Untreated Bipolar Patients." *Biological Psychiatry* 56 (7): 467–75.

Seagrave, Daniel, and Thomas Grisso. 2002. "Adolescent Development and the Measurement of Juvenile Psychopathy." *Law and Human Behaviour* 26 (2): 219–39.

Siever, Larry J. 2008. "Neurobiology of Aggression and Violence." *American Journal of Psychiatry* 165 (4): 429–42.

Skeem, Jennifer L., John F. Edens, Glen M. Sanford, and Lori H. Colwell. 2003. "Psychopathic Personality and Racial/Ethnic Differences Reconsidered: A Reply to Lynn (2002)." *Personality and Individual Differences* 35 (6): 1439–62.

Sterzer, Philipp, and Christina Stadler. 2009. "Neuroimaging of Aggressive and Violent Behaviour in Children and Adolescents." *Frontiers in Behavioural Neuroscience.* https://doi.org/10.3389/neuro.08.035.2009.

Toglia, Michael P., and William F. Battig. 1978. *Handbook of Semantic Word Norms.* Hillsdale, NJ: Erlbaum.

Vanderah, Todd W., and Douglas J. Gould. 2016. *Nolte's The Human Brain.* 7th ed. (Online edition). Oxford, UK: Elsevier.

Viding, Essi, and Alice P. Jones. 2008. "Cognition to Genes via the Brain in the Study of Conduct Disorder." *Quarterly Journal of Experimental Psychology* 61 (1): 171–81.

Vitale, Jennifer E., Stevens S. Smith, Chad A. Brinkley, and Joseph P. Newman. 2002. "The Reliability and Validity of the Psychopathy Checklist-Revised in a Sample of Female Offenders." *Criminal Justice and Behaviour* 29 (2): 202–31.

Webster, Christopher D., Kevin S. Douglas, Derek Eaves, and Stephen D. Hart. 1997. "Assessing Risk of Violence to Others." In *Impulsivity: Theory, Assessment, and Treatment*, edited by Christopher D. Webster and Margaret A. Jackson, 251–77. New York: Guilford Press.

Webster, Christopher D., and Stephen J. Hucker. 2007. *Violence Risk: Assessment and Management*. New York: John Wiley and Sons.

Wheeler, Sarah, Angela Book, and Kimberly Costello. 2009. "Psychopathic Traits and Perceptions of Victim Vulnerability." *Criminal Justice and Behaviour* 36 (6): 635–48.

Williamson, Sherrie, Timothy J. Harpur, and Robert D. Hare. 1991. "Abnormal Processing of Affective Words by Psychopaths." *Psychophysiology* 28 (3): 260–73.

SECTION III

CHANGING RISK PRACTICES
IN CRIMINAL JUSTICE
INSTITUTIONS

The final three chapters in this volume examine evolving risk and security practices on the ground, and some of their challenges in contemporary criminal justice institutions: in policing (Schneider, chapter 6), in jails (Doyle and McKendy, chapter 7), and in border security (Côté-Boucher, chapter 8). Themes woven throughout this volume interact and refract in these diverse institutional settings. While a spectrum of efforts to govern uncertain futures is evident across these diverse sites, what is also noteworthy is the messiness and endemically limited success of these risk governance efforts in practice, and the double-edged role of technology, which may be presented as a "silver bullet," but can, in practice, work both in the service of security and to introduce new insecurities.

The chapters also show that change on the front lines in criminal justice institutions is far from necessarily a top-down, centrally managed process, calling into question narratives about criminal justice becoming increasingly subject to precise technical management. As Schneider (chapter 6) shows, police have been adapting in a somewhat piecemeal fashion to the revolutionary changes brought about by social media such as Facebook and Twitter, which, although they offer new openings for police surveillance, also create tremendous new risks for police. Schneider situates his chapter as building on Ericson and Haggerty's (1997) classic *Policing the Risk Society*, which reconceptualized police as knowledge workers embedded in technological webs that produced knowledge of crime but, in the same process, also created knowledge that allowed for organizational monitoring of police behaviour. Schneider extends Ericson and Haggerty's analysis by illustrating how social media produce new forms of risk knowledge both for and about police. Schneider's chapter illustrates that while some other new technologies are introduced specifically to manage risk in the criminal justice system, there are other simultaneous technological shifts underway in the broader society that can create sweeping and unsettling changes that undermine established institutions like the police. This is similar to how the rise of television news in the 1950s and 1960s, and, for example, the presence of television cameras on the front lines of the policing of public protests destabilized established authority (Doyle 2003; Meyrowitz 1985). Likewise social media promote new forms of visibility and critical discourse that add to the climate of doubt characteristic of risk society.

Doyle and McKendy (chapter 7) describe what is also a profound, but largely hidden, shift in the penal system in Canada. This dramatic shift is in the balance of the incarcerated population, as the number of sentenced prisoners is declining and being replaced by more and more prisoners held for lengthier and lengthier periods for preventive security prior to being convicted of crimes for which they have been charged. This shift is not tied to new technology, but it does fit with the broader trend towards preventive security, surveillance, risk management and "pre-crime" (Zedner 2007) documented throughout this book; although, as Doyle and McKendy suggest, the remand population explosion also has some unique properties. One of the most striking things about the massive growth in preventive detention in Canada is that it has occurred due to patterns of risk-averse behaviour among police and legal officials emerging spontaneously on the front lines, in spite of, and working counter to, concerted top-down efforts by the Ontario government to reduce the remand population. One impact of this is massively spiralling costs, undermining claims that preventive security is a way to be cost-conscious.

Côté-Boucher's chapter 8 opens up the little-examined world of border service agents. The chapter is an excellent example of how field research into practices on the front lines complicates narratives of new risk technologies being neutral tools that simply enhance precision in risk management. Côté-Boucher's work on how technologies contour "smart borders" highlights the extent to which the impact of risk technologies in practice shapes and is shaped by organizational dynamics on the ground, leading to shifts in division of labour and loci of decision making, and unintentionally complicating power dynamics within border agencies, as well as how they interact with other security institutions. Front-line actors such as the border officers she studies will struggle to preserve their own autonomy and resist de-skilling if new risk technologies are introduced. Côté-Boucher argues that these tensions create openings to question the effectiveness and justice of "smart borders."

Across all three chapters are illustrations of how concerns of different individuals and agencies to avoid personal and organizational risk can be in tension with, and run against, the current of reducing risk to the public. More broadly they show many of the conundrums of institutional efforts to outrun risk in the risk society, and that these efforts to control risks often themselves produce substantial new risks.

REFERENCES

Doyle, Aaron. 2003. *Arresting Images: Crime and Policing in Front of the Television Camera*. Toronto: University of Toronto Press.

Ericson, Richard V., and Kevin D. Haggerty. 1997. *Policing the Risk Society*. New York: Oxford University Press.

Meyrowitz, Joshua. 1985. *No Sense of Place: The Impact of Electronic Media on Social Behaviour*. New York: Oxford University Press.

Zedner, Lucia. 2007. "Pre-crime and Post-criminology?" *Theoretical Criminology* 11 (2): 261–81.

6 Policing and Media: Social Media as Risk Media[1]

Christopher J. Schneider

By increasing exposure of personal information, social media has raised the threat level. This new entity has a unique nature that makes it powerful and unpredictable. Several characteristics combine to make it especially threatening to law enforcement.
    —*San Bernardino Police Department Captain Gwendolyn Waters*

INTRODUCTION

Ulrich Beck's "**risk society**," a term coined in his book *Risk Society: Toward a New Modernity* (1992), initiated a significant paradigm shift responsible for directing our analytical focus toward the concept of risk. Attention to risk is now a dominant agenda in the social sciences. According to Beck (1992), risks are products of the social transition from industrial to modern society. Management of risks, particularly those associated with security, has become a central concern in many modern professions. According to Nikolas Rose (2000, 198), "risk classifications tend to become the means by which such professionals think, act and justify their actions." As risk expands and becomes a dominant preoccupation in modern society, "governments are no longer able adequately to tackle the issue of risk" (Matton 2004, 383), a task, according to Ericson and Haggerty (1997), that has been taken up by police.

Risk has been established as leading to significant changes in policing (Ericson and Haggery 1997; O'Malley 2015). The thesis that Ericson and Haggerty develop in their highly regarded *Policing the Risk Society* (1997) concerns the idea that policing shifts from order maintenance to the gathering and dissemination of knowledge that police share with various social institutions and players concerned with security—the management of risk. This shift toward risk management has contributed to the reframing of police work to focus principally on the brokerage of information. In other words, policing becomes concerned with strict management and regulation of risk information in relation to the security concerns of various social institutions.

Scholarship has mostly failed to engage in depth with the basic thesis presented in *Policing the Risk Society* (O'Malley 2015). In fact, O'Malley (2015, 427) has even suggested that "the highly controversial nature of its broad-ranging thesis should have spawned a criminological agenda that exposed its central propositions to sustained examination and further development." In an effort to contribute to such an agenda, albeit even if in a very minimalist way, I explore some of these developments in relation to social media. I investigate the process by which social media is reported to present risks to the institution of policing as it develops in news media reports. In doing so, I wish to illustrate social media platforms as the newest and most widespread "**risk media**" format. According to Ericson and Haggerty (1997, 106),

> Risk media formats make risks visible and subject to assessment and management. They typically include some combination of electronic and print media that effect surveillance, distribute knowledge, and provide risk analysis.

Rather than brokerage of information to other social institutions (see Ericson and Haggerty 1997), I explore how social media have developed into a new type of risk media, one in which the public management of risk information has turned to police (i.e., police control and regulation of their own security-related information in the public sphere [e.g., in news media stories]) due to new risks that emerge from advancements in mass communication. In the last decade, social media has very quickly developed into a significant risk media for police agencies across the globe (see Goldsmith 2015; Lee and McGovern 2014; Schneider 2016).

Unforeseen risks to police attributed to social media can include credibility and legitimacy issues, officer privacy (both public and private), and, ultimately, the loss of control of the circulation of select information online (Goldsmith 2015). Further, in "Police Use Twitter as Crime-Fighting Public Relations Tool" (2014), social media are identified as spaces to hold police accountable, wherein members of the public can post negative or critical comments about police (see also Kudla and Parnaby 2018). The concerns in these areas for law enforcement agencies have expanded well across the criminal justice landscape. In "Social Media and Law Enforcement: Potential Risks" (2012), Captain Gwendolyn Waters of the San Bernardino Police Department explains:

> Personal credibility is essential for law enforcement. Through social media, people easily can attack a police officer's character. If an officer's integrity is compromised, courtroom testimony and investigations are at risk. Law enforcement officers can find their honor under serious attack online at any time. Even erroneous information can reach a significant audience, to include potential jurors and internal affairs investigators, possibly causing irreparable damage to officers' reputations. Cases have occurred where comments posted online by officers have led to disciplinary actions. These behaviors have been the key focus of social media policies currently in place. Postings by the public—over which departments have no control—can be more damaging. Regardless of their level of truth, negative comments create lasting impressions.

The above quote speaks to two of the three specific types of risk identified by Ericson and Haggerty (1997, 43–44): risks to *careers* and *personal identities*. Two key points are worth noting about how these risks are different than those articulated by Ericson and Haggerty. First, many of these risks are fully visible online in the public realm, and, for this reason, can be the subject of discussions in news media reports. Police posts on social media, as an officer or a private citizen, can just the same become a news story or featured topic in news media reports. Such circumstances are the next phase in the *post-journalism* era where "issues that journalists report about are themselves products of media" (Altheide and Snow 1991, x). Numerous examples can be provided to illustrate the point; consider the following post made by a Royal Canadian Mounted Police (RCMP) constable on a private personal social media account: "How come every chick I arrest lately refuses to put clothes on and they're the ones you never want to see naked" (*Daily News* 2010). This post, along with others made by the constable, was featured in a *Daily News* report titled "Nanaimo Mountie Red-Faced over Public Facebook Posts." The posts initiated an RCMP professional standards review. Second, as this example shows, social media presents new risks to police *careers* and *personal identities* of officers that turn the public risk spotlight upon the institution of policing itself.

With some exceptions (see Goldsmith 2015), little scholarship has systematically addressed these risk issues, and work in this area continues to remain necessary to empirically understand this process; "what is clear, however, is that technologies have changed the ways in which the police view themselves and they [*sic*] way in which others view the police" (Lee and McGovern 2014, 175). Existent research, while in its infancy, has shown that when compared to earlier media technologies, social media has had a "far more profound impact" yet remains "poorly understood" and, nevertheless, "poses major risks" to police legitimacy and operational effectiveness (Goldsmith 2015, 249). Research illustrates that police agencies continue to respond to negative materials on social media by issuing official statements through news media (Schneider 2015a, 2016, 2018a). When and how police respond to social media materials in news media signals a "focal point" for "the selection and definition of risks" (Ericson and Haggerty 1997, 9).

Social media are an expanding form of information media. According to the Pew Research Center, "Nearly two-thirds of American adults (65%) use social networking sites, up from 7% when Pew Research Center began systematically tracking social media usage in 2005" (Perrin 2015). Further, according to a 2016 social media survey of 539 law enforcement agencies across the United States administered by the International Association of Chiefs of Police (IACP), law enforcement use of social media is diverse. The IACP reported that 91 percent of responding agencies use social media to notify the public regarding safety issues, 89 percent use it for community outreach, and 86 percent use the technology for public relations and image management (Kim, Oglesby-Neal, and Mohr 2017). These data anecdotally suggest that social media are the newest form of risk media from which police agencies produce knowledge of risk; "risk media make knowledge of risk accessible for a variety of uses" (Ericson and Haggerty 1997, 107). By locating focal points that define risks in news media reports, we can learn more about associated risks to policing by examining how the development of risk is connected to social media. A few basic questions emerge: In what ways are risks associated with social media and police discussed in news media reports? And what might this suggest about social media as an emergent type of risk media format? In the next section, I turn my attention to a brief overview of when and how police agencies first became attracted to social media platforms, before directing my focus to a discussion of research methods.

POLICE AND SOCIAL MEDIA: A BRIEF HISTORY

The first social media site launched in 1997 (boyd and Ellison 2007) and in just a few years this number quickly ballooned into hundreds of sites. Police would not regularly publicly appear on social media platforms until nearly a decade later. This observation is not meant to imply absence from social media in police surveillance or undercover work; however, because this work is often secretive, it is difficult to detect. MySpace is significant because it was the first social media platform to attract public attention from police across the United States, beginning in 2005.

MySpace launched in 2003; in July 2005, News Corporation acquired the site from Intermix Media for $580 million. At the time of the News Corporation acquisition, MySpace had a reported 16 million users.

Reports that spotlighted the sale helped to attract increased attention to MySpace—the number of MySpace users would nearly double by the end of the year. At this time, a considerable percentage of MySpace users were teenagers, an age demographic often associated with delinquency and deviance. At the end of 2005, police attention to MySpace intensified in response to news media coverage of the high profile murder of a 17-year old first-year university student.

When public tips produced no leads for investigators, police turned to MySpace as an information source. This is an early example of police gleaning publicly accessible information from MySpace to aid in a private investigation—what police referred to at the time as a "virtual tip machine." Prior to MySpace, police were largely able to manage and control information from criminal investigations, including associated risks of crime, fear, and danger that were then shared with organizations like news media. Consistent with Ericson and Haggerty's (1997) thesis, the proliferation of social media contributed further to the lessening of crime control efforts in lieu of increased police surveillance online, developing first on MySpace and, later, across all social media platforms.

Police surveillance efforts intensified on social media in 2006 following a *Dateline NBC* report that put the figure of sexual predators online at any given moment at 50,000. The number later turned out not to be supported by evidence; nevertheless, the statistic was cited in speeches given by such prominent claims-makers as politicians and also in news media reports. Police were quickly bombarded by complaints from concerned parents from across the United States. Some police agencies joined MySpace in hopes that their presence on teen profiles would deter would-be predators. Police also turned to MySpace for information disclosure in response to the online sexual predator moral panic (Marwick 2008). A confidential document issued by MySpace for law enforcement only, leaked in 2009 by whistle-blower site WikiLeaks, explains:

> In order to assist law enforcement in narrowly tailoring its requests and ensuring the necessary process is provided, we identify below the specific categories of information and corresponding process required to lawfully produce that information under ECPA [Electronic

Communications Privacy Act]. When drafting subpoenas, court orders, or search warrants, please be as specific as possible about the
profile at issue, and the nature of the information sought. Clearly
worded requests will reduce confusion, enable MySpace to respond
more quickly, and ensure that no other issues arise under ECPA
limiting MySpace's ability to comply. (MySpace.com 2006)

At the dawn of the social media age, MySpace provided a new and
uncharted avenue from which police were able to collect and manage
risk-related information. Regulation and access of information generated by MySpace was often publicly available to anyone and constantly
changing. As noted in the above-referenced law enforcement guide:

For public profiles, law enforcement may access and save screen shots
of publicly available information without involvement of MySpace.
Because users can change the content on their profile and change the
status from public to private at any time, MySpace encourage law
enforcement to preserve the content on public profiles themselves by
using screen shots. (MySpace.com 2006)

Social media affects police surveillance in new ways unlike other social
institutions. Social media is difficult to define and goes by other names, including new media and social networking. All of these share the following
basic characteristics: they enable creation, rely exclusively on audience par-
ticipation relative to the production of content, and involve varying degrees
of user engagement (see Mandiberg 2012). Knowledge and information
collected from social media platforms is non-linear and multidirectional;
can be available to everyone, everywhere; and is evolving 24 hours a day.
In the early years of MySpace, police activity on MySpace was in direct
response to social media–produced knowledge of risk (e.g., sexual predators
online and safety of teenagers). As social media expanded and new media
platforms launched (e.g., Facebook in 2004, YouTube in 2005, and Twitter
in 2006), counter citizen surveillance on social media turned against police,
thereby initiating an unprecedented form of risk media.

As one example to illustrate the point, consider the 2007 Montebello summit protest in Quebec, Canada. An innocuous video posted by a citizen to YouTube showed three suspicious and seemingly out of place people at the protest. These people were later revealed to be undercover police officers. The officers were accused of trying to incite a riot in order to end an otherwise lawful protest. While not the first video or social media post to profile police in a negative matter, this circumstance is unique as it was among the very first instances in Canada where police provided an official and therefore authorized account *because of* discrediting materials circulating on YouTube.

Police work, along with a host of other activities on social media platforms, has now become visible and subject to assessment in the public realm. Understanding police visibility and assessment on social media is an emerging area of research, and for this reason, little scholarship has examined how policing develops in response to social media. In the balance of this chapter, my attention will focus largely, but not exclusively, on how police respond publicly in news media reports to perceived risks because of social media. A qualitative media analysis of news documents can help provide some insight into the development of social media as an emergent risk media format for police agencies.

METHODOLOGY

Qualitative media analysis (QMA) involves the collection and analysis of documents, defined as any symbolic representation that is recorded and retrievable for analysis. This method provides a framework from which to define, organize, and examine relevant documents as identified by the researcher during the research process, which occurs over a series of 12 steps (Altheide and Schneider 2013, 39–73):

1. Identify a specific topic to investigate.
2. Learn the information source and review any existing literature on the topic.

3. Become familiar with examples of relevant documents (about a half a dozen or so).

4. List several categories (i.e., variables) on a data collection sheet (protocol).

5. Test the data collection sheet by gathering data from separate documents.

6. Update and modify the protocol to reflect additional cases.

7. Employ sampling rationale and strategy (e.g., theoretical sampling, outlined below).

8. Collect data examples using preset codes, add additional categories to the data collection sheet (if necessary), and complete data collection.

9. Conduct an analysis of the data.

10. Locate significant differences in each category, and compare and contrast any extremes and write summaries.

11. Amalgamate written summaries with typical examples of the key differences.

12. Integrate these materials with your findings and interpretations in a draft that will become your manuscript.

The first three steps concern the pursuit of the topic of investigation and developing a familiarity with the information source. Since my concern is with understanding how police respond publicly to social media as risk media, as outlined above, I directed my attention to focus on news media documents concerning police and social media. These documents were retrieved from the LexisNexis database.

Searches were limited to the *New York Times*, as this news publication is recognized as an agenda-setting national paper of record. Additionally, the New York Police Department (NYPD) is the largest urban police force in the United States. Given these two details, we can surmise that coverage of national issues related to police and social media, as well as those specific to the NYPD, would be represented. According to Nancy Kolb, program director of the Center for Social Media at the International Association of the Chiefs of Police, an "exponential increase" of law enforcement on social media platforms occurred between 2009 and 2011 (Knibbs 2013), with the NYPD joining the most popular site, Facebook, in February 2012. These materials provide a basic timeframe for searches. Preliminary searches of the LexisNexis database included "social media" and "police." Between 2005 and 2010, searches yielded 127 results, whereas between 2011 and March 7, 2016, the same search criteria returned 2,551 results. These search results suggest that the increased use of the phrase "social media"[2] in the last five years coincides with a broader shift in the cultural acceptance of the phrase in reference to a host of interactive media platforms, notably Facebook, YouTube, and Twitter. These social media platforms were added to the data collection sheet and then tested against further searches to ensure categorical consistency across the searched data. These data were then downloaded from LexisNexis and converted into a 7456 PDF file. Further review of these data revealed identifiable key terms and phrases that were entered into the PDF document search function as a way to continue to review these collected data for emergent themes and narratives, an approach consistent with QMA. Examples included the following search terms: "social media," "comment(s)," "account(s)," "tweet(s)," "post(s)," "threat(s)," and "smart phone(s)."

Steps 4 to 6 involve the construction of a protocol or data collection sheet. Protocol categories including date, topic, focus, sources, and social media platform were added to the protocol sheet to help further guide and categorize collected data materials. Searches of these data continued until the point of saturation (i.e., additional searches produced no new results for collection). Consistent with QMA, theoretical sampling was selected as a relevant sampling strategy (step 7). This strategy refers to the purposeful selection of materials based on the understanding of the topic, prior to actual data collection (step 8).

> Qualitative data analysis is not about coding or counting, although these activities can be useful in some parts of fulfilling the goals of the quest for meaning and theoretical integration. . . . The goal is to understand the process, to see the process in the types and meanings of the documents under investigation, and to be able to associate the documents with conceptual and theoretical issues. This occurs as the researcher interacts with the document. . . . [Therefore] it is best to rely on the more straightforward "search-find-replace" options on most word processing programs. (Altheide and Schneider 2013, 70)

Analysis (step 9) allows the researcher to then begin to understand the characteristics and organizational elements of theoretically identified documents. The next step (10) is to identify the range or "extremes" in the collected data. This process involved short summaries that highlighted these differences that were then added to the protocol sheets under a "Notes" category. Concepts and themes were developed by drawing key comparisons between protocol categories. Step 11 is when these materials were brought together into a more cohesive narrative, which developed as an early version of a final manuscript (step 12). I now turn my attention to three basic themes that each illustrates social media as form of risk media, one that is visible and in need of assessment and management.

SOCIAL MEDIA AS RISK MEDIA

Threats to Social Order

As discussed across the examined news media reports, various threats to social order (i.e., the status quo) circulated on multiple social media platforms. These threats were largely consistent with crime matters and, later, with terrorism. In 2011, reports highlighted crime on social media as an emergent phenomenon, but one, nevertheless, that was quickly expanding as a useful and vital information source to police and prosecutors. The topic and focus of these reports was usually crime related with a discussion of various specific crimes (i.e., examples from social media). An excerpt from a report with the headline "'On tha Run for Robbin a Bank' and Other Online Postings That Investigators Love" helps illustrate the point:

> But a year later, while [Rodney] Bradford, 20, was out on bail on a charge that he had assaulted a relative of his girlfriend, prosecutors hauled him back before a judge to explain a disturbing message that had appeared on the girlfriend's Facebook account. . . . As Twitter, Facebook and other forms of public electronic communication embed themselves in people's lives, the postings, rants and messages

that appear online are emerging as a new trove for the police and prosecutors to sift through after crimes. Such sites are often the first place they go. The phenomenon arose again this week, when investigators went online to make sense of a stabbing in an East New York, Brooklyn apartment. A few clicks away, some of the clues were there for the world to see. (Goldstein 2011)

As occurrences of crime on social media become featured more regularly across news reports, there is a shift in discourse from *reactive* to *proactive* discussions of crime. This shift appears to signal the recognition of social media by police as an information source. In other words, raw data is produced on social media, and these data are converted into a new type of risk data that is shown to influence *proactive* police actions.

Lt. James Perez of the Fairfield Police Department said that nonspecific threats of protests at the funeral home, coupled with "stupid comments" on the Internet and on social media, had prompted the unusually large police presence. "You have to prepare," the officer said. "Newtown wasn't warned either." (Barry 2012)

Not only does the statement made by Perez indicate the conversion of social media data into useful knowledge for the mobilization of police officers, it stresses unspecified threats to public safety. Perez connects "stupid comments" with the Sandy Hook Elementary School shooting in Newtown, Connecticut, in December 2012, where 20 school children and 6 staff members were shot to death. We can surmise that these "stupid comments" were likely not criminal in nature, because if they had been, these comments would have been labelled and treated by police as criminal threats, and thus subsequently reported in news media as criminal threats. The pervasiveness of social media as a decentralized media format and as connected with existent fears of crime helps contribute to the more widespread perception of risk. Across reports the extraordinary (i.e., isolated events on social media) become routine. The normalization of unspecified threats starts to expand risk and the scope of police control and surveillance efforts.

In June 2013, Facebook (currently the world's largest social media site with more than two billion monthly users) disclosed for the very first time law enforcement requests for data. The public disclosure by Facebook was a topic in news reports and illustrates how social media sites such as Facebook, Twitter, and YouTube acquire institutional identities, each with their own "**population identities**" to be managed (Ericson and Haggerty 1997).

> The social networking company said that in the last six months of 2012, it had 9,000 to 10,000 requests for information about its users from local, state and federal agencies. Those requests covered 18,000 to 19,000 user accounts. "These requests run the gamut—from things like a local sheriff trying to find a missing child, to a federal marshal tracking a fugitive, to a police department investigating an assault, to a national security official investigating a terrorist threat," the company's general counsel, Ted Ullyot, said in a blog post disclosing the data. (Goel 2013)

Reports of law enforcement requests for raw data produced on social media sites like Facebook, as the above thematic example illustrates, conflate various specified (e.g., missing children, assault) and unspecified (e.g., terrorist threats) actions. These actions are not linked to time or place, thereby expanding the parameters of threats to order, including, notably, crime. Social media platforms operate as new accessible spaces where publics can publish unfiltered raw crime data—unfiltered risk data. The highly visible, online meaning-making process that surrounds these raw data is a multi-faceted, multidirectional, and public affair—one that complicates the management of these data for the purposes of law enforcement. For instance, research has traced the online meaning-making process of raw crime data as these data were circulated by citizens on Facebook in response to the 2011 Vancouver riot (see Schneider 2015b). The interpretation of these raw data, without the assistance of police, influenced how publics then aided police criminal justice efforts in response to the riot itself (Schneider and Trottier 2012, 2013).

Another recent and much less explored development involves how social media companies, as data-producing institutions, control access to their own data, especially data that have been deemed by police to pose a threat to order. Reports in the examined documents of threatening tweets on Twitter provide one thematic example. A series of tweets made in specific reference to an alleged planned shooting at a Broadway theatre in New York City caught the attention of police. According to one reported tweet, "I got 600 people on my hit list and that's gonna be a mass murder for real." Police sent an emergency request to Twitter for account information. Twitter responded as follows:

> "We appreciate the timeliness and sensitivity of this matter, and have reviewed the reported Twitter account," the company wrote in an e-mail to the police. "While we do invoke emergency-disclosure procedures when it appears that a threat is present, specific and immediate, this does not appear to fall under those strict parameters as per our policies." (Ruderman 2012)

Twitter was eventually forced to comply by court order to surrender the requested information. While similar challenges to law enforcement by withholding information are certainly nothing new (e.g., privacy laws), the manner in which this occurs in public spaces on social media, and subsequently in news media, is a more recent development, and one that can sometimes leave the police out of the equation altogether. News reports that highlight the absence of police in such situations present the police as inefficient at best, and incompetent at worst.

> A teenager in Los Angeles had posted a tweet saying that the pop music heartthrob Justin Bieber had been arrested. CNN's Los Angeles bureau followed up on the tip by calling the appropriate local precinct. *The police said that they were pursuing an attempted robbery complaint against Mr. Bieber, but wanted to know how the cable news network could possibly have known that.* (Kaufman 2014; emphasis added)

This example illustrates a loosening of police control over crime (i.e., threat) because of materials circulating on social media. The above circumstance is just one of numerous similar examples of a "crime story" that can develop simultaneously online and in news media *ahead of police control* (see also Chermak 1995).[3] This example illustrates that news journalists are no longer forced to rely exclusively on police as knowledge brokers or even as the "authorized knowers" (Fishman 1980) of crime information. This is not to suggest that police have lost relevance—they have not—but rather that because of social media, police have lost control over how "recently discovered crimes get presented" (Chermak 1995, 33). This disruption to police control and inability to manage risk data is among a list of growing threats, as noted in the epigraph of this chapter, to police both at the organizational and individual levels. I now turn to a discussion of the organizational level.

Organizational Threats to Police

Threats to the police as an organization linked to social media as an emergent form of risk media began to increase in frequency in 2014. Risk media makes risks visible, and because of heightened visibility, risks become subject to assessment and management (Ericson and Haggerty 1997). At the organizational level, threats to public police that were associated with social media were usually presented in one of two ways in the examined documents. First, threats were linked to risks of perceived weakened police effectiveness to combat crime and terrorism in online spaces. Second, risks associated with concerns over police accountability were connected to the citizen documentation and circulation of depictions of police deviance (e.g., brutality) on social media platforms (see Schneider 2018a). These organizational threats problematize police control over their public image as the legitimate authority (Ericson 1982) since police "presentational strategies" (Manning 1978) require explicit promotion in news media (Fishman 1980).

In a risk society, "the onus is placed on organizations and individuals to be more self-sufficient, to look after their own risk management needs" (Ericson and Haggerty 1997, 6). The organizational response by police has been to incorporate the logic of social media into contemporary police practices. The Federal Bureau of Investigation National

Executive Institute Associates, a United States law enforcement organization that focuses on training, perhaps summarizes this position best: "the question is no longer whether the police will use SM [social media], it is just how quickly and how well we will do it!" (Major Cities Chiefs Associates et al. 2013, 7).

The NYPD first joined Facebook in 2012, but it was not until late 2014 that officers were provided with NYPD-issued devices capable of accessing and managing social media. It was announced in October 2014 that all 35,000 NYPD officers would be equipped with smartphones for law enforcement purposes. This was to include a total of 41,000 devices as well as 6,000 tablets installed in police cars at a total cost of $160 million. In the words of New York City Mayor Bill de Blasio, "[police] must have 21st-century tools to deal with 21st-century threats" (Schlossberg 2014). These devices were provided by the organization to individual officers to "look after" risk management needs in order to address social media threats to social order (i.e., crime).

> Each device will hold several applications, such as a mobile version of the Domain Awareness System, a computer surveillance system that joins video feeds from thousands of closed-circuit cameras to law enforcement databases, allowing them to track and gather information about criminals and possible terrorists. The devices will also ensure access to relevant 911 data, including notes by call-takers and information about the location of the call, the statement from the district attorney's office said. The office is looking into adding GPS features to the devices, it said, which could help in coordinating backup. The program also anticipates adding the capability to scan fingerprints in the field, sometime next year. (Schlossberg 2014)

This thematic example speaks to the first of the two above-mentioned risks made to police at organizational level by appearing to strengthen the perceived police inability and ineffectiveness to combat online crime and terrorism. The report citing the above announcement discussed this development as an "update [to] the patrol beat for the digital age" and referenced police body cameras. The NYPD announcement that it was providing smartphones and tablets to officers was reported just weeks after the force initiated a **body camera** pilot program. The death of New York resident Eric Garner is noted, but no specific context was provided in the above-referenced article. Garner's name, however, appears across the examined reports and speaks to the broader topic of organizational police risk management issues that reflect police accountability concerns, the second of the two above-noted thematic threats to organizational police activity.

Garner died on July 17, 2014, after being placed in a chokehold by NYPD Officer Daniel Pantaleo while the officer attempted to arrest him for allegedly selling cigarettes illegally on a street corner. Bystander Ramsey Orta captured the confrontation and death on his cellphone. "The main role of the police with respect to knowledge of death is to profile people who die in unusual circumstances" (Ericson and Haggerty 1997, 243); death as a result of police action is unusual, but the profiling of these deaths online is increasing. Orta's video of Garner's death went viral on social media within hours. Characteristics of *viralness* include "stories and videos that [quickly] gain traction in social media" (Broxton et al. 2013, 242). The video of Garner's death was "seen around the world" (Goodman and Baker 2014) and "viewed by millions of people" (Yee 2014). The video is significant, as it was "the first in a wave of recordings of African-Americans in violent confrontations with white police officers to command national attention [in the United States]" (Sanburn 2015). Perhaps most importantly for our purposes here, according to an anonymous senior NYPD officer, "We didn't know about the chokehold or hands to neck until the video came out … *we found out when everyone else did*" (Baker, Goodman, and Mueller 2015; emphasis added).

Circumstances such as Garner's death profiled publicly on social media compel police agencies to develop technologies in response to these growing external pressures for knowledge and management of risk (Ericson and Haggerty 1997). Law enforcement agencies across the United States began equipping officers with body-worn cameras in September 2014, just months after Garner's death. This was extensively profiled in news media (see Schneider 2017). As noted in one report, "Amateur videos of police officers doing their jobs have become part of the fabric of urban democracy, with embarrassing or violent images spreading via social media in minutes" (Johnson 2014). The report further illustrates new risk management concerns for police:

> But the spread of police body cameras is also raising concerns about what is recorded, when and how video might be released to the public, and how the millions of hours of video will be archived and protected from leaks and hackers. Some police unions worry that videos could become tools of management, used by higher-ups to punish an officer they do not like, or that private conversations among officers could go public. (Johnson 2014)

While little empirical evidence is available concerning the use of police body cameras across police services, the quick introduction of this technology to front-line policing seems to at least anecdotally address a few of the issues related to social media as a form of risk media. First, as an organization, police are able to assert that their body camera recordings are the complete (i.e., unedited or altered) depiction of any given event, thereby rendering all social media viral videos unofficial, though not necessarily insignificant. Body camera data also provide police with the ability to offer an official counter-narrative without necessarily releasing any video to the public, an existent police practice in response to social media materials. Second, in terms of the brokerage of information, body camera data are not subject to the same legal scrutiny as materials (e.g., evidence) collected from social media platforms, materials that may or may not have been altered or manipulated by online users. The expedient introduction of body camera data into the legal process (i.e., courtroom) in advance of various third-party data materials circulating on social media platforms helps reaffirm the police control over crime narratives that has loosened in recent years because of social media. I now turn my attention to the police control and management of social media as risk media at the individual level.

Individual Threats to Police

Two types of risks that emerge in a risk society, as noted above according to Ericson and Haggerty (1997), are those risks to *careers* and *identities*. Career-related risks focus on how police manage risk data for other institutions. Career risks are those that occur over the lifetime of an individual, whereas individual risks are defined as those risks to personal identities (Ericson and Haggerty 1997). Examined news media reports started focusing increasingly on social media risks in relation to individual officers beginning in 2011. This date also coincides with existent research that documents an increased police presence on social media. News reports in the examined documents, circa 2011–12, are framed in terms of risks to careers rather than personal identity characteristics associated with individual officers. Two central themes ran concurrently throughout these reports. Social media was presented as either a valuable police tool or serious problem to be dealt with, as this example illustrates:

> Social networking tools like Facebook and Twitter can be valuable assets for law enforcement agencies, helping them alert the public, seek information about crimes and gather evidence about the backgrounds of criminal suspects. But the Internet can also get police departments into trouble.... The problem is serious enough that departments across the country are scrambling to develop rules to govern what officers can and cannot do online. "This is something that all the police chiefs around the country, if you're not dealing with it, you better deal with it," said Mark A. Marshall, chief of police in Smithfield, Va., and the president of the International Association of Chiefs of Police, which has developed its own model policy. (Goode 2011)

The report from which the above quotation is taken also featured examples of what were described as "public gaffes" by police officers on social media. Other risks to individual officers were also highlighted:

> A careless posting on a networking site, law enforcement experts say, can endanger an officer's safety, as it did in Santa Monica, Calif., last

year when the Police Department went to great lengths to conceal a wounded officer's identity and location, only to have a retired officer inadvertently reveal them on Facebook. (Goode 2011)

Risks in news media connecting police and social media were initially reported at the individual level. The reporting of police risk management strategies to govern the use of social media begins with public gaffes (e.g., inappropriate posts) and then shifts from internal (i.e., police leakage of information as noted above) to external public threats to individual officer safety. The need for police to manage risk associated with social media moves away from careers and identities to safety concerns. The catalyst, it seems, stems from developments following the death of Michael Brown as a result of police action in Ferguson, Missouri. Following his death, it was reported that the Ferguson Police would not release the officer's name directly because of unspecified threats on social media:

> Chief Jackson said a provision of state law allowed police departments to withhold an officer's name if there were concerns about personal safety. Normally, a department has 72 hours to disclose a name. The rash of threats on social media, Chief Jackson said, led to his decision. (Bosman and Williams 2014)

The deaths of Eric Garner (July 14, 2014) and Michael Brown (August 9, 2014) spurred various national protests across the United States. Reports that covered the protests were largely framed in the context of police accountability and reform. One recurrent theme of these reports included growing threats to police on social media. An October 31, 2014, *New York Times* report with the headline "On the Other Side of Ferguson's Protest Lines, Officers Face New Threats" helps to illustrate the point.

> The animosity, found on social media and in protests just outside police headquarters, had been so virulent at times that she listened more carefully these days to calls requesting assistance before she sent an

officer—for fear of a possible ambush. "You want to make sure your officers are O.K.," [police dispatcher Marione Johnson] said. (Barry 2014)

The report continues:

> Even a simple stop for a soda at the Circle K has become unsettling, because of what the police describe as social media talk about catching Ferguson officers off guard at the convenience store—and shooting them in the head.
> "You are constantly wondering," Sgt. Mike Wood, a Ferguson native, said. "I know I didn't sign up with Burger King, but . . ." (Barry 2014)

The situational context of these threats against police is the Ferguson protests while the broader context is social media platforms. Risks on social media are non-linear, multidirectional, and anonymous. Reports of the association of social media with threats against police intensified in December 2014 following the deaths of two NYPD officers:

> [NYDP Police Commissioner William J. Bratton] conceded that the shootings appeared to be a "direct spinoff of this issue" of the recent protests. The gunman, Ismaaiyl Brinsley, had alluded to the cases of Michael Brown and Eric Garner on social media, the police said. (Flegenheimer 2014)

For a short time in the examined documents, social media as risk media was attributed mostly to police careers and officer identities. The management of these data in these contexts was left up to individual officers. Following national protest on social media related to police accountability, a shift occurred to officer safety concerns. These threats against individual officers were contextualized in reports as threatening to police more generally. This is largely due to the anonymity of social media and what has become the "epidemic of facelessness," as one 2015 headline read, an epidemic that reportedly "provokes and mitigates the inherent capacity for monstrosity" (Marche 2015).

DISCUSSION AND CONCLUSION

Social media are a recent addition to the media landscape. These platforms are an emergent type of risk media understood as media forms that "make risks visible and subject to assessment and management" (Ericson and Haggerty 1997, 106). How police respond to social media materials in news media signals a "focal point" for "the selection and definition of risks" (Ericson and Haggerty 1997, 9). Because of risk media, policing shifted from order maintenance to knowledge gathering and dissemination to share with other institutions. Social media as risk media initiates a new type of shift that includes the police management of these risk data, data that circulate online in public spaces. I now return to a brief discussion of the questions posed at the outset of this chapter: In what ways are risks associated with social media and police discussed in news media? And what does this suggest about social media as an emergent type of risk media format?

Risks associated with social media and police were first discussed in news media as threats to social order. These threats were associated with the expansion of crime and, then, later, terrorism online. As crime on social media is featured more regularly in news reports, a shift from *reactive* to *proactive* police response to risks has occurred. These risks are associated with the perception of weakened police effectiveness. As communication and information media expand, social media as risk media, as reported in news media, spotlights instances of police deviance and the need for police to now manage these risks by incorporating social media technologies into front-line police work. Career and identity risks, once prominent concerns, shift to a focus on officer safety concerns. All of this seems to suggest that social media as risk media helps to contribute to the expansion of police social control efforts because risks on social media are non-linear, multidirectional, and anonymous.

This chapter contributes to scholarship on the management of risk by examining how risk is presented in select news media reports. Documents are products of culture. The collection and analysis of documents can provide some insight into various "focal points" of risk definitions. What has been presented in this chapter is just a small piece of a much larger risk puzzle. Future research in this area may consider ethnographic work with police officers for a more complete understanding of police management of social media as risk media. This can include data created through police use of social media as well as the management of these and other social media data internally by police. Other work might also consider examining police body camera data as an emergent type of new visibility associated with risk (e.g., the circulation of body camera footage on social media; see Schneider 2018b). I look forward to such future endeavours.

DISCUSSION QUESTIONS

1.   In what ways do social media platforms represent an emergent type of risk media? Provide a few examples from the chapter to help support your response.
2.   What are some specific risks that social media materials pose to law enforcement officers' *careers* and *personal identities*? Can you think of others not covered in this chapter?
3.   Should police officers be subject to professional standards on their private social media accounts? Why or why not?
4.   Risks on social media are "non-linear, multidirectional, and anonymous." How do these factors contribute to the ways in which law enforcement professionals might think, act, and justify their actions in the contemporary risk society?

ACKNOWLEDGEMENTS

The workshop in which an earlier version of this chapter was presented and related activities were both professionally and personally stimulating. I am grateful to the workshop participants, co-editors, contributors, and three anonymous peer reviewers for their helpful comments and suggestions on earlier versions of this chapter. I would also like to acknowledge Stacey Hannem for taking the lead on both organizing and editing this volume.

NOTES

1. This chapter draws on and develops some arguments and materials in earlier work dealing with policing and social media (Schneider 2015a, 2016, 2018a).
2. Other terms sometimes are used interchangeably with social media such as "social networking" and "new media"; however, these terms appeared just 151 and 21 times respectively across the collected data.
3. For other examples, see Schneider 2016.

REFERENCES

Altheide, David L., and Christopher J. Schneider. 2013. *Qualitative Media Analysis.* 2nd ed. Thousand Oaks, CA: Sage.

Altheide, David L., and Robert Snow. 1991. *Media Worlds in the Postjournalism Era.* Hawthorne, NY: Aldine de Gruyter.

Baker, Al, J. David Goodman, and Benjamin Mueller. 2015. "Beyond the Chokehold." *New York Times*, June 14, 2015, A1.

Barry, Dan. 2012. "With the Why Elusive, Two Boys, Two Burials." *New York Times*, December 18, 2012, A1.

———. 2014. "On the Other Side of Ferguson's Protest Lines, Officers Face New Threats." *New York Times*, October 31, 2014, A12.

Beck, Ulrich. 1992. *Risk Society: Toward a New Modernity.* Newbury Park, CA: Sage.

Bosman, Julie, and Timothy Williams. 2014. "Police Cite Threats in Deciding Not to Name Officer Who Shot Missouri Teenager." *New York Times*, August 12, 2014, A14.

boyd, danah m., and Nicole B. Ellison. 2007. "Social Network Sites: Definition, History, and Scholarship." *Journal of Computer-Mediated Communication* 13 (1): 210–30.

Broxton, Tom, Yannet Interian, Jon Vaver, and Mirjam Wattenhofer. 2013. "Catching a Viral Video." *Journal of Intelligent Information Systems* 40: 241–59.

Chermak, Steven. 1995. "Image Control: How Police Affect the Presentation of Crime News." *American Journal of Police* 14 (2): 21–43.

Daily News (Nanaimo, BC). 2010. "Nanaimo Mountie Red-Faced over Public Facebook Posts." http://www.canada.com/story.html?id=14b1672a-6ae7-44d8acdafbe6d5839f1c.

Ericson, Richard V. 1982. *Reproducing Order: A Study of Police Patrol Work.* Toronto: University of Toronto Press.

Ericson, Richard V., and Kevin Haggerty. 1997. *Policing the Risk Society.* New York: Oxford University Press.

Fishman, Mark. 1980. *Manufacturing the News.* Austin, TX: University of Texas Press.

Flegenheimer, Mark. 2014. "De Blasio Fights to Find Balance after 2 Killings." *New York Times*, December 23, 2014, A1.

Goel, Vindu. 2013. "Facebook Offers View of Requests for User Data." *New York Times*, July 15, 2013, B2.

Goldsmith, Andrew. 2015. "Disgracebook Policing: Social Media and the Rise of Police Indiscretion." *Policing and Society* 25 (3): 249–67.

Goldstein, Joseph. 2011. "'On tha Run for Robbin a Bank' and Other Online Postings That Investigators Love." *New York Times*, March 3, 2011, A25.

Goode, Erica. 2011. "Police Lesson: Network Tools Have 2 Edges." *New York Times*, April 7, 2011, A1.

Goodman, J. David, and Al Baker. 2014. "New York Officer Facing No Charges in Chokehold Case." *New York Times*, December 4, 2014, A1.

Johnson, Kirk. 2014. "Today's Police Put On a Gun and a Camera." *New York Times*, September 28, 2014, A1.

Kaufman, Leslie. 2014. "Tool Hunts for News in the Din of Twitter." *New York Times*, September 24, 2014, B5.

Kim, KiDeuk, Ashlin Oglesby-Neal, and Edward Mohr. 2017. "2016 Law Enforcement Use of Social Media Survey: A Joint Publication by the International Association of Chiefs of Police and the Urban Institute." http://www.theiacp.org/Portals/0/documents/pdfs/2016law-enforcement-use-of-social-media-survey.pdf.

Knibbs, Kate. 2013. "How Police Use Social Networks for Investigations." *Digital Trends.* https://www.digitaltrends.com/social-media/the-new-inside-source-for-police-forces-social-networks/.

Kudla, Daniel, and Patrick F. Parnaby. 2018. "To Serve and to Tweet: An Examination of Police-Related Twitter Activity in Toronto." *Social Media and Society* 4 (3). https://doi.org/10.1177/2056305118787520.

Lee, Murray, and Alyce McGovern. 2014. *Policing and Media: Public Relations, Simulations, and Communication*. New York: Routledge.

Major Cities Chiefs Associates, Major Counties Sheriffs Associates, and Federal Bureau of Investigation National Executive Institute Associates. 2013. *Social Media: A Valuable Tool with Risks*. https://www.majorcitieschiefs.com/pdf/news/soc_media_tool_with_risks.pdf.

Mandiberg, Michael. 2012. *The Social Media Reader*. New York: New York University Press.

Manning, Peter K. 1978. "The Police: Mandate, Strategies and Appearances." In *Policing: A View from the Street*, edited by Peter K. Manning and John van Maanen, 97–125. Santa Monica, CA: Goodyear.

Marche, Stephen. 2015. "The Epidemic of Facelessness." *New York Times*, February 15, 2015 (Sunday Review section).

Marwick, Alice E. 2008. "To Catch a Predator? The MySpace Moral Panic." *First Monday* 13 (6). http://firstmonday.org/article/view/2152/1966.

Matton, Dirk. 2004. "The Impact of the Risk Society Thesis on Environmental Politics and Management in a Globalizing Economy—Principles, Proficiency, Perspectives." *Journal of Risk Research* 7 (4): 377–98.

MySpace.com. 2006. "Law Enforcement Investigators Guide, 23 Jun 2006." http://wikileaks.org/wiki/MySpace.com_Law_Enforcement_Investigators_Guide,_23_Jun_2006.

O'Malley, Pat. 2015. "Revisiting the Classics: 'Policing the Risk Society' in the Twenty-First Century." *Policing and Society: An International Journal of Research and Policy* 25 (4): 426–31.

Perrin, Andrew. 2015. "Social Media Usage: 2005–2015." *Pew Research Center*. http://www.pewinternet.org/2015/10/08/social-networking-usage-2005-2015/.

"Police Use Twitter as Crime-Fighting Public Relations Tool." 2014. University of Guelph. https://news.uoguelph.ca/2014/05/police-use-twitter-as-crime-fighting-public-relations-tool/.

Rose, Nikolas. 2000. "Government and Control." In *Criminological and Social Theory*, edited by David Garland and Richard Sparks, 187–208. London: Oxford University Press.

Ruderman, Wendy. 2012. "Court Prompts Twitter to Give Data to Police in Threat Case." *New York Times*, August 8, 2012, A14.

Sanburn, Josh. 2015. "Eric Garner Witness Ramsey Orta Has Regrets One Year Later." *Time*, July 16, 2015. http://time.com/ramsey-orta-eric-garner-video/.

Schlossberg, Tatiana. 2014. "New York City Police to Be Equipped with Smartphones and Tablets." *New York Times*, October 24, 2014. https://www.nytimes.com/2014/10/24/nyregion/new-york-city-police-to-be-equipped-with-smartphones-and-tablets.html?mcubz=0.

Schneider, Christopher J. 2015a. "Police Image Work in an Era of Social Media: YouTube and the 2007 Montebello Summit Protest." In *Social Media, Politics and the State: Protests, Revolutions, Riots, Crime and Policing in an Age of Facebook, Twitter and YouTube*, edited by Daniel Trottier and Christian Fuchs, 227–46. New York: Routledge.

———. 2015b. "Public Criminology and the 2011 Vancouver Riot: Public Perceptions of Crime and Justice in the 21st Century." *Radical Criminology* 5: 21–46.

———. 2016. *Policing and Social Media: Social Control in an Era of New Media.* Lanham, MD: Lexington Books/Rowman and Littlefield.

———. 2017. "Body Worn Cameras and Police Image Work: News Media Coverage of the Rialto Police Department's Body Worn Camera Experiment." *Crime, Media, Culture.* https://doi.org/10.1177/1741659017721591.

———. 2018a. "Police Deviance and New Media: The Death of Eric Garner." In *Handbook on Deviance*, edited by Ophir Sefiha and Stephen Brown, 337–47. New York: Routledge.

———. 2018b. "An Exploratory Study of Public Perceptions of Police Conduct Depicted in Body Worn Camera Footage on YouTube." *Annual Review of Interdisciplinary Justice Research* 7: 118–48.

Schneider, Christopher J., and Daniel Trottier. 2012. "The 2011 Vancouver Riot and the Role of Facebook in Crowd-Sourced Policing." *BC Studies* 175 (Autumn): 93–109.

———. 2013. "Social Media and the 2011 Vancouver Riot." *Studies in Symbolic Interaction* 40: 335–62.

Waters, Gwendolyn. 2012. "Social Media and Law Enforcement: Potential Risks." *FBI Law Enforcement Bulletin.* https://leb.fbi.gov/2012/november/social-media-and-law-enforcement-potential-risks.

Yee, Vivian. 2014. "'I Can't Breathe' is Re-echoed in Voices of Fury and Despair." *New York Times*, December 4, 2014, A1.

7 Risk Aversion and the Remand Population Explosion in Ontario

Aaron Doyle and Laura McKendy

INTRODUCTION

In this chapter, we consider the processes that have led to the tripling of the pretrial population in Ontario jails at a time when the sentenced population is decreasing in parallel with a long-running decrease in official crime rates. As the **remand population** has come to constitute the majority of provincial prisoners, Ontario jails are more crowded than ever, when they could be emptying, due to the fact that there are fewer sentenced prisoners. Why is the remand population explosion occurring? We consider claims of a **culture of risk aversion** influencing the bail and remand process, leading to changing practices that make it increasingly difficult for criminally accused individuals to await their court dates in the community on bail (Deshman and Myers 2014; Webster 2015). This empirical case leads us to reconsider various current theories of punishment.

On any given day, approximately 24,000 people are held behind bars in Canada's provincial jails. Over half are on remand, that is, awaiting a court date of some sort. The remainder are serving sentences of less than two years, as prisoners serving longer sentences enter Canada's federal penal system. In Ontario, out of an average daily count of around 8,000 provincial prisoners, approximately 60 percent are on remand, compared to about 40 percent who have been found guilty of an offence and sentenced in court (Statistics Canada 2016). The current situation represents a dramatic departure from the historical makeup of the provincial custodial population, and reflects a trend of rising rates in the use of pretrial custody. At the turn of the last century, there remained more sentenced than remanded prisoners in daily counts (10,842 versus 7,392), but the number of prisoners on remand has since continuously climbed, and in 2005–06 surpassed the number of sentenced prisoners in average daily counts for the first time (10,875 versus 9,560) (Porter and Calverley 2011). Numerous reports (e.g., Deshman and Myers 2014; John Howard Society of British Columbia 2013; John Howard Society of Ontario Standing Committee on Prison Conditions in Ontario 2007; Porter and Calverley 2011; Tilley 2012) suggest that Canada is experiencing a crisis in its provincial jails as a result of the population explosion of remand prisoners, even though official crime rates have been decreasing for many years. Indeed, remand populations have been rising around the world, although Canada has the highest remand rate of any common-law country (Myers 2016). Here, we focus on our home province of Ontario.

Although the remand crisis in Canada is well documented (Deshman and Myers 2014; Friedland 2012; Mitchell 2015; Myers 2013; Webster, Doob, and Myers 2009; Weinrath 2009), it is under-analyzed in relation to broader socio-cultural trends and theories of punishment. As Hannah-Moffat and Maurutto (2012, 202) note, "scholars have yet to connect the vast body of literature about mass imprisonment and penal change to the range of pre-trial detention practices." Hence, we explore the extent to which the rise in pretrial detention can be understood using recent theorizing on punishment, including the **punitive turn thesis** (Garland 2000), the "**new penology**" framework (Feeley and Simon 1992), and theories of jails as managing the underclasses (Irwin 1985; Welch 1999).

ONTARIO'S BAIL CRISIS

Within influential bodies of criminological literature focusing on incarceration, the distinction between sentenced and remand prisoners is often not accounted for. This is surprising given that the remand population constitutes the fastest growing component of the prison population, and that the jails within which they sit often feature the harshest conditions in the penal system (Deshman and Myers 2014; Irwin 1985; Porter and Calverley 2011). While a significant amount of the remand population growth can be explained by increasingly clogged courts, leading to remanded prisoners spending lengthier stints incarcerated while awaiting court dates, Canadian analysts have also attributed the remand crisis in large part to the growth of a risk-averse mentality in the criminal justice system, making it more difficult for prisoners to get bail (see, e.g., Myers 2013; Webster, Doob, and Myers 2009; Weinrath 2009). Webster, Doob, and Myers (2009, 99), for example, argue that "an increasing culture of risk aversion" can be seen throughout various stages of the Canadian legal process in relation to bail. This mentality of risk aversion, they explain, begins with police who are sending more cases to bail hearings rather than employing their discretionary powers of release. This means that more individuals are waiting in custody, rather than in the community, for their bail hearings. The risk-averse mentality, they argue, is paralleled in the courts, where, for example, adjournments—which push cases to another day, and decisions to another actor—have become standard practice, leaving individuals detained for longer as they await a bail decision (Webster, Doob, and Myers 2009, 100).

Trends making it more difficult to get and keep bail are well captured by a 2014 report by the Canadian Civil Liberties Association (CCLA; Deshman and Myers 2014), which studied bail patterns across Canada. In Ontario, the report notes, an average of nine conditions are now attached to bail for each accused. Conditions attached to bail release often criminalize otherwise legal behaviour, may have no connection to the original charges, and often extend far beyond what is necessary to ensure court attendance and/or protect public safety (Deshman and Myers 2014). Examples of conditions described by Deshman and Myers include alcohol abstinence orders placed on alcoholics, residency conditions on homeless people, no-contact orders between family members, and strict curfews. These restrictive bail conditions "set people up to fail" (Deshman and Myers 2014) and, by criminalizing otherwise legal behaviours, have the effect of producing crime. In fact, administrative offences—such as failure to comply with conditions—are now the most common criminal charges in Ontario, representing 27.3 percent of all cases, with the most common being "failure to comply with order," representing 15.5 percent of all cases (Ontario Court of Justice 2015).

Although the conditions attached to bail release are not intended to be punishment, in practice they constitute a form of "pre-punishment" (Hannah-Moffat and Maurutto 2012). Hannah-Moffat and Maurutto (2012) examine **pre-punishment** as intensified governance of those on bail in the community in a way that is punitive in effect, although occurring prior to any formal pronouncement of a penalty; however, another form of pre-punishment affects those remanded in jails awaiting court dates. This form of pre-punishment, enabled by the current bail system, is in direct contradiction to the principles underlying laws guiding bail, which place the least restrictive release option (i.e., release without conditions) as the default starting point, allowing further restrictions only where deemed necessary (Friedland 2012). Furthermore, the nature of many bail conditions violates Section 515(10) of the Criminal Code, which states that conditions must be related to the grounds on which the accused would otherwise be detained (i.e., to ensure court attendance and that the accused does not commit another offence or interfere with the administration of justice) (Myers 2009).

In addition to placing numerous other restrictive conditions on bail release, Ontario judges also increasingly require surety supervision (Deshman and Myers 2014). A surety is someone close to the accused who agrees to supervise them while they are on bail to ensure that they comply with the conditions of their release and attend court. The surety takes on considerable responsibility; the accused is sometimes required to live with and be chaperoned by their surety, and the surety risks losing money to the court if the accused person violates a condition of their release. In a sense, the use of sureties extends the disciplinary powers of the state to the community. Myers (2009, 132) explains: "Sureties are thus charged with a quasi-policing function. They are jailors in the community." In Ontario, over 50 percent of accused people are required to have a surety, yet there is no evidence demonstrating that surety supervision enhances adherence to bail conditions. The inability to secure a proper surety can result in the denial of bail (Deshman and Myers 2014).

Difficulties obtaining bail mean pretrial detention is increasingly being used, incarcerating people waiting for trial. The risk-averse mentality behind the growing use of remand, according to Webster, Doob, and Myers (2009), involves weighing the potential costs associated with releasing an accused against the possible benefits. Of particular importance is the fact that blame for serious consequences—such as the accused person committing an offence while on bail—may be borne by the individual decision-maker. Where the possible negative consequences of releasing an accused might be highly visible, the benefits of such releases are less visible and less direct; these include respecting the rights of the accused, allowing cost savings to taxpayers, and greatly reducing the interruption to and effects on the accused person's life, thus aiding in reintegration.

The culture of risk aversion is presumably underpinned by an assumption that risk can be minimized through restrictive bail conditions and pretrial detention. This logic, however, threatens the underlying principles of the legal system and has produced serious adverse consequences, including the surge of administrative charges caused by unreasonable bail conditions, and the flooding of provincial jails with pretrial prisoners. As Webster, Doob, and Myers (2009, 101) lament, "it would appear that we are willing to risk sacrificing the fundamental principles underlying the bail process (e.g., presumption of innocence, a determination of bail without reasonable delay, due process) in the name of risk avoidance." Due to court backlog, individuals on remand in Ontario will spend weeks, months, and even years in institutions designed only for short-term stays. In such institutions, akin to human warehouses because of their lack of programming or means to pass the time, prisoners experience extreme crowding and harsh conditions (John Howard Society of British Columbia 2013; John Howard Society of Ontario Standing Committee 2007; Public Services Foundation of Canada 2015; Tilley 2012). Furthermore, Kellough and Wortley (2002, 187) argue that "the detention of accused persons appears to be a rather important resource that the prosecution uses to encourage (or coerce) guilty pleas." They note that, in comparison to those on bail, individuals on remand may be more inclined to plead guilty for a variety of reasons. For example, individuals who might not receive prison time, or who will be credited for time served, might plead guilty in order to be released. Others may plead guilty in order to escape the harshness of jails and be transferred to prisons (Kellough and Wortley 2002; see also Feeley 1979).

While the notion of a culture of risk aversion may be useful for explaining trends in bail courts, its emergence has not been contextualized in terms of broader theory in the sociology of punishment. Why have actors within the criminal justice system become increasingly risk averse? Why now in particular? What broader social and cultural trends might be at play? Below, we begin to consider this trend in relation to theories in the sociology of punishment to consider the extent to which they can help explain, and be informed by, these tendencies.

CONTEMPORARY PENAL THEORIES

Over the last several decades, criminologists have spent much time analyzing how crime and punishment are being socially reframed, with a particular focus on the apparent decline of the rehabilitative ideal, and a corresponding rise of harsh policy measures (Bottoms 1995; Crewe 2015; Feeley and Simon 1992; Garland 2001; Kazemian, McCoy, and Sacks 2013; Pratt 2000; Pratt et al. 2005; Shichor 1997). Some scholars have described an ideologically driven "punitive turn," fuelled by penal populism (Pratt 2007), while others point to the emergence of a "new penology," oriented around actuarial policies and risk-based models of population management that, without intentional punitiveness, produce a harsh penal system in effect (e.g., Feeley and Simon 1992). While theorists in these camps emphasize changes to the nature of punishment as it plays out for those found guilty of an offence, equally important to consider is the growth of "pre-punishment" (Hannah-Moffat and Maurutto 2012), which takes place in spaces like the community and the jail. Note, we are making a distinction between the jail and the prison, with the jail being the entry point of the penal system, the holding tank for those awaiting trial or sentence, the final destination for some prisoners serving short sentences, and a residual container for an assortment of other socially troublesome people. Prison by contrast holds mostly sentenced prisoners. Jails are often officially called "remand centres" or "detention centres" in Canada.

Other accounts of the jail (Irwin 1985; Welch 1999) suggest that the punitive practices that occur prior to sentencing reflect not only a net-widening process, but relate to the broader and more long-standing social function of jails as warehouses to deal with a wide array of social problems. Below we draw on these different bodies of literature in more detail to assess their usefulness in understanding the remand crisis in Ontario.

The Punitive Turn Thesis

The "punitive turn" thesis describes a shift away from a welfarist and rehabilitative model and towards "tough on crime" measures. Garland (2000, 349–50) pointed to numerous policies that signalled such a punitive turn:

> "three strikes" and mandatory minimum sentencing laws; "truth in sentencing" and parole release restrictions; no frill prison laws and "austere prisons"; retribution in juvenile court and the imprisonment of children; the revival of chain gangs and corporal punishment; boot camps and "supermax" prisons; the multiplication of capital offences and executions; community notification laws and pedophile registers; zero tolerance policies and sex offender orders.

Garland (2000) attributed changing sentiments toward punishment in part to a higher visibility of crime starting in the 1960s and 1970s. To him, a declining faith in rehabilitation, combined with other socioeconomic and political factors, led to the so-called resurgence of punitive impulse: to harm, rather than reform, those who come into conflict with the law. For the state, the ability to appear "tough on crime" becomes an opportunity to appear to be "doing something" about the crime problem.

In this context, punishment comes to serve an expressive rather than instrumental function—it is meant to convey a message (Garland 2000). Rather than merely serving public safety ends, this expressive element aims to mark those deemed criminals as other through a variety of shaming and segregation practices.

To what extent can the punitive turn thesis explain the surge in pre-trial detention that has occurred in Ontario? At the level of both political rhetoric and practice, something of a punitive turn did occur in Ontario in the 1990s at the hands of Conservative Premier Mike Harris. The government pursued a so-called "common sense revolution," which sought to "rationalize" various government services and programs and promote cost-efficiency. At the same time, the government vowed to get "tough on crime" and develop a "no frills" penal regime (Moore and Hannah-Moffat 2002). In this context, existing detention centres were removed of all "frills"; almost all programming was cut and prisoners were confined to cells for 16 to 24 hours a day (Moore and Hannah-Moffat 2002). McElligott (2007, 43) explains:

> Ontario's approach was to roll back anything resembling a "privilege" for prisoners, while railing at Ottawa's alleged coddling of major offenders in "Club Fed" institutions. Rehabilitative programmes, recreational facilities and "perks" such as TVs, video games and smoking—and even time spent outside the cell—were drastically curtailed in provincial institutions. In scenes reminiscent of Southern chain gangs, inmates were dressed in bright orange jumpsuits to pick up trash from roadsides.

At the same time, several local jails in Ontario were closed and replaced with "super-max" jails, which were "deliberately designed to be cheap and harsh" (McElligott 2007, 33). In the name of security and order, these super jails are physically structured to reduce the contact and mobility of prisoners, and rely greatly on routine lockdowns and extensive use of solitary confinement (McElligott 2007). The jails are "designed to manage prisoners rather than . . . change them" (McElligott 2007, 45) and are concerned with "neutralizing risk, minimizing prison incidents, and efficiency management systems rather than wider social goals" (Liebling and Crewe 2013, 284).

What might be dubbed a punitive turn also occurred at the federal level in Canada under Conservative Prime Minister Stephen Harper, who came to power in 2006. The Conservative government enacted a series of a "tough on crime" measures that extended the scope and severity of punishment. Drawing on the repertoire of reforms in other jurisdictions that Garland (2000) describes as indicative of a punitive turn, the government enacted new mandatory minimum sentences and eliminated the standard practice of double credit for time served on remand (the Truth in Sentencing Act), among many other reforms (Mallea 2010).

The policy approaches taken at both the provincial and federal levels of government seem to substantiate claims of a drift away from the rehabilitative ideal; however, an important distinction often exists between stated penal policy and practice (Hutchinson 2006; Moore and Hannah-Moffat 2005; Phelps 2011). Some argue that a number of the "tough on crime" reforms enacted in Canada at the federal level have been largely symbolic (Webster and Doob 2015). While "tough on crime" laws under the Conservative provincial government of Mike Harris certainly led to a worsening of conditions in Ontario remand centres, they do not seem to account for changes in the operations of the bail system. Although statutory changes, such as an increase in the number of "reverse onus" offences for which the presumption is against bail, have fed into the remand explosion, by and large it has not occurred as a result of top-down influences. As various reports note (e.g., Deshman and Myers 2014), the trends in the operation of the bail system that have led to the massive increase in prisoners locked up pretrial have emerged largely spontaneously from the front lines, rather than from explicit government policy. Indeed, in Ontario, for a number of years the previous provincial Liberal government, which relied much less on law and order rhetoric, had explicitly stated the goal of reducing the remand population. The Liberal government's long-running Justice on Target project represents a failed provincial effort to reduce the remand population. More recently, in October 2017, the Ontario provincial government introduced a new bail policy, which attempted to reduce reliance on sureties and to provide more "realistic" bail conditions, and directs Crown prosecutors to favour the least restrictive alternative. Former Ontario corrections minister and provincial attorney-general Yasir Naqvi repeatedly invoked anti-punitive rhetoric, calling for "transformation" to a system with more emphasis on rehabilitation and condemning "warehousing." For example, Naqvi said in October 2017 that "A large number of people in our system are not a danger to society. . . . They are people who are low risk[;] . . . they are vulnerable by virtue of their mental health or addiction issues, or they are Indigenous or racialized" (Lofaro 2017). It remains to be seen whether these provincial government measures will endure under the newly elected Conservative provincial government and whether they will be successful at stemming the remand population explosion that has occurred under the watch of the previous Liberal government, despite its frequent rhetoric proclaiming against excessive pretrial detention.

Throughout the remand population increase, federal laws protecting the right to bail have remained intact. More specifically, the laws governing bail stipulate that most people should be granted bail, and only in certain circumstances is pretrial detention warranted. The right to bail is protected in the Canadian Charter of Rights and Freedoms, which states in Section 11, "Any person charged with an offence has the right not to be denied reasonable bail without just cause." The Criminal Code further states that the detention of an accused is only justified in certain situations, namely (1) to ensure court attendance, (2) to protect public safety, (3) to maintain confidence in the administration of justice, considering the following circumstances: (a) the strength of the prosecution's case, (b) the seriousness of the charge, (c) the circumstances of the offence, and (d) the length of the potential sentence of incarceration.

Even if one were to agree with the argument that the punitive policy changes that occurred both provincially and federally might have been more symbolic in the short run, they may contribute to a cultural context that is more tolerant of the inhumane consequences associated with pretrial detention (Webster and Doob 2015). Political discourse is a central force in shaping cultural values on crime and punishment.

Hence, even if not the cause of Ontario's remand boom, punitive ideologies might help legitimize the human costs of this trend. In this sense, while the punitive turn thesis might not explain the birth of risk aversion in Ontario's bail courts per se, it might shed light on the cultural context that helps sustain it.

The New Penology

Of course, punishment is continuously shaped by a multiplicity of competing forces, rather than a single all-encompassing ideology (Goodman, Page, and Phelps 2015; Hutchinson 2006; O'Malley 1999). While the punitive turn thesis has gained much traction in criminological thought, so too has another—seemingly somewhat contradictory—account of changes in the punishment landscape. The new penology framework, associated most closely with the works of Feeley and Simon (1992, 1994), attributes the changing penal landscape not to the return of retributive desires, but to the rise of private-sector, risk-based logics of management within the realm of public services. Feeley and Simon (1992) suggest that this approach has increasingly shaped both punishment policy and prison management. The new penology does not explicitly seek vengeance or harsh punishment, but rather, through cost-effective strategies of control, aims to minimize the risk posed by classes of people deemed dangerous. Abandoning faith in the reform projects associated with the welfare state prison, the approach involves the development and implementation of risk-based schemes and techniques to identify and incapacitate risky subjects (Feeley and Simon 1992). The incapacitation of "habitual offenders," through, for example "three strikes laws," and the growth of indeterminate sentences, are reflective of the risk-containment goal of the new penology.

The new penology framework might be tied to a broader trend dubbed the rise of "risk society" (Beck 1992; Ericson and Haggerty 1997), whereby the notion of risk has become increasingly central to government, business, and private individuals. Risk-based governance is in turn tied to the rise of neoliberal governance and the corresponding responsibilization of individuals and communities for social problems, such as crime. In theory, at least, the application of actuarial logic to the realm of human action can manage risk through scientific and mathematical models that predict it, minimizing the role of extraneous factors (such as emotion, morals, and political ideologies) in shaping the nature of decisions. Indicators of risk are supposedly used to sort individuals along a continuum, with different risk levels corresponding with different degrees of intervention. Risk-based calculation supposedly enhances objectivity, accountability, and security by using scientific knowledge to formulate responses.

There might seem to be a contradiction between the punitive turn and new penology accounts insofar as the former emphasizes the emotional and expressive (irrational) aspects of contemporary punishment, while the latter emphasizes its apparent scientific, morally neutral (rational) character (Hallsworth 2000). Brownlee (1998, 327) writes, "the punitive language of much of the official discourse on crime is, in reality, at odds with the aims of the new penology and managerialism more generally, and threatens to undermine them." Illustratively, the cost-efficiency concern of the new penology is at odds with the "excesses" associated with the punitive turn (Brownlee 1998). While "the punitive discourse heightens the expectation among the public that a tough, unmistakably punitive response can be provided for every infraction, no matter what the cost," the new penology managerialist approach would "foster a 'normalization' strategy towards crime, seeking to play down its impact in order to promote less expensive responses" (Brownlee 1998, 328, 334).

Rather than seeing punitive and managerialist forces as contradictory, others see them as complementary (e.g., Garland 2001). For example, Cheliotis (2007, 317) writes that actuarial practices can "facilitate retributive punishment" by separating out the "unruly" populations who are then the subjects of expressive punishment. Moreover, punitive sentiments can help justify and perpetuate the inhumane consequences of an actuarial approach to punishment policy and prison management, whether those consequences are intentional (i.e., expressive) or the unintentional by-products of a risk-based, actuarial mode of governance. Along these lines, Hallsworth (2000) discusses how the bureaucratic rationalism at the root of the new penology works together with the anti-modern logic of punitivism. He argues that both "rational" and "irrational" forces are at play in contemporary systems of punishment. At first glance, the new penology framework seems to resonate with the mentality of risk aversion in Ontario bail courts, and, in particular, the use of containment strategies (pretrial detention) to warehouse those deemed risky. As Feeley and Simon argued, the central goal of the new penology is not punishment or reform, but the minimization of risk through containment. Bail courts are one of the first opportunities for incapacitation (Kazemian, McCoy, and Sacks 2013), and, at the time of bail, the most effective way to eliminate future risk is to contain the accused person. Remand is the quintessential form of incapacitation, or warehousing, since the sole purpose is to hold a person to prevent them from a committing a crime (preventive detention) and to ensure that they attend court.

At the same time, the Ontario remand context raises questions about the supposed cost concern associated with the new penology, given that incarceration is an incredibly costly endeavour. As Brownlee (1998) notes, insofar as the principle of cost-effectiveness is, in fact, a guiding principle of the new penology, we might expect to see a movement towards alternatives to incapacitation, including more diversion strategies and community-based sentences, which are significantly cheaper. In Ontario, the cost is about $200 per day, per prisoner (Statistics Canada 2015b). With around 8,000 prisoners on any given day, this translates into $1.6 million per day to hold remand and sentenced prisoners.

In addition to the apparent disregard for cost, there is another key element of the new penology that might be questioned by looking at Ontario bail courts. If the new penology is concerned with identifying and managing risk, one might expect to see standardized assessment techniques for determining the level of risk posed by an accused person, and hence their bail outcome. In practice, however, the evaluation of individual cases does not appear to be tied to such procedures. As Myers (2009, 130) writes, in bail courts,

> there are no objective predictive instruments available for routine cases such as there are for release decisions made by parole boards. Instead, assessments of risk are based almost entirely on personal,

subjective judgments of an accused's risk. The only semi-structured measures that are used are the accused's criminal record and the number of times, if any, the accused has "failed to comply" with previous court orders or has "failed to appear" for court hearings.

Those who are denied or lose bail as a result of administrative charges are often not "high risk" on the basis of their criminal charges, evidenced by the fact that administrative charges are the most serious for over 20 percent of all cases (Porter and Calverley 2011). How then are bail decisions determined? Kellough and Wortley (2002) argue that it is primarily through character evaluations and moral assessments of individuals that bail is decided, contrary to the notion of the new penology, which would suggest the downplaying of such characteristics and instead employing seemingly objective classificatory techniques to measure risk. The role of human subjectivity in determining bail decisions would seem to contradict the morally neutral orientation of the new penology, whereby rule-based decision making supposedly transcends emotional and subjective forms of reasoning. Such decisions may be shaped by cultural notions of risk that are fused with racist and class-based stereotypes. While the new penology might account for the use of containment strategies to manage risk, the Ontario bail context raises questions about the nature of risk assessment. It appears that efforts to manage risk are not directed at a small number of people deemed risky, but, instead, are applied more generally through the imposition of numerous bail conditions, which are theoretically intended to reduce the likelihood that a person will commit an offence, as well as the use of remand to prevent future crimes through incapacitation. It may be argued that this represents a blanket approach to uncertainty in the absence of calculable knowledge of risk. These practices have led to local remand centres being overcrowded and the rise of administrative charges as a result of extensive bail conditions and massive court delays, as well as astronomical costs. Importantly, however, the bail crisis is unequal in its effects: there are certain groups that are disproportionately impacted by the dysfunctional bail system. Below we draw on Irwin's (1985) seminal account of the jail to consider how the bail system might be linked to the use of jails to deal with a wide array of social problems, including poverty, homelessness, mental illness, and addictions.

The Jail and the Rabble

Jails, as institutions distinct from prisons, have been given relatively little academic attention for many years (the small number of exceptions include Irwin 1985; McElligott 2007; Moore and Hannah-Moffat 2002, 2005; Piché 2014; Welch 1999). In Canada, Friedland's research in the 1960s on the Don Jail in Toronto revealed that conditions at the holding facility were much worse in comparison to institutions where sentenced prisoners were held, suggesting a subplot to Ontario's supposed rehabilitative past (Moore and Hannah-Moffat 2002). Jails have a higher turnover, tend to be more chaotic, and have even fewer amenities than prisons, given that they are holding tanks that are ostensibly meant for short-term stays only—although due to clogged courts, the length of remand stays in Canada has increased dramatically. Across Canada, problems common to jails include crowding due to the remand population explosion, minimal programming or recreational opportunities, and limited access to medical, dental, and psychiatric care (Deshman and Myers 2014; John Howard Society of Ontario Standing Committee 2007; Porter and Calverley 2011; Tilley 2012).

Within contemporary theories of punishment, the distinction between types of penal institutions is often obscured. Some authors (Irwin 1985; Welch 1999) have pointed out how the neglect of jails leads to an incomplete account of punishment, since jails are distinct from prisons in their official and unofficial purposes. The unique function of jails is not captured by accounts that focus on policy rhetoric or the official laws guiding punishment. To Irwin (1985), jails are fundamentally related to the class politics of contemporary cities. More specifically, he sees jails as serving the key purpose of holding society's disruptive "underclass," whom he describes as highly visible, yet relatively non-dangerous, social groups.

Like Irwin, Welch (1999) similarly views jails as having an unofficial social purpose that targets the poor and marginalized. He argues that jails facilitate a process of "social sanitation," whereby police clean the streets of people who are "offensive," but not "dangerous." He argues the jail is primarily a "warehouse reserved mostly for the urban underclass" (Welch 1999, 89). Hence, like Irwin, he argues that the unofficial aims of jails are related to existing forms of social inequality. Despite the crowding and harsh conditions in jails, Welch (1999, 92) argues that "like the persons detained there, jails are the most neglected institutions within the criminal justice system."

This social function is a refashioned take on the state's historical role in dealing with social problems like poverty, addictions, and mental health issues. Particularly since the demise of the welfare state, the jail has become a "social warehouse" that holds an array of individuals who are adversely impacted by social inequality and oppressive social structures (Irwin 1985; Welch 1999). In discussing his research on American jails, Irwin (1985, xiii) stated, "my critical discovery was that instead of 'criminals,' the jail receives and confines mostly detached and disreputable persons who are arrested more because they are offensive than because they have committed crimes."

Irwin argued that the role of the jail was to manage society's "rabble," comprising disadvantaged groups who engaged in minor yet highly visible crimes. In Irwin's terms, couched in the argot of his time, included in the rabble were petty hustlers, derelicts, junkies, outlaws, crazies, corner boys, lowriders, aliens (immigrants), gays, and square Johns. Irwin argued that the jail functions to "manage" these groups, who are disruptive and offensive on city streets. In the contemporary context, numerous reports suggest Ontario jails are similarly being used to warehouse socially and economically vulnerable individuals. For example, the CCLA report states, "the revolving door of pre-trial detention—arrest, release with conditions, re-arrest for breach of conditions—has its most devastating impact on individuals with marginal social support, who are already struggling with addiction, health problems, poverty and discrimination" (Deshman and Myers 2014, 72). A study in Toronto found that the number of people jailed with "no fixed" address had increased by 64 percent between 2001 and 2004, and about 97 percent of those people were males. It also found the jail to be a revolving door for homeless people: 4 out of 10 of those jailed had been jailed before

(Novac et al. 2006). According to the CCLA, bail is less accessible to those who are poor; the average bail is set at a mean of $2,669 and a median of $1,000. The authors note that "individuals without a job, property, strong family support or ties to middle-class social networks" often cannot find a surety and do not have stable housing, which are increasingly required to get bail (Deshman and Myers 2014, 74).

Kellough and Wortley (2002) also found pretrial detention in jail is disproportionately used to detain Aboriginal and Black individuals in comparison with non-racialized groups. Based on their study of bail decisions in two Toronto bail courts, they found that the rate of pretrial detention was 35.5 percent for Black individuals, compared to 23.4 percent for non-Black individuals. Across Canada, Aboriginal people are overrepresented in jails, comprising one out of every four admissions to remand, despite constituting only 3 percent of the Canadian population (Statistics Canada 2015a). This trend is particularly pronounced among Aboriginal women, who represent 37 percent of women on remand (Perreault 2014). Deshman and Myers (2014) also identify the overuse of bail conditions—breach of which results in administrative charges— as a major contributing factor to the over-arrest and over-incarceration of Aboriginal people. As a report by the Public Services Foundation of Canada (2015, 47) states, "the over-representation of Aboriginal men and women in correctional centres is an indictment of the Canadian justice system that tells us something is deeply wrong in how our society treats Aboriginal people."

Jails are also increasingly used to house those with mental health problems. The criminalization of mental illness in Canada coincided with deinstitutionalization in the late 20th century, which was not coupled with the development of adequate social alternatives (Public Services Foundation of Canada 2015; Tilley 2012). Although deinstitutionalization reflected the idea that "persons with mental illness would be better served in the community," an adverse consequence has been "the increased contact between persons with mental health issues and the police" (John Howard Society of Ontario 2015, 7). The Public Services Foundation of Canada (2015, 7) states, "as community-based mental health services have disappeared, far too many people with serious to severe mental health problems have been scooped up into the criminal justice system." Because those suffering from mental health issues have a high likelihood of encountering police, jails have become de facto "warehouses for the internment of the mentally ill," and places where individuals are punished, not treated (Tilley 2012, 18).

The use of jails as a mechanism to deal with visible manifestations of social problems—such as homelessness, poverty, addictions, and mental health issues—is not an explicit nor apparently intentional function of official punishment policies, so much as a result of how the jail functions in practice. Although this function pre-existed more recent shifts in punishment philosophy, it has apparently taken on greater prominence with the ideological and structural shifts away from welfarism that have occurred concomitantly, that have led, for example, to the increase of mentally ill individuals on the streets. That is to say, alongside changing styles of governance—manifested in the criminal justice system in the form of punitive reforms and risk aversion that responsibilize individuals for the crime problem—has been the dismantling of welfare state functions and the erosion of the social infrastructure intended to deal with social problems in a more humane manner. These changes have not only undermined the ability of the state to buffer the effects of inequality, but also rendered techniques of criminalization the standard response to dealing with social problems (Ericson 2007).

CONCLUSION

In this chapter, we considered how a variety of factors are at play in shaping Ontario's bail crisis, calling into question the applicability of any single theory of punishment and social control to account for trends on the ground. While the punitive turn thesis might help explain punishment reforms at the federal level, and the worsening of jail conditions at the provincial level, it cannot to any great extent explain shifts in the use of remand, which are not linked to formal legislative changes or policy directives, but appear to have emerged on the front lines of the court system. The cultural impact of punitive discourses, however, may help legitimize the inhumane consequences of the bail crisis, even if those consequences are not punitive in intention. Another popular paradigm, the new penology, emphasizes a shift towards threat containment through depersonalized techniques of risk-calculation and threat containment. This framework resonates with the growing use of jails to warehouse those deemed too risky to be granted bail; however, risk calculation does not appear to be informed by standardized assessment processes that rely on "objective" markers of risk. To the contrary, efforts to discern individual levels of risk have been replaced by a generalized assumption of uncertainty (Ericson 2007), evidenced by the standardized use of extensive bail conditions and growing reliance on pretrial detention. At the same time, understandings of risk appear to be fused with cultural stereotypes that disproportionately target marginalized groups. In this regard, Irwin's (1985) pioneering account of the jail remains useful for understanding jail's unofficial social function of managing visible social groups deemed a nuisance in city streets. Particularly in the current neoliberal context, the role of the jail posited by Irwin in 1985 takes on added importance, and jails are even more used to deal with a wide assortment of social problems, including poverty, homelessness, addiction, and mental illness.

The growth of pretrial detention at a time when the sentenced population is decreasing reflects a temporal reorientation of punishment. In Ontario bail courts, the imposition of numerous bail conditions and widespread use of pretrial detention signify a shift in focus from action that has taken place to action that could transpire. This temporal reorientation fits with Zedner's (2007) analysis of an emerging pre-crime society, in which crime is anticipated and action is taken pre-emptively to reduce risk. Within this context, she argues, "the possibility of forestalling risks competes with and even takes precedence over responding to wrongs done," meaning that "the post-crime orientation of criminal justice is increasingly overshadowed by the pre-crime logic of security" (2007, 262). As such, the explosion in pretrial detention can be situated in a much broader trend in Western democracies towards a wide and diffuse ramping up of attempts at preventive control of crime and other risks and uncertainties through a panoply of measures, a number of which are documented in this book, ranging from the innocuous accretion of mundane surveillance to sweeping counterterrorism initiatives (Crawford and Evans 2017; Ericson 2007; McCulloch and Wilson 2016). However, in the particular case of the boom in remand custody we have examined, this kind of control has some distinctive features: it is spontaneously emerging, bottom-up not top-down, inefficient and anti-managerial, and not closely tied to punitive rhetoric—indeed, it is occurring despite the previous Ontario government's stated goal to reduce the remand population through more effective and humane functioning of the courts and bail system. In fact, it seems that the spontaneous, bottom-up, anti-managerial tendencies that drive this form of control actually make the remand population problem more intractable, as opposed to attempting to reverse punitiveness that might be occurring as a result of top-down deliberate policy that occurs in some jurisdictions.

As we have discussed, central to this trend is that the prerogative to punish those who have committed criminal acts is backgrounded by a desire to prevent future crimes from occurring. In the Ontario remand context, for many people, the bulk of punishment that is suffered now takes place before they are ever found guilty. If not punitive in intention, it is manifestly punitive in effect. Ironically, partially because jail conditions are so harsh, judges often grant extra credit for time served on remand when calculating sentences—time in preventive detention is actually deemed more punitive than the time that sentenced prisoners will serve.

The temporal reorientation of punishment undermines the fundamental right to the presumption of innocence. Detention before trial operates as a form of pre-punishment, often in harsher conditions than experienced during actual prison sentences. Understanding the various forces contributing to the remand crisis is necessary to develop strategies for change. Addressing the ways in which jails are used to house marginalized social groups and reproduce inequalities requires, among other transformations, the decriminalization of mental illness, addiction, and poverty. Incarceration is a highly costly, inhumane, and ineffective solution to these social issues.

DISCUSSION QUESTIONS

1. Given the increased number of prisoners held in jail in Ontario before trial, and the decline in the number of prisoners serving sentences after being convicted of crimes, how is the nature of punishment changing? Does it make sense to call it "punishment" if the prisoners are held in jail before being convicted of anything?

2. How much does the trend towards holding more and more prisoners in jail before trial have in common with some of the other developments in criminal justice discussed in other chapters in this book?

3. Criminologist John Irwin (1985) argued that the jail created "social disintegration." A similar observation could be made in the current Ontario context. What social consequences might pretrial detention have for individual prisoners, even in cases where they are found not guilty?

4. What changes are needed to address the use of jails to house socially marginalized individuals, including those with mental health and addiction issues? What steps could we take to help bring about these changes?

REFERENCES

Beck, Ulrich. 1992. *Risk Society: Towards a New Modernity*. London: Sage.

Bottoms, Anthony. 1995. "The Philosophy and Politics of Punishment and Sentencing." In *The Politics of Sentencing Reform*, edited by Chris Clarkson and Rod Morgan, 17–49. Oxford: Clarendon Press.

Brownlee, Ian. 1998. "New Labour—New Penology? Punitive Rhetoric and the Limits of Managerialism in Criminal Justice Policy." *Journal of Law and Society* 25 (3): 313–35.

Cheliotis, Leonidas K. 2007. "How Iron Is the Iron Cage of New Penology? The Role of Human Agency in the Implementation of Criminal Justice Policy." *Punishment and Society* 8 (3): 313–40.

Crawford, Adam, and Karen Evans. 2017. "Crime Prevention and Community Safety." In *The Oxford Handbook of Criminology* (6th ed.), edited by Alison Leibling, Shadd Maruna, and Lesley McAra, 797–824. Oxford: Oxford University Press.

Crewe, Ben. 2015. "Inside the Belly of the Penal Beast: Understanding the Experience of Imprisonment." *International Journal for Crime, Justice and Social Democracy* 4 (1): 50–65.

Deshman, Abby, and Nicole Myers. 2014. *Set Up to Fail: Bail and the Revolving Door of Pre-trial Detention*. Canadian Civil Liberties Association and Education Trust.

Ericson, Richard. 2007. *Crime in an Insecure World*. Cambridge: Polity.

Ericson, Richard, and Kevin Haggerty. 1997. *Policing the Risk Society*. Toronto: University of Toronto Press.

Feeley, Malcolm M. 1979. *The Process Is the Punishment*. New York: Russell Sage Foundation.

Feeley, Malcolm M., and Jonathan Simon. 1992. "The New Penology: Notes on the Emerging Strategy of Corrections and its Implications." *Criminology* 30 (4): 449–74.

———. 1994. "Actuarial Justice: The Emerging New Criminal Law." In *The Futures of Criminology*, edited by David Nelken, 173–201. London: Sage Publications.

Friedland, Martin L. 2012. "The Bail Reform Act Revisited." *Canadian Criminal Law Review* 16 (3): 315–22.

Garland, David. 2000. "The Culture of High Crime Societies: Some Preconditions of Recent 'Law and Order' Policies." *British Journal of Criminology* 40: 347–75.

———. 2001. *The Culture of Control: Crime and Social Order in Contemporary Society*. Oxford: Oxford University Press.

Goodman, Philip, Joshua Page, and Michelle Phelps. 2015. "The Long Struggle: An Agonistic Perspective on Penal Development." *Theoretical Criminology* 19 (3): 315–35.

Hallsworth, S. 2000. "Rethinking the Punitive Turn: Economies of Excess and the Criminology of the Other." *Punishment and Society* 2 (2): 145–60.

Hannah-Moffat, K., and P. Maurutto. 2012. "Shifting and Targeted Forms of Penal Governance: Bail, Punishment and Specialized Courts." *Theoretical Criminology* 16 (2): 201–19.

Hutchinson, Steven. 2006. "Countering Catastrophic Criminology: Reform, Punishment and the Modern Liberal Compromise." *Punishment and Society* 8 (4): 443–67.

Irwin, John. 1985. *The Jail: Managing the Underclass in American Society*. Berkeley: University of California Press.

John Howard Society of British Columbia. 2013. *Factsheet: Remand and Overcrowding*. http://www.johnhowardbc.ca/images/jhsbc-factsheet-remand-overcrowding.pdf.

John Howard Society of Ontario. 2015. *Unlocking Change: Decriminalizing Mental Health Issues in Ontario*. http://www.johnhoward.on.ca/wp-content/uploads/2015/07/Unlocking-Change-Final-August-2015.pdf.

John Howard Society of Ontario Standing Committee on Prison Conditions in Ontario. 2007. *Second Report to the Board: Remand in Ontario*. John Howard Society of Ontario.

Kazemian, Lila, Candace McCoy, and Meghan Sacks. 2013. "Does Law Matter? An Old Bail Law Confronts the New Penology." *Punishment and Society* 15 (1): 43–70.

Kellough, Gail, and Scot Wortley. 2002. "Remand for Plea: Bail Decisions and Plea Bargaining as Commensurate Decisions." *British Journal of Criminology* 42 (1): 186–210.

Liebling, Alison, and Ben Crewe. 2013. "Prisons beyond the New Penology: The Shifting Moral Foundations of Prison Management." In *The Sage Handbook of Punishment and Society*, edited by Jonathan Simon and Richard Sparks, 283–307. Thousand Oaks, CA: Sage.

Lofaro, Joe. 2017. "Ontario Issues New Bail Policy to Ease Strain on Jails." *CBC News*, October 30, 2017. http://www.cbc.ca/news/canada/ottawa/attorney-general-changes-ontario-bail-policy-1.4378273.

Mallea, Paula. 2010. "The Fear Factor: Stephen Harper's 'Tough on Crime' Agenda." (November) Ottawa: Canadian Centre for Policy Alternatives.

McCulloch, Jude, and Dean Wilson. 2016. *Precrime: Pre-emption, Precaution and the Future*. London: Routledge.

McElligott, Greg. 2007. "Negotiating a Coercive Turn: Work Discipline and Prison Reform in Ontario." *Capital and Class* 31 (1): 31–53.

Mitchell, Megan. 2015. *Risk Aversion in the Bail Setting: An Examination of the Predictive Validity of an Ontario Bail Supervision Program's Risk Assessment Tool*. MA thesis, University of Ottawa.

Moore, Dawn, and Kelly Hannah-Moffat. 2002. "Correctional Renewal without the Frills: The Politics of "Get Tough" Punishment in Ontario." In *Disorderly*

People: Law and the Politics of Exclusion in Ontario, edited by Joe Hermer and Janet Mosher, 105–21. Halifax: Fernwood.

———. 2005. "The Liberal Veil: Revisiting Canadian Penalty." in *The New Punitiveness: Trends, Theories, Perspectives*, edited by John Pratt, David Brown, Mark Brown, Simon Hallsworth, and Wayne Morrison, 85–100. Portland, OR: Willan Publishing.

Myers, Nicole M. 2009. "Shifting Risk: Bail and the Use of Sureties." *Current Issues in Criminal Justice* 21 (1): 127–47.

———. 2013. *Creating Criminality: The Intensification of Institutional Risk Aversion Strategies and the Decline of the Bail Process.* PhD diss., University of Toronto.

———. 2016. "Eroding the Presumption of Innocence: Pre-trial Detention and the Use of Conditional Release on Bail." *British Journal of Criminology.* https://doi.org/10.1093/bjc/azw002.

Novac, Sylvia, Joe Hermer, Emily Paradis, and Amber Kellen. 2006. *Justice and Injustice: Homelessness, Crime, Victimization, and the Criminal Justice System.* Research Paper #207. Toronto: Centre for Urban and Community Studies, University of Toronto.

O'Malley, Pat. 1999. "Volatile and Contradictory Punishment." *Theoretical Criminology* 3 (2): 175–96.

Ontario Court of Justice. 2015. "Offence Based Statistics, All Criminal Cases, Ontario Court of Justice Provincial Overview, January 2015 to December 2015." http://www.ontariocourts.ca/ocj/files/stats/crim/2015/2015-Q4-Offence-Based-Criminal.pdf.

Perreault, Samuel. 2014. "Admissions to Adult Correctional Services in Canada, 2011/2012." *Juristat.* https://www.statcan.gc.ca/pub/85–002-x/2014001/article/11918-eng.htm.

Phelps, Michelle S. 2011. "Rehabilitation in the Punitive Era: The Gap between Rhetoric and Reality in US Prison Programs." *Law and Society Review* 45 (1): 33–68.

Piché, Justin. 2014. "A Contradictory and Finishing State: Explaining Recent Prison Capacity Expansion in Canada's Provinces and Territories." *Champ pénal/Penal Field* 11 (26).

Porter, Lindsay, and Donna Calverley. 2011. "Trends in the Use of Remand in Canada." *Juristat.* http://www.statcan.gc.ca/pub/85–002-x/2011001/article/11440-eng.htm.

Pratt, John. 2000. "Emotive and Ostentatious Punishment." *Punishment and Society* 2 (4): 417–39.

———. 2007. *Penal Populism*. New York: Routledge.

Pratt, John, David Brown, Mark Brown, Simon Hallsworth, and Wayne Morrison, eds. 2005. *The New Punitiveness: Trends, Theories, Perspectives*. Portland, OR: Willan Publishing.

Public Services Foundation of Canada. 2015. *Crisis in Correctional Services: Overcrowding and Inmates with Mental Health Problems in Provincial Correctional Facilities*. https://publicservicesfoundation.ca/sites/publicservicesfoundation.ca/files/documents/crisis_in_correctional_services_april_2015.pdf.

Shichor, David. 1997. "Three Strikes as a Public Policy: The Convergence of the New Penology and the McDonaldization of Punishment." *Crime and Delinquency* 43 (4): 470–92.

Statistics Canada. 2015a. "Adult Correctional Statistics in Canada, 2013/2014." *Juristat*. http://www.statcan.gc.ca/pub/85–002-x/2015001/article/14163-eng.htm.

———. 2015b. "Operating Expenditures of the Adult Correctional System by Jurisdiction, 2013/2014." http://www.statcan.gc.ca/pub/85–002-x/2015001/article/14163/tbl/tbl05-eng.htm.

———. 2016. "Adult Correctional Services, Average Counts of Offenders, by Province, Territory, and Federal Programs (Provinces and Territories)." http://www.statcan.gc.ca/tables-tableaux/sum-som/l01/cst01/legal31b-eng.htm.

Tilley, Kevin. 2012. *Justice Denied: The Causes of BC's Criminal Justice System Crisis*. Vancouver: BC Civil Liberties Association.

Webster, Cheryl M. 2015. *"Broken Bail" in Canada: How We Might Go About Fixing It*. Ottawa: Justice Canada.

Webster, Cheryl Marie, and Anthony N. Doob. 2015. "US Punitiveness 'Canadian Style'? Cultural Values and Canadian Punishment Policy." *Punishment and Society* 17 (3): 299–321.

Webster, Cheryl Marie, Anthony N. Doob, and Nicole Myers. 2009. "The Parable of Ms. Baker: Understanding Pre-trial Detention in Canada." *Current Issues in Criminal Justice* 21 (1): 79–102.

Weinrath, Michael. 2009. "Inmate Perspectives on the Remand Crisis in Canada." *Canadian Journal of Criminology and Criminal Justice* 51 (3): 355–79.

Welch, Michael. 1999. "Jail Overcrowding: Social Sanitation and the Warehousing of the Urban Underclass." In *Punishment in America: Social Control and the Ironies of Imprisonment*, edited by Michael Welch, 89–106. London: Sage.

Zedner, Lucia. 2007. "Pre-crime and Post-criminology?" *Theoretical Criminology* 11 (2): 261–81.

8 Smart Borders? Customs, Risk Targeting, and Internal Politics in a Border Agency[1]

Karine Côté-Boucher

INTRODUCTION

Contemporary borders now represent one of the many security apparatuses concerned with establishing the ordered circulation of things and
people (Kotef 2015). This governance of movement involves submitting
designated individuals to more scrutiny while facilitating mass mobility. To that effect, border security depends on targeting, data sharing,
pre-emptive screening, and the remote identification possibilities embedded in a wide array of technologies. The border is thus envisioned
as an extended space of control, one that is heavily reliant on bodily
screening and governance of mobility through data—a set of security
practices reliant on the collection, analysis, and storage of personal data
for investigative and surveillance purposes.

Given the complexity of their mandates, decision-makers in border organizations often see technologies as a silver bullet. Displaying
a quasi-magical belief in the inherent capabilities of technologies,
decision-makers often perceive these tools as offering tangible solutions
to various social and political issues framed as "security problems" (from
terrorism to drug trafficking), and to the real challenge presented by
increasing flows of goods and people. Yet, beyond the

> fantasy of total security . . . at the heart of the bordering process . . . is
> an important structuring tension between the belief that technology
> can provide total security on the one hand, and the everyday practices
> of human/technological assemblages that are riven with competing
> agendas, unexpected failures, tangents, and miscommunications, on
> the other. (Bourne, Johnson, and Lisle 2015, 313)

Yet, many critical works on border security unwittingly echo security agencies' and technology providers' views when they avoid a more careful examination of the everyday enactment of these technologies in specific security settings (Orlikowski 2000). Border technologies are not only shaped by variables such as data users with various levels of training, and diverse IT configurations—including sometimes incompatible and unconnected information systems—but also, and more importantly for this chapter's argument, by the decisional actors and the "political networks" within and outside security agencies that shape the choice and use of technologies (Manning 2008, xi).

This chapter thus proposes shifting the reflection about border technologies from its preferred field, pre-emptive border control, to the examination of their impact on the power dynamics within border agencies. The analysis presented here pays particular attention to the context in which technologies are deployed, as well as how technologies not only modify border officers' dispositions—that is, how they act and learn how to act—but also legitimate their action(s) (Amicelle, Aradau, and Jeandesboz 2015, 302). It especially highlights how technologies, which propose a new division of labour and shift decision making to centralized settings and away from ports of entry, become embedded in the organizational tensions and negotiations shaping border agencies. In short, this chapter is interested in the ways in which the governance of borders through databases disrupts "the power balance" (Manning 1996, 54) in border policing administrations.

The second shift proposed by this chapter concerns its empirical anchoring. It is set in the little studied domain of customs, that is, where border authorities are concerned with the traceability of goods and the mobility of transport workers. The flows of travellers and migrants are often taken synonymously with circulation—the facilitation of the mobility of goods remains a fundamental aspect of contemporary border control. Yet trade facilitation calls upon risk logics different from those involved in the interception and high-risk screening of individuals (Côté-Boucher 2010) and has recently given rise to a transnational security infrastructure much influenced by logistical needs. Given the increase in international trade and a global adoption of free trade policies, goods are seldom physically inspected by customs agencies. With the view of expediting the movement of goods at borders, the intersection of economic and security rationalities, as well as the meeting of private and public aims in customs, produce a permeable border. In this context favourable to circulation, border technologies are not only tasked with intercepting illicit goods, but also, more importantly, they are meant to remove impediments to cargo mobilities.

Drawing on field research, this chapter examines the case of the centralization of targeting at the Canada Border Services Agency (CBSA), where the risk management operations formerly located in ports of entry were amalgamated and centralized in Ottawa. It sheds light on the unsteady integration of surveillance and information technologies in the customs labour process, and its concrete effects upon the internal politics of a border agency.[2] To do so, the chapter first reviews the interdisciplinary literature on borders and technologies, then revisits its conclusions through empirical insights drawn from existing fieldwork research on the topic. Drawing on this literature, the chapter argues that technologies beget intricate dynamics of **appropriation** and reshape the logics of competition characteristic of security and police organizations.

The chapter then quickly expounds the current trend towards the automatization of customs, as well as the increased involvement of the private sector in data collection and sharing with border authorities. The redistribution of power relations within border administrations inaugurated by the technological reshaping of officers' tasks is experienced by these front-line security professionals as a form of deskilling. Officers respond to these changes with mixed feelings and a high level of distrust toward headquarters, which is held responsible for such transformations in customs governance.

The chapter thus addresses how technologies have enabled the re-configuration of the border security field by bringing new registers of action into the policing of borders. By doing so, it provides a different insight into the complex relationship between technologies and border control. This insight contradicts the simple assertion of improved efficiency and enhanced neutrality in border security and reveals how profoundly political the "smart border" is for border agencies.

SECURITY TECHNOLOGIES AND "SMART BORDERS"

If you are a traveller, chances are you have noticed that border authorities around the world are heavily investing in security technologies. Our personal data circulates between private actors (e.g., airlines, trucking companies) and border authorities for risk analyses. Countries are embedding passports, visas, and pre-clearance cards with biometrics. It is difficult to visit an airport in North America or Europe and avoid detection technologies—from X-rays to body scanners.

This significant technological presence indicates the expansion of new functions in border control. Screening, data sharing, risk assessment, and biometric identification sustain novel representations of borders. Historically, borders have been vital revenue-producing tools for states through the collection of taxes and duties. If this remains the role of borders for developing states, it has slowly faded for richer countries with the introduction of liberalized commerce and increases in income taxation.

Further, current border policing is moving away from a territorial, Westphalian conception of sovereignty, where borders acted as geopolitical lines sustaining the international order. Borders now elude this historical logic of enclosure that equated them with walls, fences, barbed wire, and barriers (Razac 2009). Where these means remain (Brown 2010), they generally do so as "socio-technical devices," far removed from the model of the medieval portcullis, rather proceeding as apparatuses of data collection and mobility governance (Pallister-Wilkins 2016).

Accordingly, borders are no longer "lines in the sand"; they are now dispersed spaces where flows of people and things are policed (Parker and Vaughan-Williams 2009). Borders adopt a multidimensional and dispersed configuration, associating more or less loosely a series of checkpoints and filtering mechanisms that heavily rely on technologies, that are often decoupled from ports of entry, and that diffuse borders beyond and inside their traditional localization (Scherrer, Guittet, and Bigo 2010). This dispersion of borders generates a "new topography of border control" (Walters 2006)—one where borders operate as regimes of mobility control and where, as is the case for other security apparatuses, "data have become framed as the answer to contemporary security problems and their fluid, transnational and unpredictable nature" (Amoore and de Goede 2012, 3).

This governance by databases in border policing supports the categorizing of mobilities into various risk profiles, and enables the pre-emptive screening of differentiated travelling populations and things. Border risk management—this **"social sorting"** strategy (Lyon 2007)—thus allows border agents to distinguish between those mobilities that should be permitted to cross borders from those that should be intercepted for inspection or even prohibited from crossing (Aas 2011). The mobilities of irregular migrants, asylum seekers, non-citizens, and people whose nationality is equated with risk (International Civil Liberties Monitoring Group 2010; Pratt and Thompson 2008) become more arduous, slowed down by the multiplication of bordering control points (Squire 2011). Vukov (2016) argues that rather than making border policing more objective, the capacity for racialization of border crossers is displaced within the very pre-emptive mechanisms that are meant to make border security neutral. Meanwhile, borders become porous to "trusted travellers" and corporate elites (Sparke 2006) as a panoply of pre-clearance documentation and programs are adopted. Logics of risk target non-normative subjects while increasing the permeability of borders for privileged travellers and for commodities.

The role of technologies in making differentiated, diffuse border control has been well covered under discussions concerned with "smart borders." A term first found in the title of a 2001 border agreement signed between Canada and the United States, the "smart" character of borders refers to the recourse to identification and information technologies, which security rhetoric and policies portray as a sure bet for reaching efficient security (Côté-Boucher 2008). At the Canada–United States border, this means "the expansion of digital surveillance" (Topak et al. 2015), where collected information about migrants and other "risky" travellers is increasingly shared and analyzed, and new initiatives, such as an entry-exit system, are tested. European authorities have also since adopted the term to designate their data-dependent border infrastructure—for instance, Eurodac and the Schengen Information System II (Jeandesboz et al. 2013).

While border studies are primarily concerned with the securing of migrants and travellers, how border policing is accomplished in the commodity area, and the ways in which customs regimes rely on bordering technologies, is less well understood. Yet, border authorities are not only responsible for intercepting that which they consider threatening; they are also tasked with facilitating global flows of goods. The so-called "integrated supply chain management" (World Customs Organization 2012) is now the stated official objective of customs agencies around the world. This includes the securing of transportation and distribution networks by involving private actors in managing security in yards and ports, as well as in trucks, cargo planes, and ships (Eski 2016).

Much of this security devolution is made possible by customs technologies. Pre-clearance and trusted trader programs (customs programs for those companies and transportation workers deemed to represent a low security risk) depend on pre-emptive risk analyses of goods and transport workers before they ever reach a border crossing. In short, ports of entry are reconfigured into nodes within a secured global security system that, it has been argued, aims to cater to logistical needs (Cowen 2014).

Beyond a "Determinism of Tools" in Studies of Border Security

The smart border, Pötzsch (2015, 102, 108) tells us, "acquires the capacity to see, think and act by itself" and thus "establish[es] new frames that constrain agencies." Such imagining of a quasi-autonomous border rests on the assumption, oft-repeated in the critical border studies literature, that borders are interoperable entities, where algorithmic predictions and probability assessments enable the unimpeded filtering, targeting, and screening of travellers and goods.

In contrast to such approaches, the relationship between security and technology in border policing remains fraught with tensions. Notwithstanding the level or efficacy of automation and centralized targeting, smart borders cannot be taken as spaces of neutral decision making or of smooth, total security. Instead, they affect the account-ability of security processes. Risk management technologies limit opportunities for travellers and transport workers to come up with more complex and contextualized narratives about their mobility patterns: "the reliance on expert techno-scientific knowledge subordinates other forms of border knowledge based on 'everyday knowledge' . . . that ac-cumulate over years as a border guard or that are the result of personal narrative and negotiation" (Rygiel 2013, 152–53).

Accordingly, current empirical studies of border policing go beyond official "narratives of technology as a fix and a solution" (Guittet and Jeandesboz 2010, 235). To study border technologies is to enter a world where internal dissentions, as well as power relations between security actors about the adoption, appropriation, and claims of exclusivity of their use, shape technological processes and border organizations them-selves. Therefore, Pötzsch (2015, 112) aptly remarks that we must look more closely at "the often messy realities of [technologies'] day-to-day implementation." Yet, these empirical distinctions are seldom taken into account in the literature about technologies and borders. Prey to "a determinism of tools" (Cantens 2015, 11), what the border literature displays in theoretical sophistication and powerful critical insights it lacks in nuanced understanding of how technologies are embedded in hierarchical security organizations known to be little concerned with transparency.

Recent advances in border policing research come from thorough empirical investigation (Loftus 2015). This trend in scholarship has emerged from an awareness that much can be learned from studying "border security as practice" (Côté-Boucher, Infantino, and Salter 2014).

Criminological scholarship in this vein has highlighted not only the practical but also political and symbolic modalities involved in the recourse to discretionary powers by border officers as well as local policing actors who assess travellers, migrants, and cargo (Côté-Boucher 2016; Pickering and Ham 2014; van der Woude and van der Leun 2017; Weber 2011). Further, although most of the empirical research on bordering practices has focused on what Zaiotti (2016) calls the "externalization of migration control," there has been some attention given to the regulation of cargo and transport workers. In the customs area, empirically driven research has explored the neoliberal turn in cargo processing where customs' regulatory role has become geared towards the protection of private interests, investments, and cargo mobilities (Chalfin 2010). Less critical of these tendencies, mapping of private-public security networks in supply-chain choke points such as maritime ports (Brewer 2014) has shown how this neoliberal regulation now merges with logics of securitization.

While this body of work is valuable for the purpose of this study because of its interest in the nitty-gritty detail of everyday bordering practices, it has not yet shown much concern for interactions between technologies and everyday bordering practices. This is surprising given the flourishing literature concerned with the technological in border policing. Therefore, in line with these works, and with inspiration taken from the sociology of policing, the remainder of this chapter is concerned with how technologies—as they interact with new border imaginaries and restructure what the border does, how it is done, and by whom—enact new internal politics in the organizations tasked with monitoring border mobilities.

PUTTING INTERNAL POLITICS BACK INTO "SMART BORDERS"

The importance of technologies for the daily work of security professionals should not be exaggerated. In their analysis of a French intelligence agency, Bonelli and Ragazzi (2014) have shown that despite repetitive assertions that security agencies are obsessed with data, low-tech practices that accompany logics of anticipation still generate much adhesion—intelligence workers being satisfied with more qualitative and narrative forms of intelligence work. Similarly, Manning (2008) argues that analytical tools do not readily modify daily policing, which remains very much concerned with providing a rapid, reactive response to citizens' calls. The potential for actuarial preventive policing action informed by the latest technological tools is therefore not actualized in such settings (see also Sanders and Hannem 2012; Sanders, Weston, and Schott 2015).

Keeping in mind these key scholarly interventions on security and technologies, the case of border control in Canada establishes the importance of technologies for border policing. As explained above, border organizations have come to depend on technologies to help them better assess and quickly process goods and people. In this context, while the preventive aspects of technologies remain to be evaluated (and it is beyond the purview of this chapter to do so), border technologies restructure how border officers work and how they interact with other security professionals within border agencies. While technology formalizes data collection and processing, it also complicates these procedures. It adds a degree of difficulty to security practices by requiring more advanced technological skills, a factor revealed in the lack of training front-line officers may have to use information systems (see Sanders and Henderson 2013 for a similar argument about policing). In fact, databases and the collection and analysis performed by these tools produce a new materiality of border security that plays right into the internal politics of border agencies.

Technological Appropriation and a "Logic of Competition"

How technologies are enacted in border control is best examined within specific organizational contexts where work routines, professional habitus, division of labour, and games of influence shape their appropriation. A student of customs reform, Cantens (2015) aptly suggests that the appropriation of a technology cannot be explained through its mere acceptance and adoption by users. Unfolding in complex political and organizational dynamics, technological appropriation rather designates "the process by which the control technique fully participates in re-adjusting power relations inside the [border] administration, and between this administration and the outside, namely the political authority and users" (Cantens 2015, 6; author's translation).

Technologies inaugurate "a reframing of logics of competition among security professionals on security expertise and know-how" (Guittet and Jeandesboz 2010, 235). Until now, most of the literature on the topic has been concerned with how competition affects the various relations between national and transnational private and public security actors. The security field is made up of security professionals and agencies competing for the capacity to name the threat, establish security priorities, and shape security solutions (Bigo 2011). In turn, gaining such influence grants better access to security budgets and opens the possibility to claim exclusivity over the use of sophisticated and costly technologies. For instance, in his work on borders in West Africa, Frowd (2014, 231) has shown how border agencies in this region and the International Organization for Migration were intertwined in complex relations in which actors not only competed for funding, influence, and access to technologies, but also displayed a "differential in expertise, modernity and professionalism [that] was actually part of the disparity of symbolic capital" between the transnational agency and its African interlocutors, which stood at the core of the rivalry between these agencies. Field-based approaches to security thus often highlight the struggles *between* different security agencies and actors for resources and power (Dupont 2006, 87).

However, these struggles also unfold *within* security organizations. Security organizations do not operate as homogeneous entities. Security professionals at different hierarchical levels regard their mandate and the tools that can be used to pursue it differently; some are granted privileges (e.g., high security clearance, access to policy-makers) denied to others. Because they transform work routines, division of labour, and security professionals' status, the introduction of technologies also reconfigures the internal politics of border security agencies. Therefore, whether between or within agencies, security actors can form relationships and collaborate with one another, but they can also establish rivalries when it comes to technologies. In Canadian ports of entry, this logic of competition expressed itself in everyday conversations: Which port will get a scanner for truck trailers? Who will be chosen as the ports' risk targeter? Will intelligence analyses of criminal trends be left to the local port or be centralized in a risk analysis centre? These questions speak to ideological, political, and organizational divisions between sections of a border security agency.

The Case of the CBSA

Border agencies are peculiar creatures. Mixing administrative and policing rationalities, agencies such as the CBSA operate under objectives that may at times seem contradictory—attempting to both facilitate trade and ensure security; they are expected to intercept some flows while letting most go unimpeded. However, border agencies also display a concern for secrecy and an opacity more characteristic of **high policing** than low policing organizations (Brodeur 2007).

The CBSA's activities are spread out over a large territory. As a result, the border agency's headquarters are located at a distance from most ports of entry. The disconnection between high-level decision-makers and front-line personnel in border policing is therefore not only found in the difference of status and influence between border security professionals; it is often compounded by hundreds of kilometres physically separating a port from offices in the capital. I show below that this distance exacerbates border officers' feelings of being sidelined from major policy decisions.

Given this distance from headquarters, border control has traditionally been based on the "practical local expertise" (Infantino and Rea 2012; see also Heyman 2004) of several bordering actors equipped with distinct occupational cultures and working in specific organizational environments—airports, intelligence offices, land crossings, customs warehouses, risk analysis centres, immigration authorities, embassies, and so on. Bigo (2014) pushes this analysis further, exploring the diverse "social universes" (army, border guards, intelligence) making up border security. A data analyst and a border guard in the field do not necessarily share capabilities, skills, and technologies. As they envision bordering through different professional **habituses**, the possibilities embedded in technologies may or may not be "activated" (or differentially so). It is this local expertise that higher placed border officials attempt to tame with border technologies in an effort to standardize decision making.

Such local differences became particularly clear during fieldwork, even at the port level. Located in the same port compound, the traffic section (where travellers are processed) and the commercial section (where officers assess truck drivers and cargo) contrast in the differential importance they give to administrative work and law enforcement. The employees of both sections in bigger ports of entry do not know each other and seldom interact. Commercial officers often prefer working with truck drivers whom they consider more pliable and respectful than travellers. The two sections' tasks and tools also vary. For instance, some databases are specific to customs operations. Commercial officers must also oversee the completion of export-import forms as well as learn about thousands of different products and the relevant import laws concerning them; they collect more in duties than their traffic colleagues, and when they discover concealed illegal merchandise in trucks (such as drugs), they generally do so in larger quantities. Customs is more concerned with screening for illegal goods than illegitimate mobile persons, and such screening is bounded by the trade facilitation role ascribed to border officers working "commercial."

Further, if contemporary border agencies seem to undergo perpetual reform, long-learned dispositions as well as former mandates (taxation and revenue) remain important for many security professionals—a phenomenon I analyze elsewhere through the lens of the sociology of generations (Côté-Boucher 2018). Nevertheless, transformations are happening. Since its creation in 2003, the CBSA has been asked to reinforce its law enforcement and security mandates. Without showing the levels of paramilitarism displayed by US Customs and Border Protection,[3] the CBSA is now increasingly influenced by the police model, especially in field officer hiring and training. Despite their work routine primarily involving administrative customs duties, commercial officers have come to value crime-fighting and "catching bad guys" as an essential part of their work. Being able to do so on a "cold hit" (without the help of intelligence and databases) provides an officer with his colleagues' respect. By automatizing and displacing decision making away from ports of entry, information technologies reduce the possibility for officers to gain such peer recognition and take pride in their work.

Finally, and in contrast with much critical work on security and borders that assumes that data is readily accessible and freely circulates in security agencies, a politics of secrecy influences the division of data management labour in border agencies. Access to data remains heavily codified and depends on one's security credentials and position in the agency hierarchy. Border agency employees are granted different levels of security clearance, which restrict or enable access to information systems and the ability to share that information. At the CBSA, information exchange with other security organizations can only be legally undertaken by highly ranked designated personnel. The more sensitive the information, the higher the security clearance required. That being said, security professionals have been known to exchange data informally through personal contacts and other unregulated daily verbal interactions (Privacy Commissioner of Canada 2006). In contrast, front-line border officers do have access to local targeting results as well as to pre-formatted intelligence analyses circulated within the border agency (Pratt and Thompson 2008).

The internal politics of this differentiated access to information is characteristic of all security agencies. Security professionals interact with technologies within the framework provided by security bureaucracies, some of which foster a sense of loyalty, pride, and exclusivity amongst their employees. As shown by Nolan (2013) in her fascinating ethnography of the Central Intelligence Agency (CIA), access to information and sophisticated technologies is one distinction that characterizes security and intelligence agencies. In fact, data hoarding may prevent interoperability and information exchange. What does this mean in a border control context? We need to be prudent about how we theorize the role of data in border control. Borders may well be "smart" but primarily for those with the clearance and the willingness to make them so.

The case of the CBSA teaches us that the relation between technologies and bordering resists generalization. It is not enough to assume that the passing of a data-sharing agreement will automatically generate interoperability, or that acquiring a border technology will readily result in its smooth adoption by end-users. The integration of technologies in customs involves varied practices of appropriation, levels of access, and dispositions. It also reshapes power relationships within the organization and between the actors that take on the technologies, embrace them, resist them, and learn to work with them. Paying attention to these phenomena puts the human, the political, and the organizational back into the analysis of smart borders.

AUTOMATION AND CUSTOMS OFFICER DESKILLING

A new "customs regime" (Chalfin 2007) is taking form in the global push to streamline trade compliance and centralize risk assessment. This new regime does not eliminate traditional customs methods—for instance, the physical examination of cargo or the evaluation of a traveller's conduct by assessing their behaviour and other "risk indicators." However, as it is becoming increasingly common to turn to these technologies to reallocate customs and security tasks, border control is progressively breaking from these methods and attributing them less importance now that mobilities can be governed through many control locations beyond physical ports of entry.

I have described in detail elsewhere (Côté-Boucher 2016) the new technologies that reconfigure Canadian customs, the related displacement of great parts of risk management and customs release away from ports of entry, and the helplessness felt by officers in view of this loss of influence, as well as the consequences of these processes for border officers' discretionary powers. The remainder of this chapter examines anew the effects of these changes, this time focusing on their effect on the internal politics of border agencies. Accordingly, through the case of the centralization of targeting, I return to these technological transformations in the customs area that rest on two intertwined processes: the automation of customs, and private sector involvement in border security and customs compliance.

The automation of customs release and border security depends on the information transmitted by private actors to border authorities. Transportation companies, exporters, customs brokers, and customs authorities are now involved in a security assemblage mediated by databases. Because private actors perform data collection activities, responsibility for bordering is partly downloaded to private third parties that have become security regulators in their own right.

Interestingly, data collection and transmission by private actors is done without compensation; it is now part of the cost of doing transnational business. Data exchange with border authorities is structured by multiple border initiatives, from pre-clearance to trusted trader programs. For instance, carrier companies and importers can now be approved by Canadian and US border authorities to become members of trusted trader programs—the program with the most membership is the American Customs and Trade Partnership Against Terrorism. Carriers and importers become responsible for ensuring the safety of their facilities, trucks, drivers, and commercial partners; they must also share detailed information about their business activities and observation of safety measures with border agencies.

Further, the new Canadian e-Manifest electronic declaration system (which includes customs release and risk management features) requires carriers and importers to submit their customs data electronically before arriving at the border, including detailed information about the cargo and carrier, as well as the truck driver, importer, and exporter. The release of goods is often now approved prior to arrival at the border; much of this data is processed automatically while higher-risk cargo, drivers, or companies are flagged for front-line officer consideration. From the late 1990s, risk assessment on this data was conducted by local targeting systems in ports of entry but, since 2013, much of that analysis work has been centralized.

At the time of research, a highway risk assessment centre was being piloted in Windsor, Ontario. Following this project, officers expected a series of localized target centres to be created, but the CBSA has since implemented a National Targeting Centre in Ottawa. This centralization removed the bulk of risk assessment determinations from local ports of entry and, according to officers, this transition was implemented without the benefit of their experiential knowledge about border crossers, transportation companies, and criminal trends.[4]

Electronic declarations, automation, and centralized targeting have changed the work routine of "commercial" service officers. Since centralized commercial targeting alters the motives for inspection and the ways inspections are carried out, border agents are now tasked with collecting detailed information gathered during secondary inspections that are sent to other bodies to be analyzed. No longer a stand-alone examination procedure, manual inspections are now considered a method of data collection by CBSA management. Further, electronic declarations considerably reduced border officers' administrative responsibilities, including paperwork. Pre-clearance of goods requires border agents to remotely recommend shipments for clearance when giving their release recommendation—in other words, without inspecting the truck driver or cargo. These officers might now spend two to three hours of their shift in front of their computer receiving declarations and recommending releases (or secondary inspections) to other officers, sometimes located in other ports of entry. One officer who releases cargo electronically from an airport located several hundreds of kilometres from his workstation told me: "Doing the job remotely is what we found a little difficult at first. We were used to having something in front of us we could see." This new way of coordinating tasks between border crossings resulted in some officers no longer being responsible for making release recommendations as their tasks were delegated to a different officer at another crossing. In these conditions, border agents are increasingly called on to take part in inspections generated randomly or based on specific targets, but recommended by officers elsewhere in the border space.

These technological changes challenge the practical knowledge that has been accumulated collectively by border agents, including their familiarity with local carriers, economic factors, and regional criminal trends, as well as the ability to use this practical knowledge to question and examine truck drivers and goods. My research thus suggests that this extension of the border space is reinforced by what Ocqueteau and Dupont (2013, 8) call a new "division of [human]/machine labour for public security." Making this new division possible, the turn to technology in customs has significantly altered the fundamental spatiotemporal dynamics of the work routines of border officers. As these processes preside over officers' loss of traditional influence over decision making at the border, officer discontent sometimes translates into tense relations with CBSA headquarters.

"They Keep More and More of That Aspect Away from Us": Customs at a Distance at the CBSA

Upper management of border agencies adopt information technologies for a variety of reasons, including to expedite cargo assessment. Despite concerning issues for the rights of travellers such as false positives (Salter 2008) and security problems such as failures of detection (Leese 2015), risk technologies continue to be viewed by managers as tools that reduce rates of faulty decision making. Technologies can also be embraced to curtail corruption in countries where customs officers supplement their revenue through bribes or, as in the recent case involving hundreds of Transportation Safety Authority (TSA-United States) officials, through stealing from passenger luggage (Chuchmach, Kreider, and Ross 2012). All these justifications for the implementation of technology share a common rationale: the purported objectivity of the technological tool stands in contrast to officers' subjective judgment, potential dishonesty, or diminished awareness caused by fatigue.

But another justification drives the adoption of technologies: making better use of border officers' work time by eliminating binary decision making from officers' routines—for instance, decisions to let in or to intercept for further screening. In Canadian airports, automated kiosks have undertaken those tasks. In customs work where most trade is supposed to be streamlined, this has driven the adoption of algorithms to automatize the entry of low-risk cargo. The objective is to let officers concentrate on more complex decisions, such as an immigration evaluation, or to perform time-consuming secondary inspections of vehicles. These activities are time-consuming and require more knowledge of elements such as automobile and truck features, hiding places on these vehicles, and drug trafficking routes. Yet I have shown that without proper infrastructural changes to accompany such reorganization of tasks, automation has left customs officers with less to do, generating a feeling of idleness in some ports of entry (Côté-Boucher 2016).

Centralized risk management is part of these trends that aim to reach more "scientific" bordering methods. Although it may be difficult to obtain detailed information on the methods used by the CBSA's new targeting centre, the individuals who participated in our research and are familiar with these projects were frank in expressing their reservations about this change. They questioned the ability of centralized risk management to generate an accurate understanding of local risk conditions. One border officer explains:

> You're trying to . . . it would be like me trying to target a marine port. I never worked at a marine port. For me to try to target that, it's . . . you don't have a realistic understanding as to how that operation works. . . . And it's just not the best operation. Right? They keep more and more of that aspect away from us I find.

Another officer doubts that centralized targeting would in fact succeed in pointing at high-risk merchandise and persons:

> So, all the verification of commodities and imports will be done before. It is the Windsor people who will decide to send them at our docks for an exam. It's a shame because we know our clientele. And we know what is going on here at [the port of entry], we know the commodities. Whereas over there, they don't know our clientele, they will target approximately anything and everything, and it is them who will decide for us what we have to inspect. So I find that a bit lame.

Border officers are often critical of the socio-technical interactions that remove decision-making power from their local context. The comments made by the participants in this study raise questions about the assumption of improved security and more efficient decision making through the use of surveillance and information technologies.

Interviewees emphasized how border intelligence departments located in the capital might not catch some of the new criminal and security issues emerging locally.

Furthermore, border officers have doubts about the pertinence of some recommendations made by these centralized analysis departments. Some agents believed that some of the mandatory inspections required by centralized targeting recommendations were unnecessary—either because the local border service is already familiar with the targeted truck driver or carrier company and has previously inspected the subject on several occasions, or because there is not enough space at the docks. These mandatory inspections may prevent others that officers deem a higher priority from happening. Since targeters working remotely have limited knowledge of local factors, front-line officers are concerned that they may hinder the security actions taken against legitimate targets.

DOUBTING "OTTAWA"

My interviews revealed border agent dissatisfaction with the decisions made by the central administration and invite a deeper sociological analysis of the impact technologies have on security organizations. The distrust these agents display toward managers at the capital reveals their powerlessness regarding the distancing mechanisms that are transforming their jobs and taking away their decision-making power. The agents expressed repeated frustrations concerning not knowing enough about new customs procedures; some complain of not being properly trained to implement programs conceived elsewhere, while others consider themselves the guinea pigs for systems created by federal IT departments without consultation with officers about the needs and daily reality of ports of entry. An officer reveals how the transfer of targeting responsibilities gave rise to an internal debate between border regions and the capital:

> Until the debate between regions and Ottawa about targeting is closed . . . [i]t seems that for now, Ottawa is winning. In Windsor, anyway, they already have opened the national targeting centre.

> So they oppose regional or local targeting. . . . Regions fight to keep a
> part of their targeting responsibilities or at least maintain those they
> already have. . . . So, the local phenomena, Windsor won't be able to
> represent them well. Officers will probably have to note down local
> events, transmit these notes to Windsor, and it's Windsor that will
> do the targeting.[5]

Officers' sense of slowly losing decision-making powers and their related frustration were apparent in interviews through their descriptions
of "Ottawa's" lack of appreciation for their work. In such statements,
decision-makers are framed as not having the required expertise: "Ottawa
does not know how operations are conducted"; "Ottawa, they don't even
know what customs is." The references to "Ottawa"—a title designating
both politicians and border authority upper management—illustrate the
disconnect between the capital and the front line.[6] These references also
imply the inaccessibility of the centre of power that is the CBSA headquarters for most officers working in remote areas. This superior symbolic
position of the capital was frequently referred to through phrases such as
"up there," "upper management," and "the powers that be."

Of course, it is not uncommon for front-line employees and administrative authorities to be at odds regarding an organization's mandate,
the work methods to use, and the objectives to pursue (Lipsky 2010);
however, the restructuring of border work processes through technologies and front-line officers' loss of authority to enforce rules and laws at
border crossings exacerbates existing tensions between managers based
in the capital and agents in the field. Recent studies of federal employees
highlight the effect these struggles have on working conditions. Among
government employees, CBSA agents are some of the least satisfied with
their jobs, finding themselves toward the bottom of the list near corrections staff (Treasury Board of Canada Secretariat 2014).

This chapter shows that there can also be resistance on the ground
to the introduction of technology as it increases managerial control
over officers' work (for a similar argument in policing, see Meehan
1998; Tanner and Meyer 2015). Diverse tactics may be employed by
reluctant officers. Recent ethnographic research at the Canada-US

border demonstrates that automation and centralized risk targeting allow border officers to claim deniability when questioned in court about the basis for their decisions: "Don't blame me, blame the database" (Kalman 2015).

Beyond blame avoidance, I have found some border officers reluctant to adopt these new technological tools. Many doubted the efficiency of centralized risk targeting and others were sometimes unwilling (or unable, for lack of proper training and limited technological skills) to provide detailed information about their activities to feed targeting databases. This controversial situation is reflected in the tensions between these security workers and management in the capital. Thus, if some increased efficiency has been reached in improving the mobility of low-risk goods and people, the incorporation of these tools results in struggles between front-line personnel and headquarters due to the deskilling that accompanies the automation of customs work.

CONCLUSION

Going beyond the assumption of smooth technological appropriation often found in both critical border studies and policy documents alike, this chapter reconceptualizes "smart borders" starting from the empirical complexity of appropriation, implementation, and the competing logics that govern the use of bordering technologies. How, why, and by whom a technology is used raises questions of power within border agencies that reshape what used to be seen as the fundamentals of border control by front-line security professionals and border managers alike.

These dynamics are partially a result of officers' efforts to preserve their influence following the organizational and technological changes that are agitating the field of security from within. Since the introduction of technologies for the purposes of risk management and customs facilitation, some tasks that border agents used to spend a good part of their day on have been reallocated, scaled down, or simply eliminated. Understanding border agents' views of their ability to carry out their daily tasks and the progressive loss of their decision-making power allows us to better identify the concrete effects of contemporary political, technological, and organizational transformations concerning border security.

It is important to note that these internal tensions caused by the reform to customs work are also present in other nations. It was the case with the British border officers who held a strike against the UK Border Agency in 2011 following debates on reduced security controls because of the congestion at certain British border crossings. My conclusions also align with those of Brenda Chalfin (2010) who, in her ethnography of the impact of the neoliberal measures on Ghanaian customs, noticed the increased tensions between border agents and managers of border services because of a centralization of customs and the authority front-line officers lost as a result. These power struggles therefore give us reason to question the rhetoric claiming the efficiency and neutrality consistently embraced by those who glorify the automation of security processes. Instead, information technologies appear to renew the power struggles within border security organizations.

The CBSA is one of the least accountable security agencies in Canada. While it undergoes periodic, yet limited, financial audits by the auditor general, it is submitted to no independent surveillance mechanism regarding its respect of legal norms, including the effects of border surveillance on border crossers. The CBSA also remains suspicious of independent researchers. Indeed, empirical research on the CBSA is scarce and generally confined, like my own, to ports of entry (see O'Connor and de Lint 2009; Pratt and Thompson 2008). Yet billions of dollars have been invested in technologies to improve border security in Canada since 2001. When we assess their value for public security and effectiveness for regulating mobility,[7] we have to remember that the very integration of these technologies within border agencies is far from a neutral process. It involves significant internal disagreements and resistances between those who decide upon the adoption of a technology, those who will use these tools, and those who will be excluded from this novel field of technologized bordering and will interpret this exclusion as a deskilling process. These disagreements influence how and whether technologies are adopted, and by whom. This story continues to unfold at the CBSA.

DISCUSSION QUESTIONS

1.   How does the integration of database governance at borders disrupt the traditional power balance in border policing?

2.   How do risk technologies at the border reshape the logics of competition that are characteristic of security and police organizations?

3.   What are the competing logics that govern the use of border technologies, and why are these important for understanding the work of border security agents, as well as the securitization of the border?

4.   How are these new risk technologies appropriated and resisted by workers, and what, if any, impact does this have on their work processes, as well as their perception of their work?

5.   What are the new relationships developed between humans and machines in border spaces?

6.   Now that you have learned about the resistance of front-line border officers to the centralization of risk management, what do you think are the effects of the centralization of targeting on border crossers?

NOTES

1.   This chapter is a thoroughly reworked and extended version of a previously published article: Karine Côté-Boucher, 2014, "Technologies et luttes d'influence chez les professionnels de la sécurité frontalière," *Criminologie* 47 (2): 127–51.

2.   Conducted in the "commercial" section (where goods, trucks, and truck drivers are released) of five Canadian land border crossings in 2010–11, the study included 32 interviews with front-line border workers—including an intelligence analyst, a chief of operations (the main manager of a port of entry or several small- or medium-sized ports), 2 administrative assistants, 5 supervisors, and 23 border service officers (previously known as "customs officers"). My current research on border policing and the Canada-US cross-border trucking industry also informs the analysis presented in this chapter.

3.   This difference in organizational cultures between the CBSA and US Customs and Border Protection has been underscored by a few of my interviewees.

4. It goes beyond the purview of this chapter to argue whether or not officers are
    right in their assessment. I only wish to speak here of the type of debates that fol-
    low the introduction of risk technologies in a security agency in order to demon-
    strate how technologies are not automatically welcomed and adopted by all those
    working in security organizations.

    Officers' concerns were echoed by a CBSA internal audit, which was con-
    ducted after apprehensions were expressed about "the quality of targets" and wor-
    ries that "the method in which targets are created may not identify high risk
    persons or shipments." Importantly, the review assessed targeters' work but not
    whether and how the target was acted upon at port level (CBSA 2015).

5. The interviews cited in this section took place when centralized targeting was
    pilot tested in Windsor, Ontario, before the decision to move targeting activities
    to Ottawa.

6. I met with three agents who have had contracts in "Ottawa" in order to work on
    CBSA projects or were planning on moving there to pursue a career in the public
    sector. Despite these institutional efforts aimed at promoting the transfer of prac-
    tical knowledge from remote areas to headquarters, these agents witnessed how
    little field knowledge their counterparts from the capital appear to have. Fuel-
    ing intraorganizational conflicts, these stories about "Ottawa" circulate at border
    crossing offices. They do so once these agents finish their contracts and return to
    their port of entry, or during informal contacts aimed at exchanging information
    and carrying out correct procedures between the agents who hold positions at the
    capital and their former co-workers working at the border.

7. For instance, automation has been effective, significantly reducing waiting times
    of travellers in airports and trucks at land ports of entry. Yet user-technologies
    interactions generate much potential for error. A leaked report from the TSA
    reveals that 95 percent of mock explosives and weapons smuggled through air-
    port security by undercover agents were not detected by TSA officers, even when
    setting off an alarm and triggering a pat-down (Reuters 2015).

REFERENCES

Aas, Katja Franko. 2011. "'Crimmigrant' Bodies and Bona Fide Travelers: Surveillance,
    Citizenship and Global Governance." *Theoretical Criminology* 15 (3): 331–46.

Amicelle, Anthony, Claudia Aradau, and Julien Jeandesboz. 2015. "Questioning Security Devices: Performativity, Resistance, Politics." *Security Dialogue* 46 (4): 293–306.

Amoore, Louise, and Marieke de Goede. 2012. "Introduction." *Journal of Cultural Economy* 5 (1): 3–8.

Bigo, Didier. 2011. "Pierre Bourdieu and International Relations: Power of Practices, Practices of Power." *International Political Sociology* 5 (3): 225–58.

———. 2014. "The (In)Securitization Practices of the Three Universes of EU Border Control: Military/Navy-Borderguards/Police-Database Analysts." *Security Dialogue* 45 (3): 209–25.

Bonelli, Laurent, and Francesco Ragazzi. 2014. "Low-Tech Security: Files, Notes, and Memos as Technologies of Anticipation." *Security Dialogue* 45 (5): 476–93.

Bourne, Mike, Heather Johnson, and Debbie Lisle. 2015. "Laboratizing the Border: The Production, Translation and Anticipation of Security Technologies." *Security Dialogue* 46 (4): 307–25.

Brewer, Russell. 2014. *Policing the Waterfront: Networks, Partnerships, and the Governance of Port Security*. Oxford: Oxford University Press.

Brodeur, Jean-Paul. 2007. "High and Low Policing in Post 9/11 Times." *Policing* 1 (1): 25–37.

Brown, Wendy. 2010. *Walled States, Waning Sovereignty*. Cambridge, MA: Zone Books.

Canada Border Services Agency (CBSA). 2015. *Audit of National Targeting*. Ottawa: Government of Canada. http://www.cbsa-asfc.gc.ca/agency-agence/reports-rapports/ae-ve/2015/nt-cn-eng.html.

Cantens, Thomas. 2015. "Un scanner de conteneurs en 'Terre Promise' camerounaise: adopter et s'approprier une technologie de contrôle." *L'Espace politique* 25: 2–18.

Chalfin, Brenda. 2007. "Customs Regimes and the Materiality of Global Mobility: Governing the Port of Rotterdam." *American Behavioral Scientist* 50 (12): 1610–30.

———. 2010. *Neoliberal Frontiers: An Ethnography of Sovereignty in West Africa*. Chicago: Chicago University Press.

Chuchmach, Megan, Randy Kreider, and Brian Ross. 2012. "Convicted TSA Officer Reveals Secrets of Theft at Airports." *ABC News*, September 28, 2012. http://abcnews.go.com/Blotter/convicted-tsa-officer-reveals-secrets-thefts-airports/story?id=17339513.

Côté-Boucher, Karine. 2008. "The Diffuse Border: Intelligence-Sharing, Control and Confinement along Canada's Smart Border." *Surveillance and Society* 5 (2): 142–65.

———. 2010. "Risky Business? Border Preclearance and the Securing of Economic Life in North America." In *Neoliberalism and Everyday Life*, edited by Susan Braedley and Meg Luxton, 37–67. Montreal/Kingston: McGill-Queen's University Press.

———. 2016. "The Paradox of Discretion: Customs and the Changing Occupational Identity of Canadian Border Officers." *British Journal of Criminology* 56 (1): 49–67.

———. 2018. "Of 'Old' and 'New' Ways: Generations, Border Control and the Temporality of Security." *Theoretical Criminology* 22 (2): 149–68. https://doi .org/10.1177/1362480617690800.

Côté-Boucher, Karine, Federica Infantino, and Mark B. Salter. 2014. "Border Security as Practice: An Agenda for Research." *Security Dialogue* 45 (3): 195–208.

Cowen, Deborah. 2014. *The Deadly Life of Logistics*. Minneapolis: University of Minnesota Press.

Dupont, Benoit. 2006. "Power Struggles in the Field of Security: Implications for Democratic Transformation." In *Democracy, Society and the Governance of Security*, edited by Jennifer Wood and Benoit Dupont, 86–110. Cambridge: Cambridge University Press.

Eski, Yarin. 2016. *Policing, Port Security and Crime Control: An Ethnography of the Port Securityscape*. London: Routledge.

Frowd, Philippe M. 2014. "The Field of Border Control in Mauritania." *Security Dialogue* 45 (3): 226–41.

Guittet, Emmanuel-Pierre, and Julien Jeandesboz. 2010. "Security Technologies." In *The Routledge Handbook of New Security Studies*, edited by J. Peter Burgess, 229–39. New York: Routledge.

Heyman, Josiah. 2004. "Ports of Entry as Nodes in the World System." *Identities: Global Studies in Culture and Power* 11 (3): 303–27.

Infantino, Federica, and Andrea Rea. 2012. "La mobilisation d'un savoir pratique local: attribution des visas Schengen au consulat général de Belgique à Casablanca." *Sociologies pratiques* 24 (1): 67–78.

International Civil Liberties Monitoring Group. 2010. *Report of the Information Clearinghouse on Border Controls and Infringements to Travellers' Rights*. Ottawa.

Jeandesboz, Julien, Didier Bigo, Ben Hayes, and Stephanie Simon. 2013. "The Commission's Legislative Proposals on Smart Borders: Their Feasibility and Costs." European Parliament Study, PE 493.026. Brussels: Directorate General for Internal Policies.

Kalman, Ian. 2015. "'Don't Blame Me, It's Just the Computer Telling Me to Do This': Computer Attribution and the Discretionary Authority of Canada Border Services Agency Officers." Working paper no. 166. Halle, Germany: Max Planck Institute for Social Anthropology.

Kotef, Hagar. 2015. *Movement and the Ordering of Freedom*. Durham, NC: Duke University Press.

Leese, Mathias. 2015. "'We Were Taken by Surprise': Body Scanners, Technology Adjustment, and the Eradication of Failure." *Critical Studies on Security* 3 (3): 269–82.

Lipsky, Michael. 2010. *Street-Level Bureaucracy: Dilemmas of the Individual in Public Services*. 30th anniversary expanded ed. New York: Russell Sage Foundation.

Loftus, Bethan. 2015. "Border Regimes and the Sociology of Policing." *Policing and Society: An International Journal of Research and Policy* 25 (1): 115–25.

Lyon, David. 2007. "Surveillance, Security and Social Sorting: Emerging Research Priorities." *International Criminal Justice Review* 17 (3): 161–70.

Manning, Peter K. 1996. "Information Technology in the Police Context: The 'Sailor' Phone." *Information Systems Research* 7 (1): 52–62.

———. 2008. *The Technology of Policing: Crime Mapping, Information Technology, and the Rationality of Crime Control*. New York: New York University Press.

Meehan, Albert J. 1998. "The Impact of Mobile Data Terminal (MDT) Information Technology on Communication and Recordkeeping in Patrol Work." *Qualitative Sociology* 21 (3): 225–54.

Nolan, Bridget Rose. 2013. "Information Sharing and Collaboration in the United States Intelligence Community: An Ethnographic Study of the National Counterterrorism Centre." Unpublished PhD diss., Philadephia, University of Pennsylvania.

O'Connor, Daniel, and Willem de Lint. 2009. "Frontier Government: The Folding of the Canada-US Border." *Studies in Social Justice* 3 (1): 39–66.

Ocqueteau, Frédéric, and Benoît Dupont. 2013. "Introduction: Nouveaux regards sur les métiers de la sécurité." *Criminologie* 46: 2–13.

Orlikowski, Wanda J. 2000. "Using Technology and Constituting Structures: A Practice Lens for Studying Technology in Organizations." *Organization Science* 11 (4): 404–28.

Pallister-Wilkins, Polly. 2016. "'How Walls Do Work': Security Barriers as Devices of Interruption and Data Capture." *Security Dialogue* 47 (2): 151–64.

Parker, Noel, and Nick Vaughan-Williams. 2009. "Lines in the Sand? Towards an Agenda for Critical Border Studies." *Geopolitics* 14 (3): 582–87.

Pickering, Sharon, and Julie Ham. 2014. "Hot Pants at the Border: Sorting Sex Work from Trafficking." *British Journal of Criminology* 54 (1): 2–19.

Pötzsch, Holger. 2015. "The Emergence of iBorder: Bordering Bodies, Networks and Machines." *Environment and Planning D: Society and Space* 33 (1): 101–18.

Pratt, Anna, and Sara K. Thompson. 2008. "Chivalry, 'Race' and Discretion at the Canadian Border." *British Journal of Criminology* 48 (5): 620–40.

Privacy Commissioner of Canada. 2006. *Audit of the Personal Information Management Practices of the Canada Border Services Agency Trans-border Data Flows*. Ottawa: Office of the Privacy Commissioner of Canada. https://priv.gc.ca/media/1166/cbsa_060620_e.pdf.

Razac, Olivier. 2009. *Histoire politique du barbelé*. Paris: Flammarion.

Reuters. 2015. "Homeland Security Chief Reassigns Top TSA Official." *Reuters*, June 1, 2015. http://www.reuters.com/article/us-usa-security-tsa-idUSKBN0OI05D20150602.

Rygiel, Kim. 2013. "Mobile Citizens, Risky Subjects: Security Knowledge at the Border." In *Mobilities, Knowledge, and Social Justice*, edited by Suzan Ilcan, 152–76. Montreal/Kingston: McGill-Queen's University Press.

Salter, Mark B. 2008. "Imagining Numbers: Risk, Quantification, and Aviation Security." *Security Dialogue* 39 (2/3): 243–66.

Sanders, Carrie B., and Stacey Hannem. 2012. "Policing 'the Risky': Technology and Surveillance in Everyday Patrol Work." *Canadian Review of Sociology/Revue canadienne de sociologie* 49 (4): 389–410.

Sanders, Carrie B., and Samantha Henderson. 2013. "Police 'Empires' and Information Technologies: Uncovering Material and Organisational Barriers to Information Sharing in Canadian Police Service." *Policing and Society* 23: 243–60.

Sanders, Carrie B., Crystal Weston, and Nicole Schott. 2015. "Police Innovations, 'Secret Squirrels' and Accountability: Empirically Studying Intelligence-Led Policing in Canada." *British Journal of Criminology* 55 (4): 711–29.

Scherrer, Amandine, Emmanuel-Pierre Guittet, and Didier Bigo. 2010. *Mobilités sous surveillance. Perspectives croisées UE-Canada*. Montreal: Athéna Éditions.

Sparke, Matthew. 2006. "A Neoliberal Nexus: Economy, Security and the Biopolitics of Citizenship on the Border." *Political Geography* 25 (2): 151–80.

Squire, Vicki. 2011. *The Contested Politics of Mobility: Borderzones and Irregularity*. London: Routledge.

Tanner, Samuel, and Michael Meyer. 2015. "Police Work and New 'Security Devices': A Tale from the Beat." *Security Dialogue* 46 (4): 384–400.

Topak, Özgun E., Ciara Bracken-Roche, Alana Saulnier, and David Lyon. 2015. "From Smart Borders to Perimeter Security: The Expansion of Digital Surveillance at the Canadian Borders." *Geopolitics* 20 (4): 880–99.

Treasury Board of Canada Secretariat. 2014. *2011 Public Service Employee Survey*. http://www.tbs-sct.gc.ca/pses-saff/2011/introduction-eng.asp.

van der Woude, Maartje, and Joanne van der Leun. 2017. "Crimmigration Checks in the Internal Border Areas of the EU: Finding the Discretion that Matters." *European Journal of Criminology* 14 (1): 27–45.

Vukov, Tamara. 2016. "Target Practice: The Algorithmics and Biopolitics of Race in Emerging Smart Border Practices and Technologies." *Transfers* 6 (1): 80–97. https://doi.org/10.3167/TRANS.2016.060107.

Walters, William. 2006. "Border/Control." *European Journal of Social Theory* 9: 187–203.

Weber, Leane. 2011. "'It Sounds Like They Shouldn't Be Here': Immigration Checks on the Streets of Sydney." *Policing and Society* 21 (4): 456–67.

World Customs Organization. 2012. *SAFE Framework of Standards to Secure Trade and Facilitate Global Trade*. http://wcoomd.org/en/topics/facilitation/instrument-and-tools/tools/safe_package.aspx.

Zaiotti, Ruben. 2016. "Mapping Remote Control: The Externalization of Migration Management in the 21st Century." In *Externalizing Migration Management: Europe, North America and the spread of "Remote Control" Practice*, edited by Ruben Zaiotti, 3–30. New York: Routledge.

CONCLUSION

Carrie B. Sanders, Stacey Hannem, and Christopher J. Schneider

As we concluded this book, we were faced with the horrific news of a terrorist attack in Edmonton, Canada, and the largest mass shooting in United States history in Las Vegas, Nevada, taking at least 58 people's lives and leaving close to 500 others injured. As we prepared the manuscript for final submission, American youth were rallying—"marching for their lives"—in the wake of a school shooting in Parkland, Florida, that killed 17 people. These are just a few recent examples of terrible crimes, among numerous others around the globe. The impact of such catastrophic events and the loss of human lives result in growing public concern, and increasing pressure on governments and public safety organizations to think ahead and be proactive to prevent harm to citizens. In this way, the pursuit of security has become future-oriented and pre-emptive, relying on networks and partnerships. These new forms of governing are a result of the interconnectedness of insecurity and risks that proliferate in the "risk society." As O'Reilly and Ellison (2006, 643) explain, "the idea of 'risk' exploits the vulnerabilities and sense of 'panickyness' (Sparks 1992) that lie at the heart of late modern society and embraces the notion that such risks (real or imagined) can be controlled, managed or assuaged." Central to the pursuit of security and crime control is the integration and use of risk technologies. Risk technologies have been developed to assist in identifying and predicting risk with the goal of thwarting it. This ideology, O'Malley (2010, 3) argues, has become a "dominant way of governing all manner of problems" and has led to the development of a model of risk wherein "predictive statistical knowledge [is] linked to techniques of harm prevention."

As illustrated in this book, security technologies and practices have become primarily focused on, and interested in, mitigating risks, and less interested in the prevention of the conditions that cause threat, or in merely reacting to harm. This temporal shift from reactive crime control toward anticipatory, "pre-crime" logics legitimizes the use of crime science—such as algorithmic analytics, actuarial methods, and risk technologies—in the pursuit of security (Mythen and Walklate 2010; Zedner 2010). As Zedner (2007, 262) explains, "in a pre-crime society, there is calculation, risk and uncertainty, surveillance, precaution, prudentialism, moral hazard, prevention and, arching over all these, there is the pursuit of security" (see also Johnston and Shearing 2003; Loader and Sparks 2002; O'Malley 2004). Canadian investments in remand centres, algorithmic analytics (such as predictive policing), risk mitigation initiatives (such as situation tables), technologies (such as IonScan and smart border technologies), and offender registries are illustrative of this temporal shift to pre-crime.

Since the turn of the century, public discussion and social action around public safety and security has become more urgent, and as concerns about terrorism, mass shootings, and other large-scale forms of harm have escalated, security policies and practices have become more stringent (Loader and Sparks 2010). For example, the United States has implemented travel bans, and banned laptop computers from certain flights as risk preventive measures, while in the United Kingdom, the government has proposed "to change the law to bring in tougher sentences for people who repeat[edly] view terrorist content online—increasing the maximum penalty to up to 15 years behind bars" (Lomas 2017). Individuals convicted of viewing terrorist materials have not necessarily been convicted of terrorist activities, but these lengthy sentences reflect a fear that repeatedly accessing terrorist content signals that an individual is "at risk" of becoming involved in terrorist activity—these lengthy sentences and, indeed, the charge itself function as a form of preventive detention.

With increasing fear of future catastrophic events, governments and security agencies are investing heavily in risk technologies in the pursuit of security. As a result of this growing faith and reliance on technology, there is a *perception* that the uses of risk technologies (such as algorithmic and analytic technologies and crime science techniques) enhance efficiencies, effectiveness, accountability, and the pursuit of security. Yet, there are few empirical analyses of the in situ use of such technologies and their impact on criminal justice practices and security. With the growing use of risk technologies, it is imperative that researchers study the types of risk technologies, techniques, and practices that are adopted by different criminal justice organizations. It is important that we explore how those working within these different organizations understand and interact with these technologies in order to identify the obstacles, constraints, and intended and unintended consequences associated with their use. Additionally, the *ethics* of risk technologies and our responses to risk must be of concern to criminal justice scholars and practitioners. Given the increasing prevalence of big data and the capacity for social sorting, we must be vigilant to maintain our awareness of unintended consequences, particularly for already marginalized people, even as we are dazzled by the promise and possibilities of these technologies.

As demonstrated by Martin Dufresne, Dominique Robert, and Silvian Roy in chapter 5, and Aaron Doyle and Laura McKendy in chapter 7, the pursuit of security is increasingly influenced by mass media and public opinion, and is "at the mercy of ill-informed and sometimes whipped-up popular emotion" (Loader and Sparks 2010, 776). The result, Loader and Sparks (2010, 776) argue, is a "policy environment that is volatile and unstable, one in which it becomes difficult to make reason and evidence the drivers of what is said and done." It is our hope that the collective chapters in this volume will be read together as a "cooling device"—bringing empirical insight and rationality into discussions and perceptions of security practices (Loader and Sparks 2010)—so that future generations of criminal justice practitioners will demand that the effects of new risk technologies and practices be empirically validated *prior to wholesale implementation.*

The conflation of "risk" and "threat" appears to be an important factor behind the public emotions and political interests that drive the widespread development of risk technologies. Where *risk* is a function of calculations and probabilities of likely outcomes, *threat* is the source of the risk; threats exist objectively, independent of our ability to identify, calculate, or predict them (Aven 2016). But where threat may be sometimes imminent and identifiable (certain), risk is always characterized by uncertainty that is driven by fear, contributing to an "expectation that danger and risk are central features of everyday life" (Altheide 2002a, 229). At least some of the public enthusiasm for risk management is based on the assumption that risk technologies function to drastically reduce, or eliminate, uncertainty, and to thereby reduce or eliminate threats. This assumption is based on three contingencies: (1) that risk technologies are capable of identifying *specific* sites (or persons) of threat, (2) that the identification of risk factors and their related sites of threat enables the prevention of harm, and (3) that risk technologies and tools are being used systematically to maximize their predictive and pre-emptive capabilities. However, the fact remains that there is no risk technology that can eliminate uncertainty and the possibility of threat: *uncertainty remains a defining characteristic of risk* (Aven 2016). Risks can be managed and their probabilities reduced, but the pursuit of ultimate security and certainty is still the stuff of science fiction. While we have many risk technologies and security protocols, not one could have predicted (and thus prevented) the more than 500 mass shootings that took place between June 2016 and November 2017 in the United States alone (*New York Times* 2017). Knowing, then, that much risk technology functions in a way that cannot necessarily identify or reduce the threat of harm, it is incumbent on scholars, practitioners, politicians, students, and ethicists to think through the implications of risk technologies and to consider their potential costs and benefits, weighing their efficacy with such things as privacy concerns, the possibilities of racial or ethnic discrimination, and other potentially harmful consequences.

RISK TECHNOLOGIES AND THE PURSUIT OF SECURITY

To date, much of the research and scholarship available on security is largely theoretical and philosophical in nature—focusing on "what is security" or "what security ought to be" (Valverde 2014, 383)—with less attention to security as an enacted practice. As Sheptycki (2008) explains, much of our understanding of security has been shaped within a "national security framework" where the principal aim is to secure the integrity and sovereignty of the state *qua* state. Adopting a national security framework focuses on the defence of the state and is predominantly organized around the fear of an external attack directed against the state. By catalyzing public fear on external attacks, we lose sight of the ways in which the in situ use of risk technologies and practices shapes our everyday experiences of security. Yet, an alternative paradigm to national security has been developed, namely "human security," which entails protecting individuals and communities from any form of political or social violence and denotes both freedom from fear and freedom from want (Sheptycki 2008). These two approaches to security, while epistemologically and ontologically distinct, raise important questions about the complexities and difficulties associated with studying "security" and its effects.

As Valverde (2014, 383) explains, security is a ubiquitous concept that "cannot be seen and measured objectively"—it is not something that can be easily studied if we look at it as a "noun," a "thing," because such an approach "leads into normative discussions about good security versus bad security." Instead, one needs to document and reflect on a "very wide variety of *activities* and *practices* that are being carried out under the name of 'security'" (Valverde 2014, 383). Like Valverde, we believe that understanding how "security" is being constituted in a variety of realms requires researchers to focus on the *activities* and *practices* "that the participants themselves—not outside observers—describe as promoting security in some way" (Valverde 2014, 383–84). Thus, it requires not only an in-depth and up-close analysis of how various risk technologies and practices are designed or perceived to operate, but, more importantly, a detailed account of the everyday practice and experience of security practices.

CONCLUDING THOUGHTS

One aim of this volume is to address this significant gap in knowledge by presenting chapters focused on eight different empirical sites where security projects are operating. The contributions in this book not only revisit theoretical discussions of security, but, more importantly, they also update and problematize theoretical discussions within this field. Collectively they provide much needed empirical insight into the movement toward "crime science" and question the "objectivity" ascribed to security technologies and practices, all the while illuminating how broader political, economic, cultural, and organizational contexts shape every aspect of security—from its design to its implementation and enactment. While the eight chapters focus on different sectors of the criminal justice system and different risk technologies and techniques, collectively they illustrate and speak to a number of common themes, such as the shift toward pre-crime and preventive justice, the theatre and realities of technologies, the calculability and incalculability of risks, and the rhetoric and realities of cost savings and "justice on a budget." Researchers interested in studying security would be well served to further interrogate these themes of security. Further, researchers interested in understanding the use and impact of risk technologies should look outside the discipline of criminology for theoretical insights—for example, to the work being done in the discipline of science and technology studies—such as technologies in practice (Orlikowski and Gash 1994; Chan and Bennett Moses, chapter 2, and Côté-Boucher, chapter 8), actor-network theory (Latour and Woolgar 1979; Dufresne, Robert, and Roy, chapter 5), and social shaping of technology (Oudshoorn and Pinch 2003; Hannem, chapter 3; Sanders et al., chapter 4; and Schneider, chapter 6).

Research within science and technology studies has demonstrated how technologies—such as risk technologies—are powerful tools capable of connecting people, both known and unknown, to each other (Latour 1987). Research here has demonstrated how technologies are not apolitical objects, but instead incorporate the various political subjectivities of their designers and users (van den Scott, Sanders, and Puddephatt 2017).

However, the social makeup and construction of technologies, as illustrated throughout the chapters in this collection, have become "black-boxed" and rendered invisible because of the numerous ways they are unquestionably adopted and used by human actors. A "black box moves in space and becomes durable in time only through the actions of many people; . . . understanding what facts machines are is . . . understanding who the people are" (Latour 1987, 137). Thus, risk technologies and practices contain multiple memberships, negotiations, and complexities that can become "immutable mobiles," able to be transported and adapted across the various social worlds of public safety inscriptions that have the ability to travel unchanged across space and time (Latour 1987, 1999).

Although risk technologies are often assumed to be separate and distinct from the rest of society, as illustrated throughout this collected volume, technologies share much in common with other forms of culture as their very design, implementation, and use are patterned by users' economic, political, cultural, local, and organizational contexts. As Lehoux, Saint-Arnaud, and Richard (2004, 639) argue:

> Technology is not simply an assemblage of material features and functions to which varying social meanings can be attached[;] . . . [T]echnology should be examined in the context of their situated use, wherein more or less robust associations between technical and human components structure social action.

Thus, to study risk technologies requires one to "un-black-box" these technologies through understanding how they operate, observing what they do and how different users define and interact with them, and examining the experiences of those to whom the technologies are applied. In doing this, we cease to accept the surface-level discursive descriptions of the technologies, as presented by their designers, sellers, and advocates, and instead engage critically with the role of the technology in mediating human interactions directed at managing risks and threats.

By looking at the ways in which the social gets inside of and shapes risk technologies, we are able to uncover the intended and unintended consequences of their use. For example, studying the in situ use of risk technologies can uncover technological "function creep," where technology designed for one purpose takes on a new life and a different function (Curry, Phillips, and Regan 2004). This was illustrated nicely by Côté-Boucher (chapter 8) when considering how Canada Border Service Agency's implementation of smart borders affected the customs system; it not only created reforms to the agency's work practices, but also shaped how it collaborated and worked with other organizations. The possibility of risk technologies leading to function creep transforms their *power* from one of enhancing public security into technologies capable of socially sorting people and spaces into social classifications for the purpose of *disciplining* and *marginalizing* bodies and spaces (see Hannem, chapter 3; Doyle and McKendy, chapter 7). Future research and policy needs to consider the possibility that "objective" risk categorizations may operate in discriminatory ways to further marginalize and target racialized groups, and others who already comprise the "usual suspects."

Future research that builds upon this book might further consider the role that fear plays in the proliferation of risk technologies. Fear is a latent theme that cuts across all the chapters in this book. The justification for and continued use of risk technologies—even when illustrated as inaccurate predictors of risk, as done nicely in the preceding chapters—is quite often underscored by fear. As research has clearly shown (Altheide 2002a, 2002b, 2006, 2009), fear (general) rather than danger (specific) has become a dominant way that we orient to the social world. Such an orientation is evident in the numerous announcements that alert the public to acts of terrorism and crime, consumer warnings, and so on that pervade the social landscape. These and related issues give rise to a shared awareness of increased risks to our safety and continued calls for prediction and subsequent elimination of said risks. Responses, when they are offered, increasingly come in the form of technologies, as this book has demonstrated. When implemented, however, as this volume has also shown, such risk technologies are never foolproof and usually fail to accurately predict with certainty what they claim to predict. And so the cycle continues.

How then ought we to proceed? First and foremost, it is our hope that this volume will facilitate dialogue and encourage critical debate. Second, we leave the reader here to ponder the role of fear and to consider the possibility of alternative orientations to the social world. Fear does not call into question the specific conditions (dangers) of an event. There is often little judgment or reflection when fears are invoked. Fear is visceral, reactionary, and not characterized by careful thinking. We think a better way forward is to reorient ourselves to concern and to the pursuit of human security. As such, we ought to be concerned about the issues and related topics discussed in this volume. Concern quells the visceral and reactionary, and is oriented to the community. The expression of concern offers a space for dialogue where thoughtful judgments can emerge, allowing us to ask reflexive questions about the conditions that led to a specific event. How else are we to learn from such catastrophic events? Sometimes the questions are more important than the answers.

REFERENCES

Altheide, David L. 2002a. "Children and the Discourse of Fear." *Symbolic Interaction* 25 (2): 229–50.

———. 2002b. *Creating Fear: News and the Construction of Crisis*. New York: Aldine de Gruyter.

———. 2006. *Terrorism and the Politics of Fear*. Lanham, MD: Alta Mira Press.

———. 2009. *Terror Post-9/11 and the Media*. New York: Peter Lang.

Aven, Tereje. 2016. "The Reconceptualization of Risk." In *Routledge Handbook of Risk Studies*, edited by Adam Burgess, Alberto Alemanno, and Jens O. Zinn, 58–72. New York: Routledge.

Curry, Michael R., David J. Phillips, and Priscilla M. Regan. 2004. "Emergency Response Systems and the Creeping Legibility of People and Places." *The Information Society: An International Journal* 20 (5): 357–69.

Johnston, Lynne, and Clifford Shearing. 2003. *Governing Security: Explorations in Policing and Justice*. London: Routledge.

Latour, Bruno. 1987. *Science in Action: How to Follow Scientists and Engineers through Society*. Cambridge, MA: Harvard University Press.

———. 1999. "On Recalling ANT." In *Actor Network Theory and After*, edited by John Law and John Hassard, 15–25. Oxford: Blackwell Publishers.

Latour, Bruno, and Steve Woolgar. 1979. *Laboratory Life: The Construction of Scientific Facts*. Princeton, NJ: Princeton University Press.

Lehoux, Pascale, Jocelyne Saint-Arnaud, and Lucie Richard. 2004. "The Use of Technology at Home: What Patient Manuals Say and Sell vs. What Patients Face and Fear." *Sociology of Health and Illness* 26 (5): 617–44.

Loader, Ian, and Richard Sparks. 2002. "Contemporary Landscapes of Crime, Order and Control: Governance, Risk, and Globalization." In *The Oxford Handbook of Criminology* (3rd ed.), edited by Mike Maguire, Rodney Morgan, and Robert Reiner, 83–111. Oxford: Oxford University Press.

———. 2010. "What Is to Be Done with Public Criminology?" *Criminology and Public Policy* 9 (4): 771–81.

Lomas, Natasha. 2017. "UK to Hike Penalties on Viewing Terrorist Content Online." *Yahoo Finance*, October 3, 2017. https://finance.yahoo.com/news/uk-hike-penalties-viewing-terrorist-102145030.html?.tsrc=fauxdal.

Mythen, Gabe, and Sandra Walklate. 2010. "Pre-crime, Regulation and Counterterrorism: Interrogating Anticipatory Risk." *Center for Crime and Justice Studies*: 34–46.

New York Times. 2017. "477 Days. 521 Mass Shootings. Zero Action from Congress." Retrieved October 14, 2017. https://www.nytimes.com/interactive/2017/10/02/opinion/editorials/mass-shootings-congress.html.

O'Malley, Pat. 2004. *Risk, Uncertainty and Government*. London: Glasshouse Press.

———. 2010. *Crime and Risk*. Los Angeles: Sage.

O'Reilly, Conor, and Graham Ellison. 2006. "Eye Spy Private High: Re-conceptualising High Policing Theory." *British Journal of Criminology* 46 (4): 641–60.

Orlikowski, Wanda J., and Debra Gash. 1994. "Technological Frames: Making Sense of Technology in Organizations." *ACM Transactions on Information Systems: Special Issue on Social Science Perspectives on IS* 12 (2): 174–207.

Oudshoorn, Nelly, and Trevor Pinch, eds. 2003. *How Users Matter: The Co-construction of Users and Technology*. Cambridge, MA: MIT Press.

Sheptycki, James. 2008. "Policing, Intelligence Theory and the New Human Security Paradigm." In *Intelligence Theory: Key Questions and Debates*, edited by Peter Gill, Stephen Marrin, and Mark Phythian, 166–87. London: Routledge.

Valverde, Marianna. 2014. "Studying the Governance of Crime and Security: Space, Time and Jurisdiction." *Criminology and Criminal Justice* 14 (4): 379–91.

van den Scott, Lisa-Jo K., Carrie B. Sanders, and Antony J. Puddephatt. 2017. "Reconceptualizing Users through Enriching Ethnography." In *The Handbook of Science and Technology Studies* (4th ed.) edited by Clark A. Miller et al., 501–27. Cambridge, MA: MIT Press.

Zedner, Lucia. 2007. "Pre-crime and Post-criminology?" *Theoretical Criminology* 11 (2): 261–81.

———. 2010. "Pre-crime and Pre-punishment: A Health Warning." *Centre for Crime and Justice Studies*: 24–25.

GLOSSARY

actor-network theory: A form of theorizing concerned with the collective social negotiation of meanings by emphasizing action and process. Actor-network theorizing argues that the activity of humans and non-humans continually interact to help establish and maintain social order. In this approach, researchers focus on the most powerful actor as he or she makes connections and interacts with other human and non-human actants.

actuarial justice: A theoretical model of justice and crime control that Feeley and Simon (1994, as cited in chapter 1) identify as having emerged in the late 1980s. Actuarial justice is characterized by a focus on managing the risks that criminals represent, rather than attempting to transform or reform those who have broken the law. Models of actuarial justice rely on aggregated data about risks to profile offenders and identify risky categories of people/offenders in order to target them for management and incapacitation.

appropriation: A concept from science and technology studies that draws attention to the creative ways in which users take up and use technology to make it fit into their everyday activities. Appropriation draws attention to power dynamics that shape the use of technologies, as well as the uncertain and negotiated character of technology, by pointing out that users of technology may integrate it into their activities in ways that were unforeseen or unintended by its creators.

big data: Data that has been generally defined by three Vs: high volume of data, high velocity (i.e., speed at which data is generated), and high variety of data sources and formats. Other features of big data technologies include the following: it is exhaustive (i.e., representing a census of all activity), relational, and of fine resolution quality. Much of the literature and theorizing available on big data has focused on these technological aspects. Yet, more recent theorists recognize the social shaping of big data by arguing that it is a cultural, technological, and scholarly phenomenon that incorporates technology, analysis, and mythology (see, e.g., boyd and Crawford 2012, as discussed in the opening remarks for section I).

body camera: Also known as a police-worn body camera, it is a mobile video and audio technology that police officers can attach to their uniforms to record what they see and hear.

calculability: Refers to the ability to estimate or precisely mathematically determine the odds of an event. Some risks can be calculated (are calculable) in terms of percentage likelihood, such as the odds of getting in a plane crash, while other risks or dangers exist at the level of potential and are not reducible to a set of odds because they occur so infrequently as to be statistically incalculable or unpredictable, such as the likelihood of nuclear holocaust.

capital: The resources that actors (and, more specifically, nodes) have access to within security networks in order to influence security networks. Benoit Dupont identifies five different forms of capital—economic, cultural, political, social, and symbolic—that nodes (i.e., actors or organizations within a security network) can draw upon to exercise, yield, or acquire power within the broader security network (see Dupont 2004, as cited in chapter 4, for a detailed discussion).

***cordon sanitaire*:** A French phrase that literally translates into a "sanitary barrier" and refers to mechanisms used to quarantine and prevent the spread of disease. The criminologist Jock Young used this term in his 1999 book, *The Exclusive Society*, to refer to technologies and mechanisms by which "undesirables" are kept out of public and private spaces and cordoned away from acceptable society. These technologies may be physical barriers (e.g., fences, locked doors), or they may be symbolic barriers. For example, a credit card and identification are symbolic barriers that permit "undesirables" to be excluded from places like hotels, which can refuse to rent to individuals who do not have appropriate documentation and credit.

courtesy stigma: A term coined by Erving Goffman (1963; see chapter 3 for discussion) to refer to stigma that is attached to an individual by virtue of their relationship with someone else. In other words, the stigma originates with another individual and "spreads" to their associates (e.g., family, friends). A person subject to courtesy stigma need not be the bearer of a stigmatized characteristic—for example, the family member of a person convicted of a crime, who is stigmatized but has not committed any criminal act.

culture of risk aversion: A growing societal discomfort with risk such that risks, once identified, are expected to be effectively managed and minimized. Individuals, organizations, and government are increasingly unwilling to tolerate unmanaged risk or to allow potentially risky situations to go on without intervention. Failure to manage risk is viewed as irresponsible or negligent, and there is little tolerance for false negatives, wherein an individual who is deemed low risk goes on to commit harm.

distanciated governance: Defined by Anthony Giddens (1990; see chapter 4 for discussion) to explain the way in which the state diagnoses problems and mobilizes different service providers to work together to address community safety issues.

dividuals: A term coined by Gilles Deleuze (1995; see chapter 1 for discussion) to refer to the digital identity that allows citizens to be governed and processed via automated data systems, which in turn confer privileges and sanctions on to individuals. Examples of dividuals include when banks process credit applications electronically on the basis of a social insurance number and its associated credit score, or when a ticket and fine are issued in the mail to a driver on the basis of the ownership information attached to the license plate of a car that was photographed by a traffic camera.

economics of policing: Refers to economic pressures on police services to do more with less. The economics of policing refers specifically to the rising public expectations placed on police for community safety coupled with depleting police budgets.

facticity: The recognition that facts are not "objective" in nature, but are instead socially constructed and arise through a series of socio-technical relations. Facticity draws analytical attention to the way in which facts are made stronger and more durable by their social and material alliances.

false positive: A situation in which a tool or technology that is intended to identify risky persons or situations for intervention falsely identifies a person or situation who would not have been a danger. The inverse, false negative, would refer to a situation where an individual or situation identified as not risky or "low risk" then goes on to cause harm or danger.

governance or **government at a distance:** A concept developed by Peter Miller and Nikolas Rose (1990) and expanded on by David Garland (1996) (see chapter 4 for discussion), drawing on Foucault's theory of governmentality, to explain the changing role and responsibility of the state or government in controlling the behaviour of citizens. Instead of the state being solely responsible for preventing and controlling crime through direct, coercive control and punishments, responsibility is shifted to individuals and mobilized through arm's-length institutions such as education, religion, and family, and through market mechanisms like insurance. Citizens become "responsibilized" for their own safety and are expected to manage their own risks, avoiding dangerous or risky behaviour and situations. Citizens are incentivized to act in ways that conform to dominant societal expectations and to manage risk in a way that reduces the likelihood of harm.

habitus: A term coined by the French sociologist Pierre Bourdieu; the concept of habitus embodies the reflective social experiences of the individual, as well as the knowledge (including that which is taken for granted), skills, and values held within the organization or profession. Thus it is a system of dispositions or understandings that integrate previous experience to enable one to interact in a specific cultural environment.

high policing: Canadian criminologist Jean-Paul Brodeur differentiated between "high" and "low" forms of policing in his 1983 article, "High Policing and Low Policing: Remarks about the Policing of Political Activities." High policing mixes legislative, judicial, and executive powers of government in order to preserve and protect the nation-state. High policing is connected to agencies more recognizably involved in political policing, as it casts a wide surveillance net for the purposes of maintaining the existing social and political order. The goal of high policing, as compared to low (i.e., street-level) policing, is the acquisition of "intelligence" and "information" with the aim to acquire total information awareness.

informatics: A branch of engineering concerned with information management, processing, and computational analytics. Informatics are used to manage and work with large data sets to generate useable information.

intelligence-led policing (ILP): An organizational approach to policing that uses the collection and analysis of information to inform tactical, strategic, and business law enforcement decision making.

ion mobility spectrometry (IonScan): A technology used to identify substances based on the movement of its constituent particles (ions). This technology has various uses in chemistry but its commercial variant is most commonly used to identify trace particles of explosives at airport security or in military combat zones, or to identify illicit drugs in prisons.

ion mobility spectrums (plasmagrams): The visible output of the ion mobility spectrometry device. The plasmagram or ion mobility spectrum resembles a line graph and is compared against the plasmagrams of the target substances (e.g., illicit drugs or explosives) stored in the device's memory bank.

jurisprudence of risk: An orientation to legal decision making and criminalization that prioritizes the management of risk of future harm, rather than merely punishing harms already committed. Penalties for drunk driving and speeding exemplify the jurisprudence of risk since these offences are for *creating risk* (i.e., increasing the likelihood of an accident), rather than *causing harm*. Similarly, sentencing policies such as indeterminate sentences for high-risk offenders (dangerous offender designations) and parole decisions operate on a jurisprudence of risk concerned with reducing the probability of a future offence.

mass preventive justice: A form of preventive law enforcement drawing on a jurisprudence of risk that is enacted on a mass scale via the employment of surveillance and digital technologies. The stated aim of mass preventive justice is to censure potentially risky behaviour in order to prevent harm from occurring. The use of traffic cameras to electronically ticket speeders and drivers who run red lights in an effort to reduce traffic accidents is an example of mass preventive justice.

new penology: Feeley and Simon (1994; see chapter 7 for discussion) argued that in the late 1980s a "new penology" focused on risk management replaced the "old penology," which was concerned with the punishment and rehabilitation of offenders. Where the old penology was focused on identifying the guilty party (who is responsible for the crime?) and determining an appropriate treatment for that individual, the new penology takes as its aim the effective management of offender populations, classified by levels of risk. Connected to the idea of "actuarial justice," the new penology assumes that crime is a given in society—the goal is no longer to eliminate crime or rehabilitate individual lawbreakers but to effectively manage dangerous groups.

nodal governance: A way to theorize about security networks and the new plural landscape of policing. Nodal governance does not see the state (i.e., police) as holding a hierarchical or central role within the provision of security networks, but instead argues that the relationships between and among various actors within a security network take different forms and different shapes at different times. Thus, security networks are fluid and ever-changing. Governance is perceived as a complex activity that requires different agencies and organizations to act at different times.

plural policing: In reference to the changing landscape of contemporary policing, plural policing describes the way in which policing is being increasingly provided by networks of public, private, and welfare organizations.

population identities: According to Ericson and Haggerty (1997; see chapter 6 for discussion), the concept of population identities refers to social-group identities that are translated into knowledge for the purposes of classification. Once identities are classified, these groups can be organized by unique characteristics, like age and race, and subject to further risk assessment, management, and surveillance.

pre-crime: Describes the shift from reactive crime control toward anticipatory, pre-emptive crime control. A pre-crime society is one in which intelligence gathering, risk assessments, and crime science are used to inform and guide policing and security practices. It is not about preventing crime, but is instead focused on preventing individual perpetrators of crime and intervening before they act.

predictive policing: Analytic tools, computational analytics, and proactive approaches to policing that aim to forecast and predict where crime and/ or victimization are likely to occur. These predictive models are used to assign the placement of officers and patrol resources in order to be most effectively positioned to prevent, intercept, or respond to the predicted criminal activity.

pre-punishment: The act of punishing individuals for crimes that they have not yet committed, but that we predict they will commit. For example, pre-emptive detention of individuals identified as potential terrorists, who have not yet committed any criminal act, is a form of pre-punishment. This logic of pre-punishment may be extended to include the detention and punishment imposed by pretrial detention, in which individuals accused of a crime, but *not yet convicted*, are incarcerated while awaiting trial and sentencing.

preventive justice: A system of law and punishment that is oriented toward preventing *future* offences or harms. This may include preventive detention, prison release schemes (parole) based on risk calculations, and indeterminate sentences for high-risk offenders. The criminalization of risky behaviour that *may* lead to future harm (e.g., drunk driving) is also a form of preventive justice. See also *mass preventive justice*.

punitive turn thesis: A theory of justice and punishment put forward by David Garland (2000; see chapter 7 for discussion) suggesting that the criminal justice systems in Western democracies are shifting away from rational, measured responses to crime that focus on offender rehabilitation and prevention, and toward ever more punitive and harsh punishments for crime. Garland argues that this increasing punitivity is driven politically by citizen demands for a "tougher" approach to crime and a desire for retribution against individuals who do harm.

remand population: The population of incarcerated persons who are held in jail while awaiting trial. These individuals have been charged with a crime but have not yet been convicted and are still considered legally innocent until proven guilty.

risk: Refers to a measure of exposure to danger or possible harm. Theorists of risk generally assert that in order for a danger to be understood as a risk, we must be aware of it—there is no such thing as an unknown risk. Therefore, risks are understood as knowable and calculable—we can assess the likelihood of any given risk causing harm, either in a precise, actuarial/statistical sense, or in a more intuitive way. Risks may be subject to measures of risk reduction or intervention in order to reduce the likelihood of harm. Importantly, many risks may be managed through dispersion or sharing of the potential harm; for example, insurance schemes that share the cost of potential loss among many insured people (who pay premiums) disperse the risk of a large loss (e.g., their house burning down), such that no one individual must bear the entire cost.

risk media: A concept developed by Richard V. Ericson and Kevin Haggerty (1997; see chapter 6 for discussion) that refers to communication and information formats that capture and document risk. These documentations of risk then can become subject to assessment and management for the purposes of analysis and surveillance. For example, written (format) police reports that document car accidents (paperwork/documents) can be shared by police with insurance companies to calculate car insurance rates (analysis and surveillance).

risk society: A term associated with the work of Ulrich Beck (1992) and Anthony Giddens (1990) that is used to describe modern society's preoccupation with risk and risk management. Giddens sees the idea of risk as emerging from widespread concerns about ensuring future safety, while Beck (1992, 21) defines the risk society as "a systematic way of dealing with hazards and insecurities induced and introduced by modernization itself." Specifically, Beck's risk society is one characterized by a great number of new threats and concerns to be managed that are the product of modern society and technology (e.g., the threat of nuclear disaster, cancers, or global warming). See chapter 6 for a detailed discussion of *risk society*.

risk technology: Drawing on a broad definition of "technology" (see *technology*), risk technology is any kind of technology that is used to gather information and make decisions about risk or threat. Risk technology may be used for surveillance and gathering information or data about potentially risky people (e.g., traffic cameras, customs declaration forms at border crossings); to assess risk levels and sort people into groups (e.g., risk assessment checklists); to target and identify potentially risky people or situations (e.g., metal detectors at airports); or to respond to risky situations. Each chapter in this book presents an empirical example of risk technology.

security networks: Made up of different organizational and institutional actors that, either directly or indirectly, bring the actors together in the provision of security. Security networks include both public and private policing and security organizations.

situation tables: A collaborative, risk-driven, proactive approach to community safety that involve regular monthly meetings between police and social service providers—such as mental health, hospital, family and child services, and education professionals. The agencies share information with the goal of identifying individuals or families deemed at risk of engaging in, or becoming victims of, crime. Individuals or families who are identified by the table as being at risk are then offered support and services by member agencies.

social sorting: As defined by David Lyon (2007; see chapter 8 for discussion), a technologically augmented way of sorting and verifying identities. It works to sort individuals based on economic and social categories with the goal of influencing and managing people and populations.

surveillance: The observation of citizens, actors, organizations, and entities for the purposes of knowing and governing their actions. Contemporary technological surveillance includes the collection and storage of personal data for aggregated and detailed analyses, which are often carried out by computer systems. Surveillance works to sort people into categories in order to identify risk and to target interventions. (See also Foucault's work on bio-power.)

technological determinism: A theoretical orientation that conceives of technology as being developed outside of society and not being influenced and/or determined by social, economic, and political factors. Further, a technological determinist perspective regards technological change as causing societal change and views the implementation of technology as causing or *determining* specific intended outcomes or behaviours (see Wyatt 2008, cited in the opening remarks for section I, for a detailed discussion on technological determinism). Technological determinism is distinct from a social construction of technology perspective that conceives of technology as being shaped by social, economic, organizational, and political factors.

technology: A term used to describe an array of objects and tools used by human beings to facilitate their desired actions and outcomes. Technology, in this sense, incorporates everything from wheels to vehicles, pencils to computers, checklists to smartphones. Technology comprises not only physical objects and materials, but knowledge and use of these objects and materials. Technology is created, not only in the sense that it is designed and configured by humans, but also in the way it is interpreted and understood by social groups influenced by economic, political, organizational, cultural, and social factors that can change over time.

technology in practice: A theoretical framework that recognizes that technology only becomes meaningful when it is used in practice. Technology in practice also recognizes the importance of "users" and the way users can shape how technology it is used and, thus, its outputs and effects. Technologies in practice can be quite different from the ways they are designed to operate, or are anticipated to be used, and can thus lead to unintended and unexpected applications or outcomes.

theatre of security: The visible use of technological security measures that may or may not be wholly effective in producing security from harm. This show of security is used to instill public confidence and to provide an existential sense of security, reducing fear without necessarily providing real protection from possible threat.

threat: An impending danger or harm. Unlike risk, threat (or danger) can exist even when individuals are unaware of the potential for future harm. Threat may be nebulous, and cannot be managed through dispersion of harm. A threat becomes a risk when it is known, calculable, and manageable.

CONTRIBUTOR BIOGRAPHIES

Lyria Bennett Moses is director of the Allens Hub for Technology, Law, and Innovation and associate professor in the Faculty of Law at UNSW Sydney. Her research explores issues around the relationship between technology and law, including the types of legal issues that arise as technology changes, how these issues are addressed in Australia and other jurisdictions, the application of standard legal categories such as property in new socio-technical contexts, the use of technologically specific and *sui generis* legal rules, and the problems of treating "technology" as an object of regulation. Bennett Moses is currently a key researcher and project leader on the Data to Decisions Co-operative Research Centre, exploring legal and policy issues surrounding the use of data and data analytics for law enforcement and national security. She is also lead of the UNSW Grand Challenge on "Living with 21st Century Technology" and a PLuS Alliance Fellow.

Katy Cain is a PhD candidate in the Department of Sociology at the University of Toronto, specializing in crime and socio-legal studies. She received her MA in criminology from Wilfrid Laurier University in 2015. Her research interests include prisoner re-entry, stigma, wrongful conviction, and risk.

Janet Chan is professor at UNSW Law and leader of the Data Justice Stream of the Allens Hub for Technology, Law, and Innovation. Internationally recognized for her contributions to policing research, Janet is interested in the study of occupational cultures, creativity and innovation, and the impact of technology on policing and security. She is a key researcher of the Data to Decisions Co-operative Research Centre, examining the use of big data technology for national security and law enforcement. She is co-author (with Lyria Bennett Moses) of recent articles on big data for legal decisions, policing, and security in the *UNSW Law Journal* (2014), *Theoretical Criminology* (2016), *Policing and Society* (2016), and the *British Journal of Criminology* (2017). Janet is a joint editor (with Lyria Bennett Moses and Gavin Smith) of the 2017 *British Journal of Criminology* themed issue on big data and criminology. Chan was elected Fellow of the Academy of Social Sciences in Australia in 2002. In 2015, she was the joint recipient of the Australian and New Zealand Society of Criminology Distinguished Criminologist Award.

Tony Christensen is associate professor in the Department of Criminology at Wilfrid Laurier University. His primary academic interests are in social constructionist and symbolic interactionist theory. He is particularly interested in how different groups go about convincing the public to view certain acts as criminal or problematic.

Karine Côté-Boucher is assistant professor in the School of Criminology and regular researcher in the International Centre for Comparative Criminology at the Université de Montréal. Her research focuses on border control as it concerns the regulation of the mobilities of goods and persons. One of her current projects examines the securitization of the cross-border transportation industry in Canada. She has published in the *British Journal of Criminology*, *Security Dialogue*, and *Theoretical Criminology*.

Aaron Doyle is associate professor and chair in the Department of Sociology and Anthropology at Carleton University. His research interests include prisons and jails; public criminology; risk, insurance, and security; crime and media; and visual surveillance. He has published eight previous books, most recently *57 Ways to Screw Up in Grad School: Perverse Professional Advice for Graduate Students* (with Kevin D. Haggerty) and *Eyes Everywhere: The Global Growth of Camera Surveillance* (edited with Randy Lippert and David Lyon).

Martin Dufresne is associate professor of criminology at the University of Ottawa. His theoretical and methodological interests include actor-network theory, pragmatism, criminal justice history, history and sociology of science, science and technology studies, and mapping controversies. His research interests include technological and scientific controversies in neurosciences, biocriminology, criminology, surveillance, DNA, DNA data bank, and other criminal justice technologies.

Kevin D. Haggerty is a Killam Research Laureate and editor of the *Canadian Journal of Sociology*. He is also professor of sociology and criminology at the University of Alberta. In addition to the assorted journal articles and book chapters he has authored, he co-authored *Policing the Risk Society* (with Richard Ericson, Oxford University Press), wrote *Making Crime Count* (University of Toronto Press), and co-edited *The New Politics of Surveillance and Visibility* (with Richard Ericson, University of Toronto Press). His recent work has been in the area of surveillance, governance, policing, and risk. He and his co-author (Aaron Doyle) recently published the book *57 Ways to Screw Up in Grad School*, which conveys a series of professional lessons for the next generation of graduate students.

Stacey Hannem is associate professor and chair in the Department of Criminology at Wilfrid Laurier University. Her research interests are broadly linked theoretically around the experience of stigma and marginality, particularly the implications of crime and the criminal justice system for families, sex work legislation and policy, and the use of law and policy to regulate risk. She is co-editor (with Chris Bruckert) of *Stigma Revisited: Implications of the Mark* (University of Ottawa Press, 2012). She has recently published in *Symbolic Interaction*, the *Journal of Contemporary Ethnography*, and *Deviant Behavior*.

Taylor Knipe is a PhD student in the Department of Sociology at the University of Guelph. She completed her MA in criminology at Wilfrid Laurier University in 2017. Her research interests include policing networks, risk classifications, and community safety and well-being.

Debra Langan is associate professor in the Department of Criminology at Wilfrid Laurier University. Guided by critical theorizing and qualitative methodologies, her current research projects focus on women in policing, families and intimate relations, gendered violence, and risk technologies.

Laura McKendy recently completed her PhD in sociology at Carleton University. Her dissertation was entitled *The Pains of Jail Imprisonment: Experiences at the Ottawa Carleton Detention Centre.*

Pat O'Malley is distinguished honorary professor in the Research School of the Social Sciences at Australian National University and is a fellow of the Academy of Social Sciences in Australia. Previously he was professorial research fellow in law at the University of Sydney (2006–13) and Canada research chair in criminology and criminal justice at Carleton University (2002–06). From 1992–2002 he was professor of law, director of the National Centre for Socio-Legal Studies (1990–92), and deputy dean in the Faculty of Law and Management (1996–2001) at La Trobe University, Melbourne. Recent publications related to the topic covered in this volume include (with Gavin J. D. Smith) "Driving Politics: Data-Driven Governance and Resistance" in the *British Journal of Criminology* (2017), and "Policing the Risk Society in the 21st Century" in *Policing and Society* (2015).

Dominique Robert is associate professor of criminology at the University of Ottawa. Along with her students, she conducts research inspired by pragmatic sociology and science and technology studies, specifically actor-network theory. She researches the scientific and public controversies about the most recent biological turn (new genetics and neurosciences) in criminology, as well as technologies of ordering such as early childhood prevention programs and automation of risk evaluation.

Silvian Roy graduated with an MA in criminology from the University of Ottawa. He is an institutional classification/rehabilitation officer with the Ontario Ministry of Community Safety and Correctional Services, and a Fanshawe College professor of abnormal psychology. His research is inspired by science and technology studies and, more specifically, actor-network theory. His research interests include neuroscience, neurocriminology, criminal risk assessment technologies, and mental health and justice.

Carrie B. Sanders is associate professor in the Department of Criminology at Wilfrid Laurier University. Using interpretive theories and qualitative methods, her research investigates policing and technological change, police cultures, big data and data analytics in policing, and surveillance.

Christopher J. Schneider is associate professor of sociology at Brandon University. His research and publications focus on information technologies and related changes to police work in Canada. He has written or collaborated on five books and has published dozens of articles and chapters. His most recent book is *Policing and Social Media: Social Control in an Era of New Media* (Lexington Books/Rowman & Littlefield, 2016). Schneider is the 2017 recipient of the Canadian Criminal Justice Association's Public Education Award. Other recognition includes the 2016 Society for the Study of Symbolic Interaction's Early in Career Award; a 2013 Distinguished Academics Award, awarded by the Confederation of University Faculty Associations of British Columbia; and more than a dozen teaching awards and related distinctions. His research and commentary have been featured in hundreds of news reports across North America, including the *New York Times*. In 2019, he will hold the Endowed Chair of Criminology and Criminal Justice at St. Thomas University in New Brunswick.

INDEX

Page numbers ending in "g" indicate that word's glossary entry.